ROGER J.

The Lengthening Shadow

Shadow

OXFORD UNIVERSITY PRESS

Oxford   Toronto   Melbourne

Oxford University Press, Walton Street, Oxford OX2 6DP

Oxford   London
New York   Toronto   Melbourne   Auckland
Petaling Jaya   Singapore   Hong Kong   Tokyo
Delhi   Bombay   Calcutta   Madras   Karachi
Nairobi   Dar es Salaam   Cape Town

and associated companies in
Beirut   Berlin   Ibadan   Nicosia

Oxford is a trade mark of Oxford University Press

British Library Cataloguing in Publication Data

Green, Roger J.
The lengthening shadow
I. Title   II. Green, Roger J. The fear of Samuel Walton
823'.914[F]   PZ7
ISBN 0-19-271509-7

Illustrations by David Parkins

Phototypeset by Tradespools Limited, Frome, Somerset
Printed in Great Britain by Biddles Ltd, Guildford

For Carlos

Deep, O deep, we lay thee to sleep;
We leave thee drink by, if thou chance to be dry;
Both milk, and blood, the dew and the flood.
We breathe in thy bed, at the foot, and the head;
We cover thee warm, that thou take no harm;
And when thou dost wake
Dame earth shall shake
And the houses quake,
And her belly shall ake
As her back were brake,
Such a birth to make . . .

Ben Jonson *The Witches' Song,* 'Charm 4'

BOOK ONE

The Last Warning

Chapter One

They should not have been there. They had been told not to go there. And now, John Mellor, who had gone off on his own for a few moments, had seen something thick and snakelike in the deep, cold, dark well.

He was big and strong was John. He thought he was, and so did many others too. He was feared by all the other boys in school. He was always picking on the others, particularly Sam Walton. John Mellor was twelve years old in May. He would be leaving school at Christmas. He thought he was a grown man.

Down by the old well it was as black as the darkest night. John had no candle with him—that had been part of the game. He was quite alone except for the faint glow from his clay pipe, which he always smoked when there were no grown-ups about.

Something as thick and black as an oak branch had moved in the dark, deep waters. John saw a swirl of luminous circles as the waters of the well heaved and ebbed again. Then he thought he saw the gleam of a dark scale and for a brief

1

moment the sight of an eye as green as a prowling wild cat.

He cried out and stepped back from the well's edge. Then something ripped at his cheek. It was wet and cold and viciously sharp. He shouted and yelled. He began to climb up the narrow stone steps, crying and shouting as he ran in terror away from the heaving, splashing waters.

Once more something pulled at his jacket, clawing at his shoulder, pulling him backwards to the well again.

Samuel Walton, John Mellor, Tom Wilson, and Will Saltby were not supposed to be in the cellar that was underneath Will Saltby's shop. Will had been told time and time again never to go down the cellar without permission. For down from the dark, musty cellar a flight of steep, ancient steps led down to a deep and dangerous well. It was the deepest well in Derbyshire, so the old folks in Lambton said.

And there the boys, on that late afternoon of 23 July 1883, were playing a dangerous game they had made up. A game by the side of that dark and mysterious, deep and ancient well.

It was a strange well. Every now and again the circle of black water contained in a low limestone wall would shudder and move, rise and fall, lap and smack the low wall. It was as though something were moving deep in the well itself. Sam had heard Will say you could lower a lead weight on six balls of best string, all tied together and still not reach the bottom of the well.

Will's cottage and little shop and the cellar and well were in Church Alley Lambton—and that was the other mysterious fact. The well was deep under the churchyard of All Saints' Church, under all the gravestones. Will had once told Jessie Smith that he had seen a skeleton deep in the well water, and she had told Sam, for she had sat next to him at school.

Will Saltby's cellar was twenty creaking wooden steps down from the Saltby's wash-house, where Mrs Saltby kept her heavy iron-framed mangle against the cellar door to stop Will from going down into the cellar. John Mellor had pushed it away with one hand behind his back. Then, from the cellar, exactly one hundred, worn, steep steps carved into the limestone led down to the well. To get to the steps you went through a strange archway, carved and pointed at the top like the North Door leading into All Saints' Church. There was a broken carving over the door arch that led to the steps that looked like a serpent. But it was very old, it was crumbling, and it looked as if someone had tried to destroy it many years ago. Carved into the harder stone at the base of the archway was the cruel and wicked face of the Devil.

It was Will who had thought of the game: it was his cellar after all. His mother and father were both busy in the little shop, for it was market day in Lambton. If they had seen them going down they would have stopped them.

It had been so hot in school. They had all been sweating; it was the kind of afternoon when your legs stuck to the sticky varnish of the school bench. A game down by the old, cold, dark well had seemed a good idea. So, down they had crept.

They had all crept down the hundred steps to the well first of all. There, they had drunk deeply of the sweet ice-cold water that came up from deep under the Derbyshire hills from dark secret caves and long forgotten lead mines. They had watched the waters heave and shudder and swell as though alive. They had thought no more about it and gone back up to the cellar.

On the way up, John Mellor had tickled Samuel Walton's ear. 'Hey up, Sam, a water bug's crawled up out o' water and gone to nest in thy lughole.' Then he nipped the soft part of Sam's ear with his fingernail until it bled.

'Gerroff,' Sam had said. They'd thought no more about that either, for John Mellor was always playing cruel tricks. If he wasn't doing it to Sam, he was doing it to Will or to one of the girls.

Back up in the cellar Will explained his game. They sat on the cellar floor round a penny candle that Will had 'borrowed' from the shop above. The cellar was full of cold, black, jumping shadows. The shadows seemed to jump out at the boys from behind the high mounds of coal that were in the cellar. In the game, Will had said, the candle would be blown out. Then, anybody who dared would creep down the hundred steps to the well; once there, Will said, they must put their hand in the water and splash it about as proof they were

3

down there. When you returned you could have, as a reward for the ordeal, a striped penny fish that Will had also 'borrowed' from the shop above.

Will had held up the sugar fish to the swaying flame of the carriage candle, the raspberry one red as ruby, the other, cold green peppermint like the deep mill dam where the water-weed grew.

Of course, big, tough John Mellor had to go first. He was the bravest. Soon he would be a working man, earning real money. He'd show them. In the dim golden candlelight you could see the first faint shadow of a ginger moustache that would soon grow. He'd show them. He had lit his clay pipe and blown smoke in Samuel Walton's face. Then, suddenly, he took the pipe from his mouth. He spat on his finger and stooped down and dragged his finger in the coal dust. Then, moving as quick as a cobra, he wiped spit and coal dust down Tom Wilson's white school collar. Tom leaped up to get him, but Mellor had gone through the archway, laughing loudly and belching.

'Frit thy mam might smack thy bum?' he called up to Tom, who paused at the top of the steps. John Mellor had grown a lot in the last few months. Tom decided not to follow him. Will promptly blew the candle out; perhaps that would frighten him. It didn't. Mellor swaggered down the narrow steps, his shoulders bumping into the cold rock as he went down. As he walked down the hundred steps the boys above in the cellar heard a faint yet distinct knocking or tapping that seemed to come from deep in the earth.

'Hey up, lads!' Will had said in the darkness, 'That old witch next door is at it again, tapping and banging. I've heard her many a time when I've been sent down for coal.'

'Shurrup, you daft old bag!' Will yelled at the top of his voice. He had felt his way in the darkness to the cellar wall and banged and kicked the wall.

Next door to Will lived old Mrs Trotter. She was very old. Most people called her Dame Trot, for she was to be seen at all hours of the day, trotting through the streets of Lambton or searching for plants and berries in the woods. All the girls and younger children at school said she was a witch. Will found the old woman a big joke. None of the bigger boys, or

4

Will himself, believed in witches or magic. So, Will banged and kicked at the old woman's cellar wall.

'T' Witch!' he yelled. 'Mek less noise you, old cowbag!'

All the boys had laughed, even Tom, who was rubbing away at his collar. The laughter was tinged with fear however; not because they thought she was a witch, but because if they had been discovered making fun of the old woman they would all have got a good hiding.

When they had stopped laughing they heard Mellor splashing in the well below. Then they heard him calling and shouting. They relit the still warm candle and holding it high, they rushed down.

'Summat's gorrus,' yelled Mellor. When they reached the bottom of the steps they found Mellor crawling on the floor in the shadows, blood pouring from his face.

Sam stared at his enemy Mellor as he crawled towards the boys. Sam had been rubbing his ear where Mellor had cut it, not really listening to Will banging on the cellar wall. He had thought that the tapping came from deep in the earth—not from Dame Trot's cellar next door. He thought he had heard a soft hissing just before Mellor had shouted for help, but he had decided he had rubbed his ear too hard. He stared over Will's shoulder at the well. Then he too stepped back in alarm. For one moment the reflected candle flame had looked like an eye.

'There's nowt there!' said Will, his dark eyes sparkling with mischief. He was thoroughly enjoying seeing big John Mellor scared out of his wits. Will was as small for his age as John Mellor was big, and Mellor often tortured him. John Mellor snatched the dripping candle from Will. He held it high over his head, setting the shadows leaping and jumping round the old well. 'Look at me face, then, clever clogs Saltby,' roared Mellor, his hand shaking so much that tiny drops of candle-grease were scattering like pearls on the damp floor. Still holding the candle he began to elbow his way through the other boys to get to the narrow steps. Blood trickled down his face from a cut on his cheek, shaped like the crescent moon.

'You've cut thy ugly mug on them nails where we used to hang us buckets afore us had a tap!' shouted Will daringly

5

after him as he began to push his way out, for the other boys were not really helping him to get away from the well.

'Summat touched me as well!' shouted Mellor angrily, but he did not turn back to thump Will for referring to his face as ugly mug.

'That mucky old cloth fell on thee,' said Will, picking up a wet mouldy cloth from the floor. 'Me mam used to wipe out buckets wi' it,' he explained to the other boys. Will was enjoying himself greatly.

'Tha's a coward, Mellor. Frit!' said Will, very daring now, as Mellor reached the steps.

Sam was standing now on the bottom step, where he had backed to, after he had thought for a moment he had seen an eye in the water. Sam was not as easily convinced as the others. 'Look at them black slimy marks up the wall and that circle of water on the wall, as though summat's crawled up,' said Sam. 'They weren't there when we were down the first time.'

'They were,' said Will promptly. 'And anyway, how dost thou know, Sam Walton? It's not even thy cellar.'

But Sam was not so sure. He couldn't help thinking there had been something in the well. There had been the eye, the hissing, then the marks. He opened his mouth to say so, but Mellor, pushing by, deliberately pushed his elbow into Sam's stomach at that moment. He was winded and the pain sickened him.

'I'm gerring out of here,' said Mellor, kicking Sam as he crouched on the low worn bottom step. 'Thee go an' look, Sam Walton, if you're so bloody clever.'

'Tha's always been frit, Mellor,' shouted Will from the well, becoming more and more daring as the bully began to climb the steps. 'When we went exploring that mine and when we were in woods gerrin' frogs you were frit!'

Mellor said nothing as his boots scraped the old steps as he climbed up. Neither did Sam. He hated Mellor with all his heart and soul, but he couldn't help agreeing with him.

Mellor swore under his breath as he climbed the hundred curving, twisting steps. He was the biggest in the school. Grown men did not see monsters. His face was red with shame by the light of the candle flame that streamed out in the draught.

6

Once more came a soft deep tapping.

'Shurrup, you owd rat bag,' shouted Will. The tapping stopped.

When John reached the cellar above, his hands covered with beads and threads of candle wax, he was in a foul temper. His eyes gleamed white and hating in the swaying light of the candle.

Down by the old well Will and Tom were in no hurry to come up; they were not in the least bit scared or frightened by what Mellor had said. They put their hands to their mouths and made hooting owl noises, then wild dog noises, then they pretended to be goblins laughing. Will made a wind noise on the back of his hand, dipping it into the well to get it wet. The noise echoed round the well chamber.

'Eh, John, lad, there's a monster wi' belly ache just come up in well!' shouted Will.

Sam had reached the top of the hundred steps. 'Tell us what you saw, then,' said he to Mellor. They did not usually have a lot to say to each other. 'I thought I heard summat knocking or hissing, like, an' there were this slit like a moon-shaped eye, a bit like a cat—'

Mellor cut him short. He felt better now he was away from the well. 'It were nowt. I dropped me pipe in t' well an' it burned me hand an' made me jump, that's all.'

'But, you yelled out an'—,' but Sam was not allowed to finish. Mellor got hold of him, pulled him towards him, then knocked him down on the coal-stained cellar flagstones. Mellor had an urgent need to make himself feel big again.

'Art tha calling me frit, Walton?' he growled in his deepest voice. He hit Sam again, hard. Sam lost his temper and hit back. That was it. Mellor was very angry that he had been called frit and a coward. It was uncomfortably near the truth. He began to take it out on Sam. He smashed his fist into Sam's face, although Sam was a year younger and smaller. He pulled down Sam's lower lip till the flesh ripped. He twisted his arm and his little finger. He trod on Sam's other hand. All this he did with the agile speed of a striking snake. Then he pulled Sam up and pretended to hit Sam in the belly but as Sam ducked he head-butted him. Then he blacked Sam's eye.

7

The candle rolled slowly over and over leaving a rivulet of milky candle wax.

'How many times, our Will, do we have to tell thee not to come into this cellar and play about, either by thysen or with other lads? And near that well too. I thought you'd grown a bit of sense. Your father'll have to padlock it after he's given thee a belting.'

It was Mrs Saltby on the cellar head, shouting at Will, who was now grinning at her at the top of the hundred steps, idly touching with his boot the candle that had now melted into a lake of wax with the wick flickering in the middle. She began to walk over to Will.

'And have you been tapping on that wall to old Mrs Trotter? Your father said he heard something. It's not right to tease old ladies, Will. Your father will have something to say to you, young man.'

'Why?' said Will cheekily. 'Is she a witch then? Do you think she's put a boggart in t' well? John there, says there's a boggart in t' well. Do—'

His mother smacked Will across the head angrily, but it did not stop Will rolling his eyes at Mellor and grinning at the big boy. Mellor was dusting himself down, brushing coal dust off the old waistcoat he wore that had lost a button. Will made faces. He knew Mellor would not lay a finger on him while his mother was there. Will rubbed his smacked ear and grinned the more to see Mellor blushing a deep ashamed red.

'Now come on out,' said Mrs Saltby as the candle drowned its flame in the wax. 'It's as cold as death down here. It seems to get colder every time I come down here. Your mother'll have something to say when she sees your collar, Tom Wilson.' Grumbling loudly all the time Mrs Saltby watched them come up into the wash-house.

'I'm going now,' said Mellor sulkily, wiping his nose on his shirt-sleeve.

'Yes, and I'm going to tell thy mam about you smoking down our cellar,' said Mrs Saltby, sniffing the air heavy with candle and tobacco smoke. Then her face softened as she remembered that John had no father. She thought it a shame to see the lad walking round in his dad's old clothes that were too big for him, because Mrs Mellor was so short of money.

8

The waistcoat and shirt were almost in rags. Mrs Saltby remembered how she had liked John's father.

'Take a lardy cake out of the shop on thy way out, John, for thy ma,' said Mrs Saltby. 'Tell Will's dad I said so. And think on. Next time you spend money on a penn'orth of baccy, think how your ma needs the money.'

Mellor muttered something about thanks but was cut short by Will. 'See thee tomorrow, John,' said he with mock friendliness. 'It's school trip tomorrow. Don't forget we're going by train to Matlock. Hey up, John. There might be giant worms wi' claws an' bogey men wi long nails that scratch thee down them caves we're going down!'

Tom Wilson sniggered behind his hand.

'We're going in them caves at Matlock, mam,' said Will to his mother. 'Miss White says there'll be stalactites and stalagmites.' His mother looked impressed and she turned from Mellor.

Mellor took the opportunity to shake his fist at the other boys. 'It were a fish or me pipe that made me jump,' he muttered as he went. He half-believed that himself now; he wanted the whole thing forgotten.

'And as for thee, Sammy Walton,' Mrs Saltby said, seeing them out, 'you'd better get next door and see old Mrs Trotter and get thy face straightened out. She'll give thee something for that black eye from all them herbs she has and some ointment for that cut.'

Will pulled a face behind his mother's back and mouthed the word 'Witch' at Sam. Sam went. He was silent. There had been something in that well. He'd find out about it when all the other boys had calmed down. He'd ask Mellor again tomorrow, and find the truth.

Once outside in the hot, brilliant, dusty alley Sam had an idea. He would ask Dame Trot about the well in Saltby's cellar. If anybody knew if there were anything down the well she would. She was, for all Will's jokes, a wise old woman. His own father bought medicines for the sheep and cattle from her, and his Grandmother took the old woman's medicines herself. The old woman would probably know some of the old stories about Lambton ... old stories of ghosts ... and monsters and dark things that lived down the old lead mines and deep wells. Sam knew a few of these horrible old stories ... his Grandfather had told him a good few ... some of them scared you stiff ... he himself had been badly scared earlier in the year by one of the old ghost stories ... Perhaps he wouldn't ask the old woman after all. Best forget the whole thing down by the well that afternoon ...

So he stood before the tightly shut door of the old woman, wondering what to do. The hot July sun had peeled off some of the dark green paint and the flakes had fallen into the mignonette and lavender that were growing round the boot scraper. Did he really want to hear one of those frightening stories that kept him awake at night, watching and listening? The old tales were horrible and there were so many that some had to be true ... He sniffed in the scent of the mignonette that smelled like a penny chocolate violet cream. Then curiosity got the better of him. He knocked timidly. The sun beat down on his head. Nothing moved within the cottage.

He supposed he'd done the right thing. He made a little pile of dust, fallen lavender heads, and the dry spidery lime blossom that fell from the lime trees that were overhanging the cottages from the churchyard. Anyway, he'd have to see the old witch woman if only to get some ointment for his eye and cheek. If his mother thought he'd been fighting, there would be a thrashing for him when he got home. He knocked again.

He looked up to the overhanging branches of the church-yard lime trees. He was glad he was not living near the graveyard, like Will and the witch did ... that well was black and deep ... that tapping and hissing ... he remembered some of his Grandfather's stories, and then part of him could not help wondering if there was any connection between the thing in the well and the old witch. He wanted to run. A big fly settled on some blood on his cheek. It hurt. So he knocked louder. He was being stupid. He'd told himself earlier in the year not to think about the old stories and legends. He kicked at the pile of petals and dust with his boot and banged loudly. Inside someone laughed. Then he was called in.

Sam went in. The room stank in the heat; a big fire

10

crackled and roared up the chimney. A huge black cat with eyes like candles behind green glass and a bald patch on its back sat before the great fire. Big bluebottles and flies dipped, circled, buzzed, and weaved in a patch of hot dusty sunlight that poured in from a dirty window that overlooked the gravestones. A row of small skulls grinned down on Sam from a shelf.

Sam blinked. The gleam of the cat's eye and the curve of its claw as it stretched on the stained rug reminded Sam of the trouble by the well. As his eyes became even more used to the dusky gloom, he saw piles of bones, bottles, bundles of dusty herbs and flowers, grasses and leaves in old pot jam jars. In the middle of a crowded table was a beautiful old Sheffield silverplated candlestick. Writhing and curving up the stem of the candlestick was a finely carved and worked silver serpent. By its side stood a tall blue bottle and a big leather book with a brass lock on it. There was Dame Trot wrapped in dozens of filthy shawls, sitting with two other old women of Lambton, Lil Gosling and Lizzy Gomersall.

'I've come about me eye an' I'd like to ask about Saltby's well and—'

'My!' interrupted old Lizzy Gomersall, opening her toothless mouth in a round circle of gum-rimmed wonder. 'That's a shiner of a black eye, Sam Walton. But you're not pushing in t'queue to see Dame Trot. Tha mun wait thy kale. She's going to see me leg when 'er's had her grub then she'll see to thy eye an' thy questions.'

Sam stared. He had been a fool to be afraid. They were just silly old women. They were spreading tea leaves and sugar on bread and eating it with pleasure. Then they drank very black tea which Sam heard gurgling in their bellies.

'While I'm waiting, do any of you please know anything about the well—' began Sam again, but old Lizzy stood up, making her stool fall over with a crash, making the old tom cat's eyes gleam like green crescent moons in the dim heat of the room. To Sam's great embarrassment Liz began to pull up her dress. She revealed a varicose vein, red and angry like a thin purple snake, crawling up her white trunk leg. Sam blushed as the old woman hoisted her ancient black dress higher and higher about her knee.

11

There seemed to be no end to the angry red vein.

'All I wanted to ask was—' said Sam, sweating in the great heat, and the dress went higher and higher. He turned his head away at what he might see next.

'Sammy Walton'll see London if tha lifts thy pinna any higher,' said Lil Gosling, sprinkling ancient wet tea leaves on her well-sugared bread.

'Aye, well, he could see a lot worse,' snapped Liz. 'I'd the best pair o' legs this side of Derby seventy years ago.'

Sam stole a look at the tremendous leg and looked wearily out at the graveyard through the dusty window. His eye throbbed and he was getting nowhere with the questions. The gravestones cast menacing black shadows on the stubble of the churchyard grass where piles of cut grass cast longer shadows. There had been something in that well ... not surprising when you realized it was under all those dead bodies in the graves ...

'I dunna like the look o' thy leg, Lizzy, or thy eye, Sam Walton,' said Dame Trot suddenly from the shadows. 'I'll just fetch mysen a jug o' gin from The Anchor to set me up, like, then I'll get me ointments an' see to thee both.'

She vanished through the door, a white pot jug clasped to her bosom. Old Liz, despite the poisoned leg, hobbled to the dusty window.

'She's gone!' said the old woman triumphantly. 'Now Sammy Walton, canst read? Do they learn thee to read in that new school? Art a real scholard? I've allus wanted to read yon spell book but I canna read—' and she nodded to the big brown book on the table.

'It were Dame Trot's ma's book,' she went on, her hand covering her mouth as though someone were watching. 'Folks allus said her ma were a real black witch. She could raise the Devil, and folks said 'er could make great worms come up in t'graveyard when there were two full moons in a month.' Liz looked over her shoulder, as though expecting the witch or the monster to attack: she obviously believed every word.

'I don't—' began Sam. Blood was trickling from his face. He didn't want to hear one of those old tales like the ones his Grandfather told. He knew what would happen. He would

12

be too scared to sleep, he would jump at every noise and be awake half the night sweating with fear. Yet he might find out about the well . . .

Liz turned the yellow pages of the witch's book. 'Read this, lad,' said she. 'It looks like a story. She (jerking her head in the direction Dame Trot had gone) won't read us the best bits. She only reads recipes and medicines. All that witches' magic frits her!'

The old woman stuck her finger in her mouth to remove some sugar grains that had stuck in a hole where a tooth had been. She pulled out her finger with a wet plop and stabbed at the old page with a sugary spit-wet finger.

Sam sighed. He looked at the yellowing page. He hoped it was not going to be one of those horrible stories. It was the well he really wanted to find out about. He began to read aloud from the old black writing written down by Dame Trot's mother, the old witch, when she was a young woman. He read slowly at first and then with growing speed and horror.

> *I, Annie Dale, aged twenty years in this year of 1790, write down what I have been told by those who know and what I have seen for myself. There are many evil things in this parish and what is written here I got from old Rachel Gibbs and she got it from Francis Thompson who knew the Lambton Witches who were burned alive.*

Sam stopped for a moment. For in the margin, in faded inks or berry juices, was a faded drawing of the crescent moon, tinted a strange evil green. From the bottom of this protruded a cat's claw, jagged and wickedly sharp, and a drop of dark red blood.

'Gerron wi' thy reading, then,' said Lil. 'She'll be back soon.' Sam did.

> *There are many old and evil Things that lie deep in the earth below the Town of Lambton. Shadows of darkness that lie deep in caves and foul waters that pull men towards them. In the caves and tunnels are Things not imagined by men and not made by God. And there lies the creeping cold, older than time, that brings death.*

13

The two old women, finding the old spell book was not going to tell them any juicy bits of gossip about anybody who had lived or was still living in Lambton, lost interest. 'Them big buzz flies are after thy leg, Liz,' said Lil. 'Tha must be starting to rot in this hot weather.' Liz hastily covered up her vast leg from the flies. Sam ignored them and went on reading the spell book. He just could not help himself. He knew it would lead to sleepless, terrified nights, and even being too afraid to climb the stairs at night or go in the woods on his way home. But he had to find out the worst: he could not help himself.

> *Men in Lambton live their lives and do not know what lies in the earth below. But those who draw waters from the deep wells that never see the light of the stars and moon will see the waters of the wells shudder and move as the Things below stir in the darkness and follow the unspoken commands of the great Devil himself. Them that go into caves and tunnels and take the lead and silver will hear the tap and rustle of these great and evil Things. And them with a deeper sight will see the eyes of the Lord Satan ...*

Sam had to stop. There was another of the drawings. This time there was the crescent moon again, but now it was on its back, like a boat, and it looked remarkably like an eye. Again in the corner there was a drop of blood. In the margin was another, decorated with the leaves and berries of deadly nightshade and the claws of cats. Sam turned to the old women as though for help. The spell book was unbelievably frightening just to look at. But they had only been half-listening.

'It's like the Bible,' said Liz, scratching her leg. 'It's a fine thing to be learned in school like they do these days,' she added dreamily.

Sam ignored them. He went on reading in a shaking voice. Had something nearly killed them all in the well?

> *Miners hear the Things knocking and tapping their ancient language and they call it The Knocker. They do say that them that hear this strange knocking die before the year has finished.*

Sam gasped. He wished he'd never started to read the book. He had heard the tapping clearly by the well. So had the others. God, he hoped it had been Dame Trot knocking in her cellar and not one of these Things. He turned to the old women.

'I've heard knockings and tappings like that,' he said. They ignored him completely.

'I dunna know how Dame Trot can drink her gin wi' all them skulls a-watching her,' said Liz, pointing to the shelf of grinning skulls.

'They were her mam's,' said Lil. 'All old witches had skulls on their mantel shelves so t'Devil'd feel at home, like, when he came out o' flames.'

Liz moved her stool nervously away from the fire. But Sam read on aloud.

> *They do say that men worshipped these Things of the Dark before the Romans came here. The Things would appear half devil or man or cat and with the body and tail of a snake. Their black coils would stretch in the dark below for many a cave long. The caves sigh and hiss with their death-bringing cold breath.*

Sam shuddered. He must tell Will and the others. But there was more.

> *I found an old book beneath the altar of All Saints' Church when they were rebuilding it. John Daintry the vicar, he taught me my letters and let me wander the church at will. And this book tells of a Stone on the hills to the east of Lambton, close by the Turnpike Road to Chesterfield. And on this Stone is a carving of the Lord Devil himself. Men prayed to this Stone before Jesus Christ was born. It was an evil, wicked Stone. It was jealous of the new church built in Lambton in 883, and working with the Devil it destroyed the church. Men now call the Stone the Bow Cross, for it is twisted with evil power.*

Sam groaned aloud. Oh God, no, no, no. The Stone was in one of his Grandfather's fields and looked down on his own farmhouse. His Grandfather's farm was called Bow Cross

15

Farm in fact. And it was the stories about this Stone that he had been trying so hard to forget. Stories that had kept him awake and trembling all night long. He read on, praying that the witch's story was not the same one he had heard about earlier in the year. He couldn't stand it if it was. 'Oh God, please don't let it be the same, please, God, oh please,' he prayed.

'I'n't he like his Grandad up at Bow Cross Farm?' said Lil. 'Them big eyes!'

'Oh God, don't let the story be true.'

> The Stone and the Creatures of the deep destroyed the church in 883. They will do so again in 1883, for the evil is renewed every thousand years. The Devil himself will renew the power at Midsummer and the Stone will then begin to take blood. It will take three men, women, or children. If it has not had its fill of human blood by Midsummer its—

A large black beetle fell out of Dame Trot's bread oven in the wall. It hit the stone floor with a smack.

'By gum, Lil,' said Liz. 'That's a big 'un. Gerrit with thy stick.' The two old women scuttled round the dirty floor, not hearing a word.

> If it has not had its fill of human blood by Midsummer its power will wax. As the shadow lengthens, as the sun shines on it through July, August, and September those living by it will sicken and die. For its shadow is the shadow of the Devil. By Hallow Night at October's end in that year 1883 it will have killed, drunk blood, and with the creatures of the deep destroyed the great church itself. John Daintry, he would not listen and burned the book saying it was the writing of the heathen. But I told many who believed. Here ends my tale.

Sam groaned aloud, his head in his hands. The story was the same—only worse. The Stone near his farm would kill him. That was the story he had heard earlier in the year and believed for many a tormented day. Now it had all come back

16

to haunt him. Keep him awake ... eventually kill him. And the adventure by the well was just the start for him of the Devil's curse. He knew he was going to be one of the three the Stone and creatures would get.

His groans were unheard by the old women. They tossed the beetle into the fire where it crackled and snapped. The door wrenched open and there stood Dame Trot.

Desperately Sam began to tell her about her mother's book and how he believed every word about the curse on the old Stone and those who lived near it and how he believed he was going to be dead before All Hallows Night. He pushed the old leather book towards the old woman, knocking over a jampot of strange red berries. As he did so, the drawing of the moon in the spell book seemed to watch him like a warning from the past.

Dame Trot snatched the spell book, banged it shut, locked it with a key that had been hidden under the silver candlestick. Then she took the big book and put it in a corner cupboard and locked that, dropping the silver key down the front of her dress, and plucked at her dress till the key nestled securely in her vest.

'You'd no business lookin' in that book!' she shouted. She grabbed Sam and began soothing in a fragrant ointment on his eyelids.

'But it says in that book that old Stone in me Grandfeyther's field will get us. Me Grandfeyther says his dad used to say the Stone were the Devil's. It's been watching me all year. And your mam's book says it's true. It'll get—'

'Shut thy face about that book,' screamed Dame Trot. 'Now, shurrup. Them are daft owd tales that are best forgot, I tell thee. My old mam, though I says it as shouldn't, meddled with things she shouldna ... black magic ... the Devil ... Now shurrup, wilt? And there's nowt in Saltby's well I tell thee. I were gettin' some coal and breakin' up some lumps— that's what thee heard down t' cellar.'

She smeared the ointment on skilfully. She smelled vilely of ancient unwashed knickers, but the ointment was fragrant with the scent of violets. Sam shouted at her again. The old book must be true. He had heard the story many times that year from his Grandfather and even seen it in another book.

17

'I know nowt about me mam's old tales in her book, I tell thee,' wheezed Dame Trot. 'That book should be burned, but there's some grand recipes in it. She were clever with medicines. This is her recipe, made wi' violets picked under a crescent moon. I keep me neb out o' her magic and so should you, Sam Walton. No good'll come o' listening an' reading old tales. Now, thy eye'll be as good as new!'

But Sam would not be quiet. The old stories filled him with fear. Dame Trot began to push him. 'Gerrout. Go on. Gerrout. Go an' get married an' dunna come back!'

'But it says—' shouted Sam wildly.

'Shut it!' gasped Dame Trot, reaching for her stick. 'Go on. Get lost. Them tales are a load o' owd cowmuck.' But Sam would not move.

'Dunna excite thysen, Betsy love,' said Lil, enjoying every minute of the fight.

'It says that Stone an' t' Devil and them underground Things will—'

Dame Trot lashed out with her stick, narrowly missing Sam. He ran. The old woman had once split Matt Barker's head open with her stick for dropping horse muck down her cellar grate.

He must see Will. He must. They must talk. Do something. He promptly went into Will's shop. 'Can I see your Will, please?' he asked.

'No, tha canna,' came Mrs Saltby's swift reply. 'He's been in enough bother today. Get off home with thee.'

Sam ran off. He would see Will tomorrow anyway. They could talk then. Find a way of seeing if the old stories and legends were true ... all his fears and worries returned as he thought about the old Stone and the things it was supposed to do. He had the horrid certainty that the old book was right. He had the feeling that trouble was coming. And that old woman knew something about it.

Sam had a long, two mile walk home: over Lambton Bridge, then by the new railway station, then into the dark silent woods, walking alone the old road that had been abandoned because of the ghost stories and accidents, climbing higher and higher to pass his Grandfather's farm—and the Stone.

In between the trees and on bends of the old road through the woods he could see the old standing Stone. It was only a bit bigger than him, but he knew it was packed with evil force and power.

He'd first noticed it last summer. There had been a violent storm that had struck down the clump of trees that had hidden it for five hundred years. After the storm you could see the Stone ... dark and black on the top of the hill, as though watching and looking. And it had been a few days after that that Sam had got the feeling that the Stone was watching him.

The fear had grown. His grandfather had told him some old tales about men seeing the Devil hiding by the Stone or appearing in storms or blizzards. He had seen the half-devil–half-snake carved on the north side of the Stone and had for a time imagined the Monster had been roaming in the deep woods. His mother and father had laughed at him, then got angry with him. His Grandfather told the old stories and then said they were old rubbish. Even when one of his uncles had died in an accident near the Stone just before Midsummer they said the old stories were not true. And since Midsummer nothing had happened. Desperately relieved, Sam tried his hardest to forget the old legends and stories about the Stone.

But now he knew the truth. His fear had been right. The grown-ups were wrong. And the old book had said that as the shadow of the Stone grew longer, so the evil would grow. People would die. He would die. He would try again to tell his mother and father, Will and his friends.

He raced up through the dark silent woods of July where dark shadows hid the old mine shafts that led deep into the earth ... and the creatures, the monsters ... He was glad the woodmen who worked for the Duke of Blackdon, who owned the woods, were still busy chopping wood. He would not have dared walk through them alone. Not after reading the spell book. Anything could come creeping out of the deep shafts.

He paused for breath in a glade where the beeches and sycamores had been chopped down. It was cold up here. It was always colder than down in the town. The wind hissed in the leaves and ruffled a sea of blue scabious that Grandfather called devilroot. There was a lot growing this year. Petals from a tangle of wild roses that hid a mine shaft blew in the cold air. He thought of the shadows and moving Things deep underground that the old book had described, and he began to run.

The old Stone, the Bow Cross as some called it, watched and waited, black and clear against a thunder cloud where swifts wheeled like tiny flies. Sam ran for his life, past his Grandfather's farm, then down the other side of the hill to his own little farm. He arrived home, red in the face, and breathless with fear and the need to warn his parents.

'And just where do you think you've been all this time, Samuel Walton?' came his mother's voice as he stood in the doorway of the lonely farmhouse that was his home. Then, when she saw him, 'Oh, just look at you. Just look. You've been fighting. Mind those boots on that step, I only did it this afternoon. You've been messing with those boys down in Lambton again. Well, you can get yourself washed down at that pump. Then you can get yourself up to bed. There's no tea in this house for boys that fight. You get off upstairs and have a good think about it and say a prayer. I'm not having a son of mine who I'm trying to bring up decently fighting in the streets of Lambton with boys like John Mellor. Now go on. Up you go.'

Sam saw the glint in his mother's eye. He decided to go quietly. But he would have liked to have told her of the warning in the old spell book—and ask her how she knew he'd been fighting with John Mellor when she hadn't been there. He wisely kept quiet. He washed in the ice-cold water of the pump. Then he went up the narrow stairs. If he kept his mouth shut she might bring him some bread and milk at supper time. And he wanted time to think. Time to plan.

He folded up the patchwork quilt and lay on his bed. When they'd calmed down he'd talk to them about the danger. His parents and friends needed to be warned.

He'd had his bread and milk. But his mother would not allow him down. She was really angry with him for fighting in the

20

street. Now it was ten o'clock. The grandfather clock in the kitchen had struck to the darkening room. His mother and father were coming up to bed now.

He had been staring at the Stone on the hill near his Grandfather's farm. He remembered what it had said in the witch's book. He watched it blacken with the coming of night and clouds. Now he knew all about it. With a growing chill of fear, he knew it was alive and knew about him. The witch had been right. He dragged out his chamber pot from under the bed. It made a musical tinkle as he used it, and it drowned for a moment or two the dull rattle of a thunder shower on the roof and the moan of the wind round the chimney above him.

'Are you out of bed, Samuel?' came his mother's sharp voice from the other little bedroom. 'You're not staring at that Stone again? Not gaping at it? You're not starting that again, are you? I thought you'd stopped all that.'

'Bugger,' thought Sam. It was uncanny how his mother knew what he was thinking or doing or planning. 'No, mother,' he shouted, imitating the Wakes' ventriloquist and using the corner of his mouth with his fist over it to try and throw his voice to the pillow.

'You don't sound in bed to me. You're out!' She bustled in through the door in her long, white, cotton nightgown, rustling with annoyance.

'You are. You're staring at that old Stone again, worrying about its magic or some such nonsense.' She twitched at the quilt that was slumped over the end of the bed.

'Mother, I had to go to Dame Trot's today and I looked in an old book of her mother's and it said—'

'What were you doing there? And it's Mrs Trotter, or Widow Trotter to you, Samuel. The Lambton boys may choose to be disrespectful to old ladies but that's no cause for you to be. What were you doing?'

'John Mellor gave me a black eye and—' He knew he had said the wrong thing as soon as he had said it. His mother began a long lecture.

'I don't bring you up to brawl with John Mellor. And on market day too. You don't know who might have seen you. What will people think of me as a mother? And once and for all get this idea of magic out of your head and that Stone or

21

whatever. I'm sick of hearing it. We live in an age of steam trains now. All this talk of witches and magic—it's, well, it's heathen. Now get to sleep or I'll fetch your father and he'll bring his strap.'

Sam turned his face to the wall. He could see talking was useless. 'I'm only trying to help you and the family out of danger,' he muttered in a low voice.

'What has happened to our family and what will happen is God's will,' said his mother. 'Now, hush.'

Sam was silent. Well, he'd see his friends tomorrow and tell them there must have been something in the well.

'He's nearly twelve now, he shouldn't be filling his head with such old tales,' Sam heard his mother talking about him to his father. He shut his ears to her. A flicker of lightning danced round the old Stone. But there was no thunder. Counting the months to Hallowe'en on his fingers, one . . . two . . . three months . . . Sam fell into an uneasy sleep.

After midnight a thin crescent moon appeared in the sky between the thundery clouds, narrow and tilted like the drawing in the spell book. By two o'clock on that early morning of Tuesday, 24 July, the sky had cleared save for the thin silver eye of the moon. The Stone, long noticed by Sam and described by Dame Trot's witch mother, crouched in a nest of moonlit brambles and black shadows—shadows as black as those down the well that the boys had played near earlier. The thunder rain-wet green blackberries, and blossom were made silver by the slit eye of the moon. The black shadows shifted and swayed in the hiss and constant rustle around the Stone, for the Stone on the highest hill always attracted an ice-cold wind.

From the hills and moorland to the north of the Stone came a faint light, as dim as the starlight, a reflection from the far-distant midnight sun in lands far to the north and thousands of distant gaslamps in the streets of cities beyond the moors. This faint light lit up the carving on the north of the Stone, the half-devil–half-snake with its carved coils and circles. The ugly, wicked eyes looked out to the northern hills of the Dark Peak of Derbyshire. The eyes were black pools of

22

shadow hidden in black shadow from the other eye of the moon. A drifting white night cloud and a sudden slight shimmer in the faint northern light made the pools of darkness in the eye carving seem to move—and look eastwards towards the little farmhouse where Sam was now asleep.

Sam's Grandfather and Grandmother, his father's parents, lived close by the old Stone at Bow Cross Farm: the Stone had stood there long before the farm.

Just as the light from the northern hills seemed to shimmer faintly and the eyes on the Stone move, Sam's Grandfather awoke in a flurry of sheets and blankets. A long rumbling shudder was shaking the farmhouse from the cellars to the chimney pots, black against the white moon cloud.

'Eh dearie me. Eh dear me. Eh dear me. Dear me. What were that?' shouted the old man, half-awake, his nightcap slipping over his anxiously turning face.

'It were thy snoring, my little love,' said Grandmother sweetly and sleepily to the big old man. 'Or it were thy belly rumbling. I've told thee before not to eat tripe and vinegar at bedtime.'

'Eh, it weren't me snoring,' replied the old man, reaching down with a heaving grunt for the chamber pot to prove that he had been awake for another reason. But the old man was upset. Despite the blue square of moonlight from the window he wanted light.

'Light us the candle, Lucy. I'm all hot and bothered. I'm in a rate mucksweat.'

'Aye, I'm not surprised, seeing as tha's pulled all blankets and covers on top o' thee,' grumbled the old lady as she fumbled for the matches.

Once again the farmhouse shuddered as though something had moved deep in the earth. The glass vibrated and shook in the windows.

'Eh dear me, what were that?' said the old man, nearly dropping the chamber pot. A huge grotesque shadow of him bobbed in the golden candlelight against the pale sprays of forget-me-nots on the yellow bedroom wallpaper. The old man and shadow wobbled back between the sheets.

23

'It were either a train coming out of Blackdon Tunnel or a boggart coming to get thee and thy golden guineas,' said Grandmother irritably from her nest in the deep pillow. 'But seeing as t'dog isn't barking it'll be a train.' She yawned, her tired old eyes closing.

'My old dad used to frit me when I were a lad an' he used to tell me there were a giant worm lived down in earth, in mines, like, an' when it were dark you could hear it shaking the ground. He said one day it'd come out and crawl up to that old Stone in Top Pasture and get me. Aye, he did.'

'I wish it'd hurry up an' come, then,' muttered the old woman to her pillow.

'Eh?' said Grandfather, his hand cupped to his ear. A train came chugging up the valley far below.

'I said train's coming, Abel,' she shouted loudly. 'Tha's woke me up for nowt, Abel.' She sighed with fatigue. She was getting old. It had been wash-day. Looking after Grandfather and four grown-up sons was not easy.

She blew out the candle flame, pausing in her muttering. 'The last thing I want to hear after a long wesh-day is one o' thy father's daft old ghost tales. It were a train that woke thee. Them trains've been up and down this valley for ten year or more and still they wake thee. Thee and thy father's tales. He were drunk when he telled them daft tales.' She shook the feather pillow with its lace trim, then to make a hollow for her head again she thumped it with her first.

Grandfather jumped again. A feather from the bed set sail in the moonlight across the room. There was silence. But Grandfather lay breathing heavily. His father, seventy years ago, had told him some terrible old stories. He had been badly scared. He had been trying to forget them for seventy years ... He would admit to nobody, least of all to himself, that they still scared him. After a lifetime of farming and making a lot of gold, stories that were told him when King George was on the throne still scared him. They kept coming back into his mind. And now, when the memory of his childhood was as sharp as though it were yesterday, he remembered all the stories in grim detail. His own six sons, when they had been little, had just laughed at him when he tried to tell the stories to them by winter firesides.

24

'I dunna believe any of them old tales,' said the old man aloud. 'If there had been any of them things underground them navvies would have found them when they were digging Blackdon Tunnel for Midland Railway. Aye. That's right. Aye.'

That was a most comforting thought to the old man. He felt better at once. 'Give us a kiss, Lucy,' said the old man.

Grandmother snored gently. But in the faint light of the thin eye of the moon and the gentle summer stars her brown eyes gleamed faintly with amusement. Then she shut them. The feather descended gently to the sleeping old people. Again the farmhouse shook. This time neither of them heard it.

But something creeping in the shadows below their window heard and felt it.

A dark shadow moved under Sam's Grandparents' window. It moved towards the haystack. The glint of the curved moon was in its eyes and on its hairy face. It was a tramp. The tramp had not wanted to go to the big Lambton Union Workhouse. It had been a fine summer's evening until a heavy thunder shower had made him run for shelter into the woods to the east of the town.

The tramp had walked up the old road under the thick trees. He had spied on Grandfather's farm, watched the lights go out, and then dozed a little in the thick bracken. He had also drunk something from a small bottle. When the moon appeared the tramp went on the prowl. When he crept into the farmyard the dog had given a short sharp angry bark. But he stopped barking, for there was a long low rumble deep in the earth, and the dog backed into his kennel, growling softly and showing the whites of his eyes.

The tramp had been as startled by the sound as the dog and took a drink from his bottle. But when the dog did not come out of the kennel he decided to look round to see what he could find. He found a full pipe of tobacco left by Sam's Uncle Ted on the mounting block; he found the short curved hay knife with its cruel blade—that pleased him. It would sell for sixpence in Chesterfield. Then he pulled a handful of sweet new hay from the stack—and still the dog did not come out. Something had really scared it. The tramp heard another long deep movement deep in the earth and then a train far below in the valley.

Tissy, the farm cat, slunk by him, her tail pressed well between her legs. Something had scared her and Tissy was not a cat to be easily upset. She vanished silently to her nest in the hay.

The tramp had spent many years snooping round places. Never had he felt as uncomfortable as he did now in this moonlit yard with the watchful eye of the tilted moon and the silent dog and cat. He wanted to get out of the place. A cold wind blew, scattering tiny drops off the small unripe elderberries into the tramp's eyes. The wind hissed in the ash trees in the lane. Three taps from the tossing trees made the tramp freeze for a moment and then stare around. Christ Jesus. There on the top of the hill, the curved claw of the moon over his shoulder, was a figure in a cloak. The tramp blinked his rain-filled eyes and stood deathly still under the clattering ash twigs. His fingers moved round the small bottle in his pocket.

Only when the wind dropped and the trees were still did the tramp blink to clear his vision and realize it was no devil but an old stone standing on the hilltop. Sweat made grooves in the dirt on his moonlit face. He ran back into the dark black shadows of the woods. By the deserted road from Lambton to Chesterfield, haunted, so the old folk said— though the tramp did not know that—he found shelter in a cave that had once led down to a lead mine far below. He put down his bundle of hay and ate the crust of bread that Grandmother had thrown out for the birds. In the silver and black moonlit wood he thought he saw eyes as he chewed the bread. That farm cat must have followed him. Either that or it was a trick of the moonlight on the rain-wet leaves.

Behind him in the cave something moved. But above the hiss of the wind that had begun to stir in the moonlit woods, the tramp did not hear it.

High on its hill the Stone seemed to watch Sam's farm. The strange dim light from the north and the summer stars lit Sam's room. Everything in the room could be seen faintly.

There was the candlestick with its tin snuffer perched on the candle like a witch's hat, and on the folded quilt could just be seen the brown stain of strawberry Sam had taken from the garden last night. It all seemed familiar and safe.

The light seemed to fade. No longer could the Stone be seen. Sam began to toss and turn as though an unseen presence in the room was pulling at him. Sam was dreaming. He dreamed it was autumn, around the time of Hallowe'en. The sun was red and swollen. Just a few brilliant blood-red leaves clung to the bare trees. He could see the sun setting behind the Stone. Mists were rising. Sam was dreaming he was watching this from his little window. The fields were covered with the cold silver dew of autumn. As the sun vanished behind the Stone, a long shadow began slowly to reach out to Sam's farm and window. A rhythmic tapping reached Sam's ears. Then Sam saw it was no shadow that reached to him from the Stone. It was the long coiled body of a vast serpent, that same monster he had seen carved on the Stone and read about in the witch's spell book that very day. Now it was creeping out to get him.

Slowly, but with determination, the coils and tentacles of shadow reached out over the shining dew-wet fields. The fog and shadow slid and spilled into the little farmyard and began to writhe and reach up the wall under his window. Sam felt the touch of it on his throat, felt the choking grasp of its coils. He felt himself in the grip of ice-cold slimy feelers, piercing and cold, stinging yet as soft as a frosted cobweb. He tried to call out.

Sam's father had been awakened earlier by a deep rumble. He drowsily thought it must be one of the goods trains taking stone from the quarries at Dartford. The long heavy trains moved at night to keep out of the way of the daytime expresses. The countryside was getting a noisy place he thought. Then he heard Sam shout out. It was such a cry of fear, half-strangled, that he thought Sam was being attacked. He lit a candle and limped into Sam's room.

The tramp awoke in his cave. He vaguely remembered a dream where something had been scratching, knocking. Then

27

he started. Something was crawling about in the cave behind him. He felt ice-cold. Something must have been on his face, it felt wet and strange.

He rushed out of the cave, his bottle falling to the ground. He ran down the abandoned road, branches ripping at his face, his rags and tatters flying in the striped black and silver moon shadows. As he ran over the railway bridge a long goods train passed, chugging golden sparks to the silver ones of the stars.

On and on ran the tramp until he reached the great iron gates of Lambton Workhouse. He shook and rattled the gates until the grumbling night porter came. 'No vagrants after nightfall,' he growled at the tramp. Then as the moon shone on the man's face he saw he had a cut on his face. It was a curved cut, like the crescent moon in the sky, and blood was seeping from it in the moonlight.

Holding the candle high, Sam's father saw the covers had fallen off Sam. A rose, silvered by moonlight, tapped at the window. The room was full of the strong scent of the night-scented stocks his mother grew in old pots in the yard.

Sam clung to his father. In broken sentences he told him of the attack by the well and the warning in Dame Trot's mother's spell book.

'And I've known for a year or more yon Stone by me Grandfeyther's farm is magic. It killed me Uncle Edgar when he had his accident by the Stone when horse and cart ran over him and your leg. It would have killed you and me but we had to go to Sheffield to have your leg mended so we weren't here at Midsummer.'

It was true. His Uncle Edgar, his father's youngest brother, Grandfather's youngest son, had been killed in the quarry close by the Stone. The horse had seen something by the Stone and bolted, running over Edgar, and breaking his father's leg—which had nearly killed him.

'There's a curse on us this year because we live near the Stone,' said Sam.

His father's white teeth gleamed with amusement in the candlelight. 'Don't be daft, Sam. Dame Trot knows her

28

medicines and herbs. She's cured me a time or two, but nobody believes daft tales like that. I can remember her mother. She were daft in her head. What you read were just a daft old woman's tale. You'll soon be a man, Sam. You shouldna be listening to old wives' tales.'

Sam felt small, bewildered, and very frightened. 'But it'll get thee or me,' Sam tried again. 'Two more it'll kill. Uncle Edgar were the first. There's a curse on us this year.'

His father's dark eyes flashed with anger. His leg, broken six weeks ago, still pained him. Sam could see two deep lines in his cheek above his moustache that had not been there before. And he looked down on Sam with a worried frown. His father, Sam's Grandfather, had once told him that one of the Waltons had gone mad. Like all country people he feared madness.

He gently pushed Sam back down and roughly pulled the covers round him. He sat on the bed that creaked loudly. The moonlit rose tapped against the window and a cold wind made the candle flame jump. His father reached out and closed the window.

'Dunna wake thy mother,' he said as he limped away.

Sam lay still and scared and tried to plan. They must listen. Their lives were in danger. All of them. He wanted morning to come so he could tell his friends.

Something was very much wrong in one of the cottages to the north of the graveyard of All Saints' Church down in Lambton, where the moon-silvered spire cast a dark shadow over the cluster of cottages. The cottages were close by the graveyard where the graves made a silver and black chequer-board pattern and where Saltby's well lay hidden deep down.

In one of the cottages lived John Mellor and his mother. His father had been killed when he was a baby. They were very poor—very close to having to go to the workhouse and live there. But at this moment, John Mellor was standing in the torn and ragged shirt he used for a nightshirt, shouting with fear. His short, cropped reddish hair was wet with the sweat of fear from the striped pillow—there was no money for pillow-cases. He sat up in his narrow plank bed, scattering

29

the ragged blankets and old clothes he used to keep warm in bed. His mother rushed into the stuffy little room.

'Been having one of them dreams again, our John?' said she, a stub of candle flickering in a saucer. Ever since the time John Mellor had seen a monster carved on a Stone by Sam Walton's Grandfather's farm last April he had had nightmares. But what was in the nightmares he would tell nobody.

'I've not been dreaming,' snarled John Mellor at his mother. He was supposed to be the man in the cottage. Big lads like him did not have dreams, or see things swimming in deep mysterious wells.

'I've got bellyache,' he growled at her. That was part of the truth. 'I want to go to lav.' That was true as well.

'Well, our John, unlock t'door and get across the yard, then.'

'Me belly hurts too much to cross the yard, mam.' That was not true. John Mellor did not want to go out in the yard that was so close to the churchyard. Not after what he had seen earlier.

'Ye can manage to walk to petty door, our John.'

'I canna!' roared John. 'Can I use a pan or summat?'

'Don't talk daft, our John. And hush. Ye'll wake them next door.'

'Let me do it in a cup, mam.' It was hard to tell whether the dream or what he had seen in the well was really bothering him.

'Now, go on, our John. Were it a dream that frit thee?'

'There's nowt up wi' me but gut ache!' roared Mellor.

Mrs Mellor gave him a none too gentle shove in the direction of the back door. He raised his fists to her, then lowered them.

'Stand at door, mam, in case I fall.' She saw that for some reason he did not want to go out alone into the shadowy yard.

'I wish ye'd tell me, our John.'

'Shurrup, mam, wilt? It's me belly, I tell thee.'

Mrs Mellor watched him cross the yard. She held a tiny farthing candle in a saucer that twinkled like a lonely star. She heard the dry scuttle of rats. She sighed. Whatever was the matter with her John? He was the finest, biggest, strongest lad in Lambton for his age, even if he was the poorest.

'Pull t'string, John,' she called softly over the yard. The Duke of Blackdon who owned the cottages had had water closets put in a year ago after six men in the yard had died of fever.

John Mellor, meantime, sweating with fear, raced back over the yard. He half-hoped something had disturbed Will Saltby's sleep. That would show him. In the meantime he was saying nothing.

Sam awoke just after six o'clock on that morning of Tuesday, 24 July. He felt worried about everything—but glad it was the School Trip, so he could have a talk with his friends and even John Mellor, about the well and spell book. It was already very hot—the July sun was beating down on the roof and his little bedroom felt hot and stifling. He was glad to get up and go down to the kitchen where bacon was frying and the door was open to the morning.

His mother saw Sam's scared eyes, with the shadows of fatigue beneath them. 'What's the matter with you, Sam?' she asked as she gave him some bread and bacon. 'You look like something the cat's brought in. I hope you'll be all right for your trip. Do you want an egg? When you've eaten, get a clean collar and put on that new jacket. You're not going to Matlock looking like John Mellor or a tramp on his way to the workhouse. Don't tear at your bacon. There'll be plenty of the gentry on holiday in Matlock and you're not going like a rag and bone man. Do you want an egg or not?'

'Yes please. I've had a nightmare about yon old Stone up there, and in Dame—I mean—Widow Trot's book it said—'

'Don't start,' said his mother. 'We've had that Stone for breakfast, dinner, and tea and it's kept you awake at night. I'm beginning to think you're going soft in the head. Don't put your egg on the bread. Eat nicely like the young gentlemen staying at Matlock would.'

'To hell with Matlock,' thought Sam.

His father came in. 'He's not still going on about it, is he?'

31

said he as he limped over to the Toby jug on the mantelpiece. He counted out 3½d in pennies, halfpennies, and farthings and gave it to Sam. 'Buy thysen summat in Matlock,' said he.

The bacon seemed to go prickly and dry at the back of Sam's throat. His father looked so ill. Since his leg had been injured, he had not been able to work as much and money was shorter. His father looked tired. There were grey hairs showing in his hair. Sam took the money, tears brimming in his eyes. He knew why there was all this bad luck. If they'd listen, he could stop it.

'My leg hurts,' said his father. 'There's thunder brewing.'

'That's not all that's coming,' thought Sam. Then aloud he said, 'Can I call in at Grandfather's and get a penny or threepence for Matlock?'

'You'll be lucky,' muttered his mother to a brass candlestick she was sanding to a golden brilliance.

'Why is Grandfather so mean when he's got so much money?' asked Sam.

'Hush, Sam,' said his mother in a louder voice. 'You show respect and mind your betters and elders.' She banged the candlestick to loosen some wax. 'Now, off you go, Sam. Be a good boy. It'll be a fine trip to Matlock. There'll be many on the train who've never been on a train before from your class. Now, God bless. Have a good day.'

'Aye,' said his father. 'Just think. I never went to school let alone on a trip. Take these two scythe blades to thy Grandfather's on thy way up. Watch 'em. They're heavy. Keep changing hands.' Sam said goodbye. It was no good. They would not listen.

And all around him as he walked up the old road were eyes. Eyes that he could feel watching him. He had started to hate this road—now a rough lane. Grandfather had told him tales of coach crashes and devils, and when Grandfather had been Sam's age, they had made a new road far below in the valley, and this one with its strange mists, its sudden snowstorms, and accidents was abandoned.

In places the lane was sunken between the gritstone walls. In a clump of blue cranesbill a grass snake watched him, its black button eye unblinking. Sam was not in the least bit scared of snakes ... but this one reminded him of the monster on the Stone, and when it glided away you could see its long coils for a long time afterwards, wrapped round a motherdie stalk. It was hiding in the stones that hid the wreckage of a coach and horses that had crashed because the coachman had seen a ghost or the Devil, so Grandfather said.

Up and up the road, sweating in the heat, toiled Sam. The sun beat down, though it was only half-past seven. The scythe blades pulled on his arm. He saw a rat watching him from a hole in the wall where it had been basking in the sunlight. Its eyes glinted behind the spikes of a huge thistle that had grown up in front of the wall. He could feel the growing evil all around him. And they said it was all old wives' tales. Couldn't they feel it? There was a magpie watching him from the stubble of a hay field. One for sorrow ...

It was so hot. No birds sang now. The dew still glittered on the wild roses. Everything, the Stone, animals, were waiting and watching. Sam's heart beat wildly with fear and heat as he turned into the entrance at Bow Cross Farm. Little marble-size St. Swithin's apples lay on the ground and crunched under his boots. When the apples left on the trees above were ripe, he would be dead. And cold as the glittering dew and last night's rain came the thought that it might happen before Hallowe'en, before he could do anything.

Sam would have another go in a moment at making Grandfather listen. He would tell him what he had read in the old book. Of course Grandfather was very good at telling you the old stories and then promptly telling you they were rubbish. Sam did not realize the old man was trying to comfort himself. He watched Grandmother crossing the yard, carrying two pails of ice-cold spring water fastened to a wooden yoke across her shoulders. She was hot and irritable. The butter would not take this morning. It was warm even in the dairy.

'I'd get up and help thee, Lucy,' said Grandfather from the Windsor chair where he sat basking, eyes half-lidded against the sun. 'But if I took one o' thy buckets from thee tha'd lose thy balance and fall in muck.' Grandmother sniffed.

'I read an old book yesterday,' said Sam to his Grandfather. 'It were old Dame Trot's ma's spell book. It said there were a curse on yon owd Stone—'

'She were a mucky old bag—' began Grandfather loudly.

'Language, Abel!' snapped Grandmother from the dairy door.

'She were a silly owd 'ooman,' Grandfather corrected himself. 'When I were a lad, folks said she were a witch an' could see into the future. Aye, they did. I dunna believe in owd wives' tales and owd women's cackling (he looked slyly in Grandmother's direction). I dunna believe in any o' them tales. Never have.'

There was a snort of disbelief from the dairy. But Grandfather stretched luxuriously in the sun. It was warm. The sky was blue. His four 'boys'—Sam's uncles and all over twenty-one—were at work in the fields. Bees buzzed in the lavender and pinks in the stone flowerbeds. Tissy lay in a bed of catmint, rolling and purring and striking at passing bees. Grandfather saw all this and felt brave. And then Sam realized that Grandfather only told the old stories when Grandfather himself was scared on days of cloud and dark mists and howling winter winds and thunderstorms. It was no good talking to him this bright glaring morning. Well, he would soon see his friends.

'It's our school trip to Matlock. We're going by train and—'

'Eh, I mun go to privy,' said Grandfather, sensing Sam was after money. 'Raspberry pie allus gives me the runs.'

Sam sadly watched the old man trudge over the hot dung and lavender-smelling yard. The old man was undoing his trousers under his smock as he walked, for he wore a pair bought sixty years ago from a tailor in Chesterfield. They had many flaps instead of fly buttons. He grunted as he walked and struggled with the flaps and Sam smelled the hot scent of nettles as he brushed by them. Then the old man vanished into the privy with its fading honeysuckle and banged the door. A goose honked.

And neither Sam nor the old man saw the dry white eye of the moon in the west or the dark shadows in the morning sun round the Stone. And Sam sighed. Nobody listened to him. Nobody talked to him properly.

Grandfather returned, pulling up his trousers under his smock. It was clear Sam was not going to get any money or sense. 'I'm as constipated as our Nora's cat, mother. I'm hard,' said the old man to Grandmother.

'Aye. You're right. You're right hard. Hard as nails when it comes to giving a bit of silver to thy only grandson.' Then she said under her breath, 'Miserable old toad!' as she poured out Grandfather some prunes and golden juice from a jar.

'Eh?' said Grandfather.

'I said there's a toad down the well,' said Grandmother shortly.

Sam sighed. This was typical of his Grandmother and Grandfather or his mother and father. You could just not talk to them about important things.

Grandmother fished in her apron and gave Sam a silver threepenny bit.

'Where didst thou get thy threepenny joy, Lucy?' asked Grandfather, always very interested in Grandmother's money supply, fearing it may have come from his.

'I found it in the dairy,' said she. 'One o' lads have dropped it bringing in the cream.'

Grandfather removed his smock and began a long search in his waistcoat and was about to say it was his when Grandmother pushed Sam out. 'Have a good day, love,' she said.

As soon as Sam had gone, Grandfather said, 'Eh dear me.. Eh dear. I were just looking for a coin to give the lad for his trip out. I couldna find one. What could I do?'

'You could cut a halfpenny in two, my love,' said Grandmother tartly. 'Or tha could've gone to thy Fry's Cocoa tin in t'dresser drawer full o' shillings, or to yon cracked greasepot on top o' clock full o' half-crowns or thy old sock under—'

'Prunes are working, Lucy!' said the old man and fled.

Sam stood in the lane. His family were in great danger and they just would not listen. And Grandfather was the biggest fool of them all. He knew the old stories and yet he pretended they were not true. Like last year. He had been helping Grandfather with some hay and there had been a shower. They had sheltered under the pattering leaves of the giant sycamore by the gate. Suddenly, as the thunder rumbled, Grandfather had said, 'Me old dad said that on Hallowe'en you could see a long black worm creeping round yon Stone. Folks said it were t' Devil. When I were a lad this were main road to Chesterfield but folks were frit o' using it, there were so many accidents and folks saying they'd seen boggarts. Oh aye. Aye . . .' And the old man's eyes had darted to and fro as though scared. Then out had come the sun, the world was blue, silver, and green again and a rainbow had jumped out over the Stone.

'Tell us more,' Sam had urged. But the old man had shrugged his shoulders. 'They're daft old tales. They're nowt. I dunna believe 'em.' And he had stumped away to tell Ted his eldest son that he had told him it was going to rain and the hay was ruined and he'd known it would be all along.

Back in the present, Sam turned to stare at the Stone that had caused him so much fear and trouble. It was just a year now since a storm had destroyed the clump of oak trees that had kept it hidden for over five hundred years. That must have been the Devil and the Things getting ready for this year of 1883, thought Sam miserably. He thought unhappily of how he had at once got the feeling that the Stone had been watching him. He had begun to think the Stone somehow made things go wrong. He clenched his fists as he thought how right he had been. And how right he had been in thinking the monster carved on the Stone could be creeping around in the woods . . . waiting for him. And all they'd done was laugh at him, tell him not to be silly, and grow up. Not even when Uncle Edgar had been killed did they listen to the old legends and stories Sam had discovered. They had said it was all his imagination. How he had tried after Midsummer to believe that himself . . . Now all the fear was back. Because he was certain he was right—there had been something in the well, the spell book and the dream were warnings—it was much more frightening.

His Uncle Jack called from the yard. 'Hey up, Sam, lad. There's a killer tom cat about in them woods. Watch out. They'll eat owt in July.' He laughed loudly. Back in March, Sam had thought he had heard a monster in the woods. Everybody had laughed, particularly Jack. He was a big strong man, with a mass of dark hair and silly laughing lips. Sam turned away from him. It was fools like Jack that

36

stopped people taking the legends seriously. He'd see one day. And soon, by the way things were going.

Sam had to admit to himself. He was afraid. Afraid to go in the woods alone again. He stood in the deep old lane, deep in the shade of bracken, butterbur, and brambles. The scabious gleamed with dew. Behind him, in a deep blue funnel of sky between two beech trees, watched the dead eye of the crescent moon. He'd miss the trip. But he dare not go down the woods, with their caves and old mine shafts. Miserably he turned to look at the cause of his trouble, the Stone. It had turned blacker. He shivered. He had wanted to see Will today. He watched some hover flies on a yarrow flower, his mind empty with misery. He watched swifts flying low round the blackening Stone in the hot humid air.

Then the rim of the July sun flashed over the hill on which the Stone was. The old shady lane filled with a dazzle of silver and gold. As it did, the shadow of the Stone leaped towards him in a black line, darkening the flowers. The shadow was growing. It was now a month since Midsummer Day. The shadow touched him like a gloved hand. Half of his body was in the Stone's shadow. His hand, in shadow, began to tingle and go numb. He felt as if ice-cold water was running over him.

He raised his eyes in horror. He was being killed. He saw a flash of silent blue fire around the Stone. Then something caught the side of his head and bounced away. He cried out. But it was stupid Jack throwing the little St. Swithin apples at him.

'Come on, young 'un. Standing and dreaming about thy lady love. Thy Grandma says tha's going on a trip.' Jack began to trot down the steep old lane, his boots ringing and scraping on the half-overgrown stones of the old road. He was carrying a big basket of eggs for Blackdon Hall and a sack of dead rabbits. Sam could see a bloodstain on the sack as he thankfully followed Jack into the woods, walking a little way behind in the trail of blue pipe smoke.

'Carry this for us, then,' said Jack, giving Sam the sack. Sam held it with both hands. His arm throbbed where the shadow had touched it. The woods seemed a lighter place with Jack there. The gold patches of sunlight moved on the

37

tree trunks. But Sam noticed the few curled sycamore leaves on the road ... the very first of the falling leaves of autumn. He gave Jack the sack back as they reached the station. Now he would see Will.

'Have a good time, young 'un. Dunna take Fanny Gibbs down a cavern like I would've done at thy age!' Jack said, grinning and giving Sam a silver threepence. 'Buy her a lollipop instead!'

Sam thanked him coldly. He still hated him. Now to find Will and the others. He clattered down the wooden steps of the foot-bridge to Platform 2. His arm where the shadow had touched it ached dully with a sort of pins and needles feeling. All around him were signs and warnings that something would happen. Now where was Will?

Damnation and hell, he thought. He was early. The platform was empty except for Mrs Turner and Mrs Broomhead, who had come to see their Frank and Peter off on the train. Although they were not going themselves, the mothers had come to share the pleasure of this big day. Mrs Broomhead nursed a grizzling, hot, tiny baby, and a child of two and one of four clung to her skirts. She controlled the two younger children with a brush handle that she used as a walking stick. Sam watched them through the pink rambling rose that climbed over the foot-bridge. There was still dew on it. He nudged it to watch the drops of water fall on the platform. As he did so, the Stone seemed to send out invisible threads of power, for his arm tingled, and he felt a faint pain in the side of his head. He wished Will would come.

Clutching his arm he watched the two mothers adjusting their shawls and admiring a flower bed with V R made out of lobelia, snapdragons, and marigolds. Sam watched Mrs Broomhead push her little girl away with the brush handle. 'Them flowers is for lookin' at not touching, our Ivy.' Ivy's howls rose up in the hot air that seemed to throb with her cries, the smell of gas and tar and roses, and invisible warnings and messages. Sam clattered down the remaining steps of the bridge.

Mrs Broomhead, turning to look who had come down the steps, saw her Peter had climbed on the signal over the bridge. Mrs Broomhead thought herself a very respectable

38

lady and never swore in public. Instead she used a curious set of words very much like swearwords. 'Just you come down off there, our Peter, you bleaching little soda!' she screamed at her son. Sam stared in amazement, his shadow-touched hand tingling by his side. Mrs Broomhead charged angrily by Sam, nudging his arm roughly. God, it hurt. What had that Stone done to it?

'Mind thysen, then,' said she to Sam, as she tapped angrily up the foot-bridge steps to get Peter. There was the sound of ripping, tearing trouser cloth as Peter retreated from his advancing mother.

'Now you've torn your best breeches, you little sardine!' screamed the furious mother. 'And you're covered in bleaching soot. You little basket. Just thee wait. Just thee wait till I get thee home tonight. It'll serve thee right if Mester Middlemas wunna take thee to Matlock today. Tha looks like chimbley sweep.'

'And what are you staring at!' she glared at Sam. She eyed Sam in his new jacket. He was holding his arm.

'Dunna worry, lad. I'm not going to brush past and spoil thy new jacket. So tha can stop holding it. No wonder Walton's eggs are dear with thee wearing togs like that.' She grabbed an escaping Ivy.

Where, oh where was Will? He must see him.

'Kids are a bleeding menace,' said Mrs Turner, who did not share Mrs Broomhead's dislike of genuine swearing. 'They're torturin' you all day long.' She swiped at a pollen-laden bee that had emerged heat-crazed from a snapdragon and rested on her hand. It fell to the floor. 'And so are bleeding bees,' said she, crushing the bee with her boot.

At last, over the wooden bridge could be heard the sound of boots. At last, there was Will, in a new jacket and well-blacked boots, and behind him came Mellor in his patched breeches and worn waistcoat and very clean but ragged shirt. Behind them, appearing as if by magic came their headmaster, Marmaduke Middlemas, crow black, and with black trousers already edged with dust from the hot Station Road. His gold watch chain shimmered hotly.

'SILENCE!' he honked.

Then 'LINE,' he croaked. He believed that children under

thirteen needed one-word commands, like horses or dogs. And like horses and dogs with a harsh master, everybody under school-leaving age of thirteen feared him. Consequently there was much shuffling of boots on Platform 2.

Miss White, Sam and Will's teacher, appeared in a new white dress with minute red dots on it. Her eyes bulged with self-importance behind the gold wire glasses. Her nose shone in the heat.

'Look at Nelly White,' said Will, his first words to Sam as they shuffled about on the platform. 'That new dress makes 'er look as if 'ers got measles.' He pointed and mocked at the teacher.

'Will,' said Sam urgently, 'you know last night Mellor thought there was a monster in your well? Well, I've found summat out. Listen Will (Will was waving his finger at Miss White's agitated and bespotted bottom). You know I went to see Dame Trot? Well, she's got an old spell book of her ma's an' it says there are things under the ground that—'

'Please, sir, Mester Middlemas sir, can I go to lav before the train comes?' came the gruff rasping voice of Mellor three places behind.

Will bent double with more laughter and shook Sam's painful arm with glee. 'Mellor's still frit!' chortled Will. 'I bet he's been on privy all night.' A ripple of laughter passed down the platform, and Will and Tom clasped each other with merriment.

'Damn and blast,' thought Sam, clutching his shadow-touched arm. 'They're still making fun of Mellor.'

'Tha's daft, thee,' said Will, grinning at Sam and banging his back with a friendly tap that set Sam's body throbbing. 'Trot's a barmy old woman. She dries weeds and smokes 'em. They stink awful. Me mam plays hell about the stink.' Tom and Will laughed again. They were in party mood, ready to laugh at anything.

'SILENCE DOWN THE PLATFORM!' roared the headmaster. Then in a lower voice to Mr Percy Ashby, another teacher, he said, 'I will follow Mell-or into the urinal, Ashby. I expect Mell-or is used to using a hole in the earth like most people in Lambton do. I will instruct him how to use a Midland Railway urinal.'

40

Will and Tom were speechless with laughter.

'I'll try and talk to Mellor, if he's still as frightened as that,' thought Sam. He looked at Will and Tom. They looked as though they were going to be daft like this all day. He tried to move to where Mellor had been.

There was another ripple of excitement on the platform as Lady Selina Blackdon appeared. She was sister to the Duke of Blackdon and lived at Blackdon Hall and spent a lot of the family money on 'God's poor of Lambton'. She was paying for the trip to Matlock. Every penny. And the poor were going second class, not third class. An angel in a dream had told her that was what God wanted for the poor children of Lambton. She tapped down the foot-bridge, her little silver slippers clicking on the boards, her silk and muslin dress billowing about her and touching the ringlets of her faded gilt hair under a flower-filled hat. Her diamond ear-rings flashed in the heat, and the scent of lavender drifted down the platform to the children. Her maid held a parasol over her.

'How old is she?' whispered Jessie Smith to Fanny Gibbs.

'Hundred and nine,' hissed Fanny. 'Nobody does their hair like that these days.'

'What dear boys an' gels, aren't they?' Lady Selina cooed to Mrs Broomhead, who was too struck dumb to curtsy to her ladyship. Miss White, looking drab by the side of the fine silk of Lady Selina, made the children bow and curtsy to Lady Selina.

Middlemas emerged from the GENTLEMEN with Mellor following—red, sweating, and sulky. Sam began to move towards Mellor. Middlemas, seeing Lady Selina, became oily and glided towards her and made a great show of arranging groups on the platform. It gave Sam a chance to get away from Will. He was standing next to Mellor when the train steamed in.

'Dear children of the poor,' whispered Lady Selina, wreathed in hot steam from the train.

'Silence,' hooted Middlemas. 'Pray listen carefully. Many of you have never used a train before. Watch me carefully children, and I will tell you how to board a train ... You lift your right leg—thus ... Hold the door handle—so ... Then, PAUSE. Glance downwards to the platform edge to judge the

41

gap twixt carriage step and platform.' He looked round pompously at the excited restless children, his leg held up.

'He looks like a dog tiddling,' Will said to Tom softly, and they fell about laughing again. Sam heard them giggling softly.

Despite Middlemas's instructions, the screamings of Miss White, the bellowing of Mr Percy Ashby and angry porters, there was chaos when the children were allowed into the train. But Sam got his wish. He found he was in a carriage with John Mellor. Sam saw there was also Jessie Smith who sat next to him at school. She'd listen. There was also Connie Smith her cousin, but she was stupid, thought Sam. There was Fanny Gibbs—but all she thought about was John Mellor. No good talking to her, she only thought of boys. There was also Herbert Wildgoose in the carriage, one of Mellor's bullying victims. It could have been worse. He'd talk to Mellor and Jessie. Sam looked at them thoughtfully as porters, sweating heavily, shut them in their carriages. A whistle blew. A green flag waved and the train heaved, shuddered, and groaned—they were off!

Mothers waved frantically. Lady Selina waved less frantically. It had been hard work looking after God's poor. She thought of iced lemonade on the cool rose-scented terrace at Blackdon. She went.

The children were locked in the carriages. There was no corridor. At once Mellor began to fool around. He drummed on the red plush seats, causing soot and dust to fly. He flexed his muscles and told Jessie to feel his biceps. Then he thumped Herbert and the carriage seats in turn. He ignored Sam completely. The train went faster and faster, rocking from side to side. Sam looked at Mellor. There were beads of sweat on his forehead and top lip, and his eyes were wild. He is still frightened, thought Sam. Good. He looked at Jessie, her eyes bright as stars with the fun of everything. It was the first time in her eleven years she had been outside Lambton. She clutched an ancient purse of dirty rose-coloured silk where nestled six halfpennies: Jessie's parents were very poor. Jessie had never had so much money. She had cleaned the halfpennies with sand and vinegar till Queen Victoria's head shone. 'I'll talk to her soon,' thought Sam. Sam looked at Fanny—not without admiration. She was in white muslin.

Her long blonde hair was loose round her shoulders, and her red lips were parted in a smile of admiration for John Mellor.

The train gave a shriek and vanished deep into the earth into Blackdon Tunnel. Every child screamed loudly. There was only one tiny flickering oil lamp swinging from the roof of each carriage. Sam felt uneasy. He knew the tunnel went deep into the hills to avoid the estate of Blackdon Hall. He remembered what the book had said. Did these Things live in railway tunnels? He knew by the tingling in his arm that things were working against him ... Could something happen today? He thought he could hear a faint knocking above the sound of the rattling train wheels in the hot darkness of the tunnel.

In the flickering flame of the oil light, he could see Mellor was terrified—his face was twisted with fear. Again the sound of tapping came to their ears. For a moment both boys stared at each other: their eyes met, and for a short time they saw the shared fear of the other. 'Eh, John, what didst really see in that well last night?' said Sam, realizing his chance had come. For a second Mellor hesitated; he swayed towards Sam, licked his dry lips and looked away. Then looked back.

The train shot out of the tunnel into the fields before Crowley. Hot sun blazed in through the soot-smeared windows. 'Eeeh, look!' cried Jessie. 'Cows are paddling in the river.' And the moment was gone. Sam's answer from Mellor was a hefty wallop on his back. Mellor did not wish to be reminded of his moments of fear—not in front of girls. Sam would have to wait a bit longer.

'Pray be seated, Ashby,' said Middlemas, in the carriage next to Sam's, with the teachers. 'It is no good knocking on the walls to the children. We would expect these country-born and very ignorant children to scream when they went underground in a miracle of modern engineering.' He flicked a smut from his waistcoat. 'I shall get out at Crowley and discipline Samuel Walton and John Mellor.' He settled back against the red seat. Then, 'May God preserve us. Hark! That arch bumpkin Mellor is singing now ...'

And so he was. He was singing to hide his fear. He had

43

been disturbed by Sam talking about the well. As he sang he beat time on Sam's shadow-touched shoulder:

Sam, Sam, you're a mucky owd man,
Tha weshes thy face in a frying pan,
Tha combs thy hair wi' a donkey's tail,
And scratches thy belly wi' thy big toe nail.

Mellor's mean eyes narrowed as he looked at Fanny and Jessie to see if they thought that clever. They did. Encouraged and wanting to forget, Mellor sang again.

Mrs Walton sells fish
Three halfpence a dish.
Don't buy it! Don't buy it!
It stinks when you fry it!

Jessie smiled dazedly, but whether or not the deafening roar of Mellor's voice pleased her or the paddling cows it was hard to tell. Mellor thought she wanted more.

Ha ha ha, hee hee hee,
Elephant's nest in a rhubarb tree! yelled Mellor.

'Shurrup, John,' said Fanny, weak with laughter and admiration for him. 'Middlemas'll cane thee at next station!' She tossed her blonde hair with enjoyment.

'I'm not frit of Middlemas or owt else. Not like thee, Walton!' roared Mellor, beating Sam's painful arm. Mellor was feeling much better. Fanny's admiring smile was helping a lot. He began to dance in the space between the seats. He sang,

Percy Gibbs plays Church organ,
Their Jimmy plays a drum,
Fanny played a tambourine,
Till her father smacked her bum!

'Oh John,' said Jessie. The rising and falling of the telegraph poles slowed a little and the white blur on the railway bank became white patches of creamy meadowsweet and the train ground to a halt at Crowley Station. Middlemas's face appeared at the carriage window.

'John Mell-or, COME HERE,' boomed Middlemas. Mellor was marched away to the teachers' carriage. Sam turned with a sigh of relief and began to talk to Jessie.

44

Perhaps it was as well Sam could not see into the woods back home at that moment. Sam's Uncle Jack returned from Lambton, then, whistling, went in the woods with an axe over his shoulder. He walked into the woods and stopped at a clearing where some ash poles were growing, near a mine shaft and just opposite where the tramp had slept in the cave.

Jack whistled as he began to chop the young ash trees for fencing. The air was hot and heavy. He was soon sweating heavily and had to remove his shirt. A swarm of huge flies at once swarmed round him, seemingly coming from the entrance to the cave. Jack felt in his cords for his clay pipe and lit it, sitting on a rock. He hoped the smoke would clear the flies.

Jack was certainly not an imaginative man but something made him turn and look. He stared around. There must be something in that cave, he thought, to attract all those flies. Something old and rotten. How still it was. The woods were absolutely still. Then he noticed some huge curved marks in the soft leaf mould. It looked as though some big animal had been crawling about. It must be the Duke's coach that's made them deep marks, thought Jack. He knew the old Duke of Blackdon and Lady Selina sometimes were driven here in their coach to look at the fine view of Lambton far below in the valley.

On a rock Jack saw some strange swirls and markings. He puffed on his pipe. Duke's coach must have scraped against the rock, he thought. He got up. Then the only sound in the woods was the sound of Jack's axe and the buzz of flies. Jack felled his final tree—a sturdy young ash sapling. It fell across a mine shaft and stones fell into the deep hole for a hundred feet. Jack could hear the stones falling for a long while afterwards. He looked over the edge of the old shaft—he knew the danger of these old shafts. It was almost as if something was moving stones deep in the old mine. But that was impossible. The mines had not been worked for fifty years or more.

For a reason he could not explain, Jack was glad to get back to the farm. His father, Sam's Grandfather, was sitting in the farmyard, avoiding Grandmother and feeling the heat. His smock hung limply on him. 'Tha's not fetched much wood, our Jack,' said the old man. 'When I were thy age I could fell a quarter acre in a morning. I pay Duke o' Blackdon a tidy sum of gold to chop in them woods.'

Jack's dark eyes flickered in anger. 'I dunna know why tha won't let us get stone off them big piles of stone in the lane to mend walls with, instead of mucking about with fencing,' said Jack irritably.

Grandfather's pale eyes bulged with annoyance. 'You're not touching them stone piles, our Jack. Dost hear? They've been in lane since me old dad's time when this were main Chesterfield road. When folks came up this road they used to bring a stone with them an' put it over some old mines. Folks said they were keeping boggarts from gettin' out. Them piles cover old shafts. You dunna know what's under them. An' them stone piles helped folks to find their way in snow or moonlight. They used to say on moonlit nights you could—'

Jack made a rude noise in his throat. He rolled his eyes at his brother Jo who was polishing harness, sweat running on to the leather. 'He's daft, him,' said Jack, jerking his thumb at his father. 'As he gets older he gets dafter. Bloody old tales about devils and boggarts. Nobody believes owt like that these days.'

The train steamed slowly out of Crowley. Sam began to tell Jessie, in a low voice, about his fears, the spell book, the curse of the Stone ... and the Things that the book said crawled deep in the mines, tunnels, and caves.

Mellor, in the teachers' carriage, was telling a story too. About Sam.

'I will not discipline you, John Mellor, on this day of joy. Indeed no. Kindly sit still,' Middlemas was saying. 'Observe the red, white, and blue herbaceous plants the station master of Crowley has planted to honour our dear Queen Victoria. She will soon have reigned for fifty years. Ponder on that, instead of singing your vulgar songs, boy.'

John Mellor crushed a heat-crazed wasp with his boot and scowled. 'Take off that face, John Mellor,' snapped Miss White. 'We shall have no mardy mouths on the Midland Railway.'

'It's Sammy Walton, if you please, sir,' growled Mellor. 'He asked me to sing because he said he were frit in tunnel. He gave me a penny to sing and I did. I haven't any money to spend at Matlock. Me mam never gives me any.'

'Silence, Mell-or,' hooted Middlemas. 'I will see Walton at the next station. I will have no carolling in carriages. Indeed not.' He took out a silver sixpence. 'Dear Lady Selina said I was to give the poorest boy this,' said he. He gave it grandly to the smiling Mellor.

At Dartford Dale Station Middlemas got out again.

'—and I know that Stone and the Things carved on it will get me soon, even some folk in Lambton. It won't just be me,' Sam was whispering to Jessie. She looked at Sam, her eyes round with the thrill of it all. She had money in the silk purse, she was on a railway train, and she was sitting next to Sam Walton who had been telling her a right frightening tale, his big, wide, blue eyes staring into hers, and he had kept running his fingers through his hair as he told her his secret. Jessie's eyes shone.

'You will travel with the teachers, Walton!' honked Middlemas, flinging the door open. Mellor got back in the carriage grinning. Sam got out.

'I won't tell anyone thy secret,' whispered Jessie as Sam got up. Sam felt cross. That's not what he wanted at all. He followed Middlemas into the teachers' carriage, and the train rocked on to Matlock, the station before Matlock Bath where they were going to get off.

Sam watched Middlemas fidgeting. He was frowning. He turned to Miss White. 'When we were in the tunnel, Miss White, I thought I heard a tapping under the carriage. I hope there are no screws or rivets loose. One hears so many tales about accidents on the railroad. I was quite afraid in Blackdon Tunnel. There have been many mysterious accidents in it.'

Sam listened with alarm. Could anything happen in the tunnel on the way back? The Stone had shown him that morning that its power was growing. The more he thought about it, the more worried he became. Something could happen when they were in the tunnel. Dare he ask Middlemas about the strange happenings in the tunnel?

47

He cleared his throat. It was worth a try.

'Please sir, Mester Middlemas sir—' he began. But Sam had reckoned without Mellor. Mellor had returned to the carriage full of his own importance: Fanny thought him daring and he was sixpence better off. He wanted more fun to take his mind off things again.

'Us gets out here,' said Mellor as the train groaned to a halt at Matlock. He waved to a porter to let them out. Out got Fanny, Jessie, Herbert, and Connie, failing to see that this was Matlock and not Matlock Bath. Mellor watched them go and line up by the ticket barrier as they had been told. The train started.

Sam, asking his question in the teachers' carriage, heard Mellor shouting.

'Mester Middlemas, sir, sir, SIR, Fanny, Jessie, an' 'Erbert, they've gorroff at wrong station, sir, I telled them not to, but they wouldn't listen . . . '

Sam saw Middlemas explode from his seat and dangerously open the window very wide. He stuck out his head.

'Stay where you are, you purblind nitwits,' yelled the enraged man.

'Watch out Mester Middlemas,' roared Mellor—Middlemas withdrew his head and narrowly missed banging it on the wall of a tunnel that the train was now sliding into. Sam saw Middlemas turn colour from red to swollen enraged purple. He could not talk to him now.

At Matlock Bath the station master telegraphed to Matlock and Middlemas arranged that Jessie and company would come on the next train in forty minutes' time. The station master also complained that the seat in Will's carriage had been ripped. 'Who has punctured the plush?' spluttered Middlemas, shaking Will as a terrier shakes a rat. 'Was it you, William Saltby? I am waiting.'

'No, sir, please, Mester Middlemas, sir, the plush was punctured when us got in at Lambton. Honest, Mester Middlemas, sir, it were.' Will stared up at Middlemas. Will had a way of looking at grown-ups that made them believe anything. Sam wished Will would help him—Will could get anybody to believe anything. He watched Middlemas put Will down and watched him and Tom

Wilson laughing behind their hands at Middlemas.

'You will all enjoy yourselves,' commanded Middlemas to them all. 'You will perambulate Matlock Bath, survey the scenery and many sights, and you will all assemble by the fishpond at the stroke of eleven precisely. Then we will all go to the High Tor Grotto, a crystallized cavern in Matlock Dale.'

The children skipped away, glad to be free and see the wonders of a holiday town. Only Sam was not free. He would stay by Mellor and get the truth about last night. Before it was too late . . .

'Please, sir, Mester Middlemas, sir, I'll wait for Fanny and the others, while you an' Mester Ashby an' Miss White gerroff an' see the sights and enjoy yourselves,' whined Mellor to the teachers.

'What a helpful boy you are today, Mell-or,' beamed Middlemas.

'Here is a penny for a GOOD boy,' said Miss White. Then the teachers walked away, with Miss White's sunshade tilted to the blazing sun. Mellor watched them go grinning.

'I'm not waiting,' said Mellor to Sam. 'You are.' For once Sam let Mellor bully him. He must talk to him. Lives depended on it.

'Wait there,' ordered Mellor. Sam did as he was told. Mellor rushed off to the nearest ale house: he looked old for his age, more like an apprentice in his old clothes. He had no difficulty in obtaining a cool pint of Burton Ale. Then he returned to the station and Sam.

'Tha can come with me,' said Mellor. Sam could smell the beer on his breath.

'We're supposed to wait here,' said Sam. He wanted to talk more to Jessie.

'Please thysen,' said Mellor shortly. 'But while tha's wait-ing, go and wesh this in station drinking fountain.' He gave Sam a small green bottle that he had found in the gutter. Once more Sam allowed himself to be bullied by Mellor—he hated him, but he needed his help. So he went over to the fountain and washed out the little bottle for Mellor. When he got back he saw Mellor sitting on the kerb, drinking from a white pot mug.

Mellor snatched the bottle, then drank deeply from the pot mug. He gave a belch, then wiped the froth from the beer on the cuff of his jacket. 'Thee have a drink,' he said to Sam. 'Go on.' Sam took a long drink of the amber ale. It tasted cool and good.

'That'll put hairs on thy chest, Walton,' said Mellor. He grinned at Sam in a fairly friendly way. Good, thought Sam. Any minute now.

'Thee wait here,' said Mellor suddenly. Once again Sam allowed himself to be bullied. He sat on the low hot wall. It felt hot to his legs. The tree shadows were hot, dark and still. His arm ached. Now he was certain of the evil powers of the Stone he must tell people—even if it spoiled his day out. In the meantime he tried to think of other things. He looked at the fine carriages bringing the ladies and gentlemen to the station. Two ladies in swishing pale blue silk dresses walked towards him, their dresses raising small clouds of white dust on the cobbles. Their parasols were tilted to the brassy sun. Sam smelled the fragrance of violets. In front of them came a boy with their luggage on a barrow. He made a face at Sam.

'That boy sitting there reminds one of the peasant boys one sees in East Prussia, Gertrude,' said one of the women in a loud voice. 'Those large, bewildered, blue eyes, that thatch of golden hair, and the sun-browned skin.' Both ladies stared at Sam. Sam blushed under his tan from haymaking. His mother had always told him that ladies and gentlemen never stared at people. He turned away to stare over to the hills towards home.

Away over the hills of home was a dark stain in the sky— like dirty water spilled on a painting. In this stain of dirty cloud, like water, there was a whitish cloud with a furry underbelly—for all the world like a monster swimming in a pool of water. It seemed to grow as Sam stared, and the cloud seemed to turn into a hand that pointed at him. He blinked for a moment and saw a dot of blue fire like he had seen round the Stone earlier in the day. Once again he knew. He knew, from the dark midsummer wooded hills with their hot walls, the Stone was reaching out again to him. It had touched him once today. It would keep on reaching out to him until he was dead.

'Shift thy great backside,' said Mellor. He was back. He waved a bottle at Sam. 'There's gin in there, lad. I'm going to have a good time, I am.' More to the point he was going to forget his fears and dreams. They heard a train steam into the station. Fanny, Connie, Jessie, and Herbert appeared.

'Hey up, there's right bother,' said Mellor. 'Middlemas's gone to borrow a cane from school in Matlock an' he's going to cane thee all in Station Yard, lasses an' all.' Tears at once filled Jessie's eyes. Herbert's face went white. But Fanny was made of sterner stuff.

'He's not.' She hit Mellor. He hit her back. It seemed to please them both and they set off. Sam whispered to Jessie what Middlemas had really said and this cheered her up.

Sam followed Mellor closely through the streets of Matlock Bath. Mellor kept sipping the gin. They all stared in shop windows, their mouths round O's of wonder. They stared at carriages, horses, waggonettes, four-in-hands and up to the white cliffs of limestone under the hot blue sky. Sam relaxed a little. He could not see the cloud from here. Fanny bought a china cat and a bottle of fizzing lemon-flavoured Matlock mineral water. Jessie bought a hot pie from a pie man and thought she had never tasted anything so delicious. Mellor told her it was made from stray dogs when she had finished it.

Sam watched for the cloud from the Stone. Had it gone? Just another warning? Or was he being watched even in Matlock?

They climbed some hot dusty steps. They were going to visit UNTAMED WILD ANIMALS IN CAGES—LADIES AND GENTLEMEN 6d.—WORKING PEOPLE 3d.—CHILDREN 1d.&½d. They queued. Now they had climbed up the hill, Sam could see the cloud again. Something was going to happen to him. He turned to Jessie who was fumbling in her battered purse for a ½d. Sam wanted to show her the menacing cloud.

'Hey up!' roared Mellor, his voice loud with drink. 'Look at Jessie's little pink purse. She's made it from a pair of her mam's bloomers. What's that brown mark, Jess?'

'Shurrup, John,' giggled Fanny admiringly. 'Folks are staring.'

'I dunna care,' said Mellor swaggering. And he didn't. He felt better. The dream was forgotten. Nobody had asked him

51

since Lambton about the well: that was being forgotten he hoped. He poked at the animals in their hot little cages. He made faces at a threadbare monkey, ill with the heat of its cage.

'Fleabitten fly-be-night!' said he. Fanny shook her blonde hair with laughter. John was pleased, but Sam was hot and depressed. When could he tell them all, and how? Down the steps they went. And the watching, warning cloud had grown again.

They visited a petrifying well where dripping water slowly turned objects to stone. There, amidst the boots, cups, books, and beads somebody had put a dead snake and it was being turned into stone. Sam's heart missed a beat. The carving on the Stone was a bit like that. Sam turned and saw a look of fear on Mellor's face. Mellor quickly turned away. He gave Jessie's bottom a hard nip to take his mind off it.

Tired and hot they were all lined up by the goldfish pond and marched away by Middlemas, with Mr Ashby in the middle of the two classes and Miss White behind. Sam kicked the white dust irritably. Now you could see the cloud from down in the valley. The milky cloud had thickened. It was now a hot gold: a thick arm of cloud with a cauliflower head—threatening him.

They crossed the wooden bridge over the Derwent. They queued up to go into the HIGH TOR GROTTO, a treat paid for by Lady Selina. Mellor snatched Jessie's bag and dangled it over the water. It was empty. Jessie had spent her halfpennies on pop, a tin thimble with TO A MOTHER FROM MATLOCK BATH written in tiny letters, the pie, and the zoo visit. She fingered the thimble in her pocket; she thought it was very beautiful.

Fanny tickled John under the arm. The purse fell. Jessie let out a cry and kicked Mellor. But her boots were old and worn and he laughed at her. 'It were only owd rubbish, anyway,' said Fanny. 'No good for owt.' She tossed her own imitation one of gold net on its chain. They watched Jessie's purse float by a patch of foamy pink valerian, saw a trout snap at it, then it was gone.

'You're a right pair of swine,' said Sam to Mellor and Fanny. Mellor raised his big fists. 'Say that again, Walton,' said Mellor. His breath stank of gin. Sam turned away in disgust; he would never have spent the day with John Mellor and Fanny usually, but today he must find things out. He could see Will and Tom laughing away, having a good time.

Sam half-expected trouble in the caves ... none came. Perhaps they were too far away from the caves in Lambton. He noticed Mellor did not like it in the caves either, but he kept trying to kiss Fanny behind the stalagtites.

Going out was like walking into an oven. The river looked like molten lead and smelled of mud and meadowsweet. The cloud had grown. It seemed to be pushing down hot air. Even the swallows flew at head height. The fist of the cloud was growing fast. Sam's belly turned over and over. There would be a storm. It was in storms that the evil became powerful. It had been in a storm last summer when the trees near the Stone had been struck away so the Stone could begin its evil work. It had been in a thunderstorm in March when he had thought he heard the monster in the woods. It had been in a thunder shower that he had thought, back in April, he had heard Something under his bedroom window. Many of the old stories that Grandfather told happened in storms ...

They marched under the cloud in the white dust to Matlock. Sam's arm throbbed. The cloud grew higher and higher. As they approached Matlock, a water cart passed, sprinkling water on the dust, and the smell of wet dust filled their nostrils. A hot wind began to stir in the trees. It raised little spirals of the dust.

'They call these little swirls of dust "dust devils" in America. They presage a storm,' Sam heard Percy Ashby telling his class.

To Sam's dust-filled tired eyes the cloud now looked like a huge bronze model of the twisted Stone back in Grandfather's top pasture. At last they were in a park and being lined up for cake and milk fetched from the vicarage. They all collapsed on the hot prickly grass.

'Now then Fanny,' Sam heard Tom Wilson saying. 'Is John Mellor holding thy hand because he loves thee or is he still frit o' that monster he says lives down Saltby's well?'

Everybody laughed, except Sam. It was no good now. Mellor would not talk now. He wanted to cry out 'It's true,' but he knew they would all laugh the more. Will rolled over and over in some fragrant white clover, gurgling, pretending to be the monster in the well. Fanny buried her head in the grass and tried not to laugh.

'Sit up, Frances Gibbs,' said Miss White, who had appeared with the monitors, carrying big white jugs of cold milk from the vicarage. There were plates of plum cake too, brought by maids. She stared at Fanny angrily.

'Have you ants in your pants, child? No? Then please do NOT roll in the grass with your legs to the heavens. It is most unladylike.'

They were given the cake and milk, all paid for by Lady Selina. Sam watched Jessie wipe her finger in the bottom of the mug to get at the last grains of sugar, and he did the same.

Under the growing cloud a piano was wheeled out on squealing castors. Country dancing was organized. Sam, nursing his shadow-touched arm, said he felt sick. As the cloud grew the pain seemed to get worse. He was told to sit under a lime tree and watch. He saw the cloud was now like a bronze monster. It now had ugly purple tints and the milky white pool at the bottom of the cloud had turned black. He thought he saw the flashes of silent blue fire again. He shuffled his boots in the golden, dead lime flowers. He watched Miss White playing the piano. Now and again her arm would snap out like a crab's pincer and grasp a passing child that was not dancing how she wanted. Sam saw her catch Mellor's flying waistcoat and shake him while her left hand still played. The sky darkened. A robin that had been singing stopped.

'Can us play tut ball, now, please, Mester Middlemas, sir?' Sam heard Mellor whining.

'I know of no such game,' said Middlemas. 'Now, perhaps a game of ROUNDERS.' Mellor scratched his short hair. 'Tut ball' was the Lambton word for rounders.

Hotter and hotter grew the molten sun. Heat seemed to rain down. The heat stifled the sound of the horses, carriages, and carts. A loud scream tore the sullen air. It was Fanny Gibbs running over to Miss White.

'Miss White, Miss White, Miss White, I HAVE got ants in me pants, I have.'

54

'Don't be impertinent child,' spat Miss White. She thought Fanny was trying to be funny.

'But I HAVE, Miss!' screamed Fanny. 'I'm in a rate mucksweat.'

'Come over to the tree where Samuel Walton is,' hissed Miss White. 'And ladies do NOT, I repeat, do NOT discuss sweat on summer afternoons. Stand still, child! You are like a whirligig.'

'Miss, they're everywhere,' writhed Fanny.

'Don't be so vulgar, child,' snapped Miss White. But at that moment a stream of servants and maids approached from the vicarage with a picnic. Miss White gave the sobbing, scratching Fanny to a maid who took her away to the vicarage. And Sam heard a deep rumble of sound that seemed to come from deep in the earth from Lambton.

The picnic was spread. Nobody cared about the ugly cloud twisting in the sky, for it still had not swallowed the sun. And even Sam had to stare at the picnic; Lady Selina had done God's poor of Lambton proud. Strawberries, cream, slices and slices of ham, tongue, bread with its butter melting in golden pools, hard-boiled eggs, radishes, plum cakes, seed cakes, pink and yellow layer cakes, bowls of melting jelly, raspberry tartlets, Bakewell tarts, jam tarts ... The children stared. Many were only used to bread and bacon. Some not that.

They ate. Sam ate. All quarrels were forgotten. Even Sam forgot the spreading dragonlike cloud and no longer felt the gentle shaking of the earth from time to time. Laughter and the rattle of spoons drowned it. A copper tea urn, big and golden and brassy as the sun itself with sweet, fragrant, piping hot, finest Darjeeling tea, filled a hundred pot mugs.

Despite the heat Middlemas arranged games. Sam joined in a sack race. The picnic had made him feel better. They lined up. He got in a sack but he found his shadow-touched hand was too weak to grasp the sack. He had to use one hand. Miss White smacked Dolly Cresswell's wrist next to him. 'Withdraw your finger from your nose at once, Dolly. Picking your nose in a sack is most unbecoming to a young lady.'

They set off. Sam had seen that Mellor kept sipping from

the green bottle and he saw that Mellor could not hold his sack properly either. Mellor was dizzy and kept falling. His face was twisted in rage. He hated making a fool of himself.

'I beseech you, John Mellor, do not twist your face in such an unlovely way. Should the wind change direction we shall be stuck with your face like that!'

The teachers laughed at Middlemas's joke. Mellor fell over. He lay on his back and saw the ugly cloud. He was overcome with panic. It reminded him of his dream and the well. He went pale. Then his belt tore at the sack.

'Jesus Christ help me!' he said aloud.

'Did you blaspheme, Mellor?' honked Middlemas. 'Even on this HAPPY day I will not tolerate blasphemy. Pray go and swill your evil tongue in the waters of yonder drinking fountain.' He pointed dramatically.

'I have taught these country children for ten years and still they take our beloved Lord's name in vain,' said Middlemas to Miss White. 'They still do not understand the use of words in prayer!'

As Middlemas pointed to the fountain, a finger of cloud covered the sun. The earth shook gently. Heavy raindrops began to fall. It was as though a hidden hand had given the signal for something to begin. 'It will have to be the early train, Nelly,' said Middlemas to Miss White, forgetting his dignity for a moment.

Fanny Gibbs giggled. The sexton of the church ran on to the darkening field and began to push away the piano. A vicious streak of vivid blue lightning ripped open the great cloud's middle. The cloud opened—the rain began to pour down. The earth shook as though something moved it from beneath, then the thunder crashed.

'To the station NOW!' honked Middlemas wildly. 'Through yonder gate, turn left for the bridge, then turn—'

Again the blue fire ripped at the cloud and the earth shook. Sam saw it was the same violent blue and purple lightning that had struck the trees near the Stone last year. Then Sam felt something else. Each flash of lightning sent a tingling pain down the arm that had been in the shadow of the Stone that morning. It was as though the Stone and the storm were working together.

56

They all ran. Some whooped and laughed. Will and Tom shouted in excitement. Some girls screamed. 'SILENCE IN THE STORM!' roared Middlemas, but his words were lost in earth-shaking thunder.

Mellor dragged Fanny Gibbs into a shop doorway. He didn't want to be alone. The gas was lit in the shop, for it was becoming as dark as night. Jessie blindly followed Mellor and Fanny, but Mellor roughly shoved her out into the deluge. Jessie tottered off.

'Who dost love best, him or me?' growled Mellor, pointing to Tom Wilson, a shadowy form in the cloudburst.

'Thee,' said Fanny.

'Give us a kiss, then,' said Mellor. Fanny obligingly turned her rain-wet cheek. She lovingly stroked the blue china cat she'd bought with her money as he kissed her. Then they splashed on through Crown Square, now a lake, reflecting the fearsome lightning. A long line of screaming girls were running over the bridge. Fanny and John were the last to gain the shelter of the station.

'Why did you dally in the downpour?' gasped Miss White angrily. Her dress hung in heavy grey folds and the spots had faded. Her parasol resembled a collapsed dandelion clock.

'Sam Walton legged me up an' I fell an' twisted me foot,' lied Mellor.

Sam was dreading the journey back. Even if they got safely back, which he doubted, he wondered what had happened at home. Even the station was a place in a nightmare. The gas was lit, but huge spreading puddles reflected the lightning. Hail and rain thundered on the roof and the station shook with thunder and trains. A howling wind blew smoke and sparks and rain round the children.

It was too much for Sam. He asked to go to the lavatory. Middlemas did not even answer, but waved him away with a wave of his hand. The lavatories were at the end of the platform and were flooded. Ankle-deep in storm water, Sam found one that could be used. Rain thundered on the roof. Each flicker of lightning made his arm tingle. When he had finished he touched the gleaming brass knob.

At once there was a crack of thunder and lightning together and Sam felt as if his arm had been struck with a sledge-hammer. He was flung to the floor. He was trapped.

'Please, sir, Mester Middlemas, sir, can I go to lav?' whispered Frank Turner. He had had several mugs of hot sweet tea and much cake.

'Why?' demanded Middlemas irritably. He was gleaming wet like a burnished crow and his face was chalk blue in the lightning.

'It's coming,' said Frank timidly.

'I did not ask for bodily details,' barked Middlemas. Frank went but was soon back.

'Sir, please, there's only one lav working an' Sammy Walton's locked in it.'

'What nonsense you do talk, boy,' shouted Middlemas. His temper was rising fast. He was wet. His head ached and he felt tense and miserable. He shook his sticky wet shoulders crossly. He followed Frank and beat on the wooden door of the lavatory, the thunder echoing his bangs.

'Come out, Walton. Come out, I say. Lady Selina does not provide payment for picnics so that you can skulk in a water closet on Matlock Station.'

Painfully, with his good hand, Sam turned the brass knob. He walked back towards the enraged headmaster. Every flash sent quivers of pain all over Sam's body. Middlemas, thoroughly angry, took both boys by the scruff of their necks. Poor Frank was in agony. He was nearly bursting.

'Nobody will use the lavatory AT ALL,' roared Middlemas. He wagged his finger as he stood in a pool of water and golden gaslight, the lightning gleaming silver on his wet black suit. Lightning seemed part of his watch chain.

There was a chaotic rush for carriages. Jessie dared to leap in front of Mellor in a flurry of pinafore.

'Thy bloomers are as mucky as thee,' said Mellor, pushing her in a seat. Mellor was terrified. The storm reminded him of one of his dreams. Frank sat doubled up with pain.

Mellor slumped in a corner of the carriage, white and pale. He was shivering with wet, cold, fear, and drink. He kept sipping his gin, his eyes darting from left to right, as though he expected something to come in from the storm to get him. Sam looked at him. He reminded him of Grandfather when he told one of the old stories.

58

Darker and darker became the sky. Nobody spoke. Fanny sucked a stick of red and white rock, her white teeth gleaming in the gloom. Blackdon Tunnel was approaching. Sam and Mellor noticed the porters had not put an oil lamp in their carriage. Then they were deep underground. They could see nothing. Sparks from the engine floated by. The whole tunnel seemed to shake. Water spouts splashed against the windows from deep underground springs. Once Sam thought he heard falling rocks and a tapping.

Mellor kept lighting his pipe. He just wanted light. 'Me baccy's wet,' he muttered to Fanny. His shaking hand struck match after match. The train gave a lurch as though some hidden hand had pushed it. Jessie gave a scream. A wind rocked the train.

It was some time before they realized they were out of the tunnel and the dim grey outside the window was Lambton underneath a vast black cloud. A mile out of Lambton the railway passed over a graceful three-arch bridge that took the railway over the driveway, three miles long, to Blackdon Hall. As the train passed over the bridge the driver saw, by the light of the flickering and flashing lightning, that the drive had been turned into a torrent of water.

In the foaming black flood, he saw, or thought he saw, a long, black tree trunk being carried along in the black foaming floodwater. It seemed to twist and turn as though alive. The floodwater looked powerful and as the driver stared, for he had slowed the train down ready for the station, the black trunk seemed to rear up.

Then the driver was thrown violently against the fireman and they both fell against the controls. With a crash of tons of metal and the hiss of escaping steam the train left the rails. Thunder drowned the noise of the crash.

The news reached Lambton: there had been a crash. Grief-stricken parents grabbed shawls and ran down the drive. Some said all the children were dead. Lil Gosling, two shawls over her head, staggered in the torrents to Lizzy Gomersall.

'Hast heard, Lizzy? Train's crashed wi' all them lads an' lasses on. They're all dead, Lizzy.' The old woman's eyes swam in tears. 'Them railways aren't healthy. It's not natural to come an' go at that speed. Now see what happens. They should never have built them. I said so at the time. An' weather's not been right since they built Blackdon Tunnel.'

'Canst remember what it said in old Annie Trotter's book?' asked Lizzy.

'Nay,' said Lil. 'It were too daft to laugh at. I canna remember owt these days anyway. Us were too busy worritin' over thy leg,' said Lil.

'Still, it makes thee wonder,' said Lizzy. 'My old dad used to tell me some right tales about them woods near railway and fields an' road round Walton's farm. Said there were boggarts and bad luck.'

'I'll not get me eggs from Walton's any more,' said Lil. 'You never know.'

Lizzy found some cake to crumble in some tea, and the two old women sat down to work out who was dead and who had gone on the train that day.

Dame Trot had known a violent storm was coming. The swifts flew low and the dew still glittered on the churchyard at noon. And on the wall of the cupboard where she kept her shawls lived thirty black beetles. As the day had gone on, they had crawled to the top of the cupboard.

Dame Trot had lit the candle and watched the lightning play round the spire. 'It's a rum storm,' said she, stroking the fleabitten cat. The cottage shook. 'There were one like this last year. It's not right. Summat's gone wrong. There's Devil's work about. Me mam would've known.'

She poked at the bobbing black pudding and pan of herbs on the fire. But the old spell book was still locked in the corner cupboard. And she did not notice the centre of the storm seemed to be on the hill where the old Bow Cross stood.

Albert, Sam's uncle, heard about the crash while sheltering in the corn mill. He at once drove the cart back to Bow Cross Farm and then to Sam's farm. The horse was hysterical going through the woods. He had to walk with it. The thunder was deafening: the woods shook with sound. He ducked several times as fire balls split the sky. His eyes were dazzled by the blue fire. He could not understand another sound, as though rocks were moving. To his dazzled eyes it seemed as if lightning was rising up from the Stone on the hill.

He forgot all about that as he splashed into Sam's farm-yard. Sam's mother's pots of night-scented stocks and love-in-a-mist were like cups of milky coffee, the plants battered down. The rain seemed to press on Albert as though stopping him from going in to tell Sam's parents.

Rain beat down. In a carriage lay a broken vase, a small green bottle, a blue china cat, a pop bottle, a broken clay pipe and a thimble that said TO A MOTHER FROM MATLOCK.

Rain poured in through the broken window.

'Oh my God,' said Sam's mother, throwing an old shawl over her head. She and Sam's father climbed into Albert's cart.

'There's been nothing but trouble this year. Our Edgar killed up by that stone quarry, our Sam going off his head and saying ungodly things about stones and devils and the like, our Tom made lame. I don't know. There's always something. God's will be done,' said Sam's mother. She began to cry silently.

Down through the shaking woods went the horse and cart. Near a cave by the old road a stream poured out. It carried small stones and the rattle of the stones seemed to echo the rain and thunder. None of them looked up to the Stone or saw the strange marks the floodwater or something else had made in the leaf mould.

Down the railway embankment came the children, pushing, crying, slipping on the limestone chippings, pushing through the rain-heavy nettles, brambles, hemlock, and wild roses. Screams and shouts were heard over the noise of thunder and steam from the crashed train. Fanny Gibbs screamed and

61

screamed, her blonde hair in dark wet strands about her white face.

Sam was helped by a man in a cape who had a long silver-banded pipe in his mouth. Raindrops ran off the pipe in a silver stream.

The bridge had sagged and slipped. The train had got across just in time. The rails had twisted as the bridge had subsided and the train had been thrown off them.

Sam clung to the man's cloak. Under the bridge there was a deep hole, half-full of swirling floodwater. In the hole the water was churning and the water was a whirlpool as though it was being sucked down. Stones from the embankment and from the bridge were falling into the water. The guard was telling people to keep away. The bridge might collapse at any time.

Sam saw the remains of a large, deep, red pipe put in by the railway engineers ten years earlier. It had been put in to take a stream safely under the bridge. It had exploded into pieces by the force of water—or something else. The pipe had carried the stream from the entrance of an old mine. The man kept Sam well away from the gaping hole and sagging bridge. Other passengers were leading children to a low wall in the lane by some dark dripping sycamores, well away from the bridge. Sam was taken there too.

The man gave Sam a hot and fiery drink from a small silver flask he had in a pocket. The man thought Sam was going to be ill: he did not like the way Sam kept looking towards the deep hole at the bottom of the viaduct, as though he expected something else to happen. Trying to take Sam's mind off things, for he thought Sam was just scared of the train accident, he told him who he was. He said he worked for *The Times*, a newspaper, and he went round collecting stories for the paper.

'I find out exciting and interesting things,' said the man kindly, 'then I write them down in this notebook, then I telegraph the story to London, and the story appears in the newspaper next day.'

Sam tugged at the man's sleeve. This was it! His mother, father, grandparents, uncles, friends—even old Dame Trot— would not listen to his warnings. Today had more than proved him right. Well, the Stone had failed to get him today. There was still time left. He would tell the story to the man and get it published in *The Times* or whatever it was. That would show them all. That would make them look fools.

So, Sam told the story from the beginning. How he had first noticed the Stone in a storm like this last year, going right through his fears to yesterday when he read about the old prophecies in the spell book. And the man began to write in a black leather-covered pocket-book with an indelible pencil that blotched purple as the raindrops from the tree fell on the page.

The story will be in tomorrow's paper, thought Sam. That'll show 'em all!

Clambering wildly down the railway bank, Mellor had looked in the deep hole that was undermining the bridge. He was at once violently sick and he left the crowd of screaming children and ran for his life back home.

But he was spotted.

'Here boy!' shouted a voice. Hands seized the struggling, frightened Mellor and he was dragged into a huge black carriage. Lord Blackdon, of Blackdon Hall, Lady Selina's nephew, had been visiting in Lambton. He had found that he could not get home—his drive was blocked by the flood-water. The horses had refused to go into the water.

Now Lord Blackdon sat in his immaculate grey suit in a fury. Something else had happened. Far more mysterious. Lord Blackdon was a lover and breeder of dogs. He bred the famous Blackdon Bloodhounds and he still carried on the old custom of having a carriage dog: this was a splendid dalmation running by the side of his carriage. Now the horses had refused to go in the water but the dalmation had swum ahead in the flood. Lord Blackdon had sent the coachman and the footman after it. They had returned, saying there had been a train accident, closely followed by the yelping, trembling, mud bespattered dog—with a deep crescent-shape cut under its eye.

Angrily Lord Blackdon sent his servants to the scene of the crash while he mopped at the dog's cut with a white silk handkerchief. The dalmation was whimpering, there was blood on the carriage floor and all over his lordship.

Seeing Mellor running down the lane he had grabbed him: the lad must go back and tell his servants he wanted to go home now by the other way. The dog was bleeding to death.

'Damn the blasted railway. I want home NOW,' muttered his lordship and grabbed Mellor. He was a strong man and pulled Mellor half in the carriage out of the rain. Then his lordship recoiled in horror and disgust. John Mellor had been very sick with fear and gin. He was covered with mud and sick and rain. Lord Blackdon dabbed the dog gently but his other hand reached for his gold-topped cane.

'My dear Aunt Selina spends the family money on the working people and this is how they repay her.' He mopped the dog tenderly. In a black rage he made Mellor ride on the outside of the carriage and took him back to Mrs Mellor. Mrs Mellor, terrified by a visit from the noble Lord Blackdon, said yes to everything.

Yes. Her John could be sent away to a School of Christian Correction, where he would be taught a trade and fear of God in Manchester. Yes. He could go that night. Yes, she was grateful, John was headstrong and difficult to control. More to the point she would not have to find the money to feed the lad for a bit. She wept a little. Then John was sent away.

By nine o'clock that night, John Mellor was thirty miles away in Manchester, in a Home for Christian Boys of the Working People, who by privation and family poverty were falling into Evil Ways so often encountered in the homes of the Poor.

And that left Sam the only boy in Lambton who had any fear or suspicion that there was anything wrong or who took the old legends seriously.

The rain eased a little. Parents, friends, and half of Lambton were at the bridge where the stones were still cracking and falling.

Mrs Turner threw her arms round Frank, then hastily pushed him away and pulled a wry face at the smell. Peter explained to his mother how poor Frank had been unable to get to a lavatory because Samuel Walton got the door fast. This at once turned Mrs Broomhead into a rage. She had not forgotten Sam's new jacket that morning.

'Where that Sam Walton is, there's always trouble. Bad luck.' She shouted wildly to Mrs Turner. She had been very worried. 'Him and them other boys were nearly killed when they went underground in that old mine in January. Then he was messing about with thy Frank on the railway line in March by Blackdon Tunnel and they were nearly killed. Then his uncle were killed. It seems as if the lad trails bad luck. Aye. Well, I'm having none of it. I'm not buying any more grub from their farm. I'm having none of their bad luck in our house. And don't you talk or play with him, our Peter. Have nowt to do with him.'

Other mothers were nodding. It was true. Where Sam Walton was there was always bother. Keep away from him. Don't listen to anything he says. It gave the worried mothers something to think about after the tension of the accident.

There was a patch of blue sky overhead when Sam was picked up in the cart. He huddled under some dry sacks his mother wrapped thankfully round him. He was not going to say another word. He'd show them all. Mrs Broomhead, Will, John Mellor, his mother. The lot of them. Wait till they saw the paper tomorrow.

He lay in the cart and watched the clouds fade into the damp blue and saw the rose and blue mists rise from the drenched woods and fields. But as they went through the woods Sam was glad he was not alone. Strange drippings, patterings, and tappings were heard amongst the misty, dark, wet trees.

Sam saw a stream bubbling out of the cave where the tramp had slept. There were strange whorls and crescent-shape ruts in the soil and grass.

'A right torrent's been coming out o' yon cave,' Sam heard his father say. He did not attempt to argue. He knew that something had been out and about under the cover of the storm. He heard the grown-ups talking normally as they walked up behind the cart, as though nothing had happened. They'd see tomorrow.

Grandmother was in her little walled flower garden, anxiously waiting; the golden rays of the westering sun shone on her face. She kissed Sam.

'Eh lad, thank God thou art safe. Thee an' thy friends. A right end to thy first trip out!'

His mother agreed, irritation and worry still in her voice.

'Aye,' said Grandmother gently to them both, shaking the sparkling rain from weighed-down pink roses. 'There's always something that spoils the good things in life.'

She turned to glare at Grandfather pottering about in the farmyard over the wall. 'He's (she jerked her thumb at Grandfather) been as restless as a parrot wi' fleas,' said she. 'All through that storm he were like a daft parrot telling old stories about devils and whatnots until our Jack said he was going off his rocker.'

Sam said nothing. Anyway, Grandfather would not listen to him. And nobody, not even Sam, realized just how afraid the old man had been in the storm, remembering his father's tales.

So they left Grandmother to her garden, shaking rain off battered stocks and marigolds, a swarm of gnats dancing like a golden halo round her head. His mother and father were chattering to each other. It was as if the storm had never been. That was until you saw the ugly, black, standing Stone and felt the earth shake gently in the distant thunder.

Next day, Wednesday, was cool and fresh, the wind rippling silver in the dark trees of Midsummer. Sam walked to school along the new, much longer, road to Lambton. He would not go alone in the woods again. It meant he would have to get a paper after school, for it took him longer to get to Lambton than he thought, and they only had spare newspapers on the station.

Will met Sam in the yard. 'Hast heard about Mellor? Lord Blackdon found him roaring and said he needed locking up in a loony-bin. They took him away in this yellow coach last night. Him an' his monsters down our well!'

Will laughed and gave Sam an aniseed ball. Sam said

nothing. He'd learned to pick his moments for talking. Just wait till he had a newspaper.

Miss White was not in school. She was 'severely shaken'. Middlemas taught them.

'Her corsets snapped when train crashed,' said Tom to Will.

Middlemas took the unusual step of giving the class a sheet of foolscap paper instead of slates. They had to write an essay called AN ACCOUNT OF OUR MIRACULOUS ESCAPE ON THE MIDLAND RAILWAY ON TUESDAY EVENING LAST.

Right, thought Sam. I'll put down what he'll be shown in the newspaper sooner or later. He did, writing quickly, as all around him nibs dipped and scratched as the children wrote. A tortoiseshell butterfly fluttered on the dusty window and Middlemas paraded the benches, his watch chain swinging. Then the door at the back of the class flew open.

Sam's heart missed a beat. Perhaps it was the doctor, Lord Blackdon, the Archdeacon—they'd read the paper.

But it was Mrs Turner marching in. She did not hold a copy of a paper, but a pair of breeches. She threw them down on the teacher's desk.

'I've brought thee a spot of weshing,' said she to Middlemas. 'Being as tha wunna let our Frank go to lav when he wants to.'

The class put down their pens in silent delight.

'If tha had to fetch water from a trough two fields away for thy wesh tha might not be so handy in causing mucky accidents. I expect tha's got a wesh-house wi' a copper in it to boil thy smalls. Let me tell thee, Mester—'

'My good woman,' honked Middlemas, banging a fist on a desk, red with rage. 'Get out. Get out. You are trespassing on Church Property. I allow no parent this side of that door. Before you go ... take ... these ...'

He picked up the soiled breeches between finger and thumb.

'And I must tell you, madam, that on Matlock Station, Samuel Walton inadvertently imprisoned himself in the Gentlemen's Conveniences—'

Mrs Turner tossed the dirty, smelly bundle neatly back.

'Aye, trust him. He would be the cause of all the bother. I

67

know Sam Walton.' Everybody turned to Sam and grinned and nudged each other.

'Just let them wait,' he whispered to Jessie.

Middlemas called the police and collected the papers and locked them away. But Sam did not care. He ran up Station Road after school and bought *The Times*. It took all his cash: 2d. left from yesterday, 2d. from under the floorboards in his room, there were also four halfpennies Pete, the man who worked on Sam's farm, owed him. After he had bought the paper, he was lucky. He saw Jack driving up in the cart: that meant he could go through the woods—he would only go if he were not alone.

'By gum,' said Jack, 'taking a daily paper now are we? Getting right posh down at your house!' Jack, never having gone to school, could barely read. Sam said nothing. He thanked him icily for the ride and then raced off home. He rushed along until he found a sheltered spot under the walls out of the fresh wind and then he laid the paper out on a bed of white clover. He began to turn the pages. He did not miss a single article. He was there a long time: ants crawled over the pages. A bumble bee fell from a thistle. A curious cow looked over the wall at him, a thread of her saliva swinging over and then falling on the paper. Sam pulled the paper away hurriedly. She might spoil the very bit he wanted. But he could not find anything. He read it through again. Nothing. The reporter had not sent it. He had only pretended to be interested.

It was six o'clock when he walked in home.

'Why are you so late?' his mother demanded angrily. She was still on edge from the day before. 'Look at those mucky knees. Where have you been kneeling? And what's this?'

The paper was seized.

'I bought it to see if there was anything about the train crash,' said Sam dully. Everything was going wrong.

'We're short of money and you spend a whole sixpence on a newspaper. I've never heard the like. I haven't really. I think you're going soft in your head. I do really.'

Before he had his tea Sam had to cut *The Times* into small squares and thread them on a string to hang in the privy for use as lavatory paper.

'It's good quality anyway. It'll last a week or two will that. Waste not want not. But if it was left to you, Samuel Walton, we'd all finish up in the workhouse.'

Sam could not see his boiled egg or the thick slices of his mother's freshly baked bread for tears of rage and fear. The Stone had won the first battle.

It was surprising how whispers and gossip grew in a day. Mrs Turner grumbled and complained about Sam everywhere she went in Lambton. Dame Trot, sugaring bread again with Old Liz and Lil, had mentioned her mother had said you could see the Devil on Walton Pastures. That caused more gossip.

'Are them eggs from Walton's?' Lil Gosling asked loudly in a shop to her friend Ma Bagley.

'Aye,' said Ma Bagley.

'I wouldna touch anything from up there. There's a curse on anything from up there.'

Some strange twist of chance was making Lambton blame Sam and his family for what was going wrong. Nobody blamed the Stone.

On Thursday night the people of Lambton looked up to see the old Stone ringed with fire.

The cool northwest wind that had blown since the storm had dried everything nicely. The dry grass and thistles round the Stone caught fire. Perhaps it was a spark blown by the brisk wind from a train. Perhaps not. The Stone looked ugly and black in a circle of flame.

Grandfather became wildly excited and frightened. He said to everybody that a tramp had been asleep in the grass and left his pipe there. But whether or not he really believed this story it was hard to say for he told it so many times. Perhaps he was convincing himself. He rushed out with his gun. He ran into the blazing field with Ted who was anxious to see no sheep were trapped.

Grandfather fired his gun into the sky three times, then shouted, 'Bloody hobos!' at the top of his voice. It made him feel better.

'Let it burn, father,' said Ted. 'It'll kill thistles off anyhow.

69

It's nowt to worry about. I dunna know why tha's so worked up!'

'I'm not worried,' said Grandfather promptly.

Grandfather could be seen from far below in the town, a little figure firing his gun. Folk wagged their heads. 'They're all mad up there on Walton Pastures,' said they.

Grandfather found Grandmother muttering in the smoke-filled kitchen. 'If old fools like thee go on leaving thy pipes all over the place we'll all be burned alive,' she muttered. Grandfather was always losing pipes.

'Eh?' said Grandfather.

'I said apples'll soon be ripe at our place,' said Grandmother loudly, savagely stirring some fast-boiling raspberry jam.

Sam saw the flames from his bedroom window. His arm where the shadow had touched seemed to throb in time to the flames. As he watched, the northwest wind blew the black smoke in writhing, coiling, darting eddies towards his farm. As he stared at the darkening fields he was reminded of his dream. He was sure of one thing. As the shadow lengthened and summer turned into autumn things would become more and more dangerous. At the moment he could see no way of escape.

Next day they broke up from school. In the yard Fanny Gibbs organized a gang of girls and arms linked they skipped round the yard chanting:

> *Mr Middlemas is no good,*
> *Chop him up for firewood.*
>
> *When he's dead,*
> *Stand him on his head.*
> *Turn him into gingerbread.*
>
> *Hip hip hurray!*
> *We break up today.*
> *Send old Nelly*
> *Far far away!*

'What were that fire last night?' Will asked Sam. He was sucking an enormous and fragrant peardrop.

'It were grass on fire. But I think—' began Sam.

'They're all saying there's a curse on them hills up there, an' thy Grandmother Walton's a witch,' said Will. 'I know tha believes in magic. Tha's as daft as Mellor was. Well, not quite,' said Will, biting off the point of the pink peardrop and giving it to Sam. Sam shook his head.

'It's that Stone!' said Sam.

'Don't be daft,' said Will. 'You said that before on the station. Tha's barmy, like Mellor.'

'But it said so in Dame Trot's book too. I've been trying to tell thee—' But Will just stuffed the whole of the sweet in his mouth and made noises.

Jessie came up. Did she remember his warning and story?

'Eh Sam, me mam says now I've been on railway I can go by mysen to me Aunty Betty's in Derby because she'll pay an' she's married to a porter an' they've got a sink with taps an' plants in pots an' lace curtains.' Her eyes shone as Middlemas rang the bell.

So the last day passed, with whispers and giggles in Sam's direction. He was glad when it was time to go home. Only John Mellor could help. He was far away. Will just laughed. All Jessie could think of was Derby. Only Sam realized the danger.

When Sam was trudging home the long way home that night Will was sent down the old cellar.

'Will, go an' get us some real cold water from bottom well. Be careful,' said his mother. 'I want to stand a jug of cream in some right cold water so we can have it with them strawberries.'

Will took a candle and went, only too gladly. He liked strawberries. When he was at the bottom of the steps a huge bubble burst in the well. Then another. Will stared. The candle flickered in a draught. The water in the well rose, then fell. Will lowered the bucket thoughtfully. He looked round. There was a lot of water on the floor and walls.

A tiny seed of doubt was sown in Will's mind. He went

71

back up quicker than he had come down. Did he ought to tell Sam Walton? No—he wouldn't see him for weeks now. He grinned to himself. He was getting as daft as Walton and Mellor.

'Can I have a dish of strawberries now, mam?' said Will when he was back.

'Wait thy hurry,' said Mrs Saltby. 'Let me cool the cream first.' The water was so cold that she let out a cry as she lowered the jug into it. But, like Will, she fancied a dish of strawberries, so thought no more about the ice-water.

But in the night Will woke up and found he was thinking of the well and the bubbles. He remembered an old story his grandfather had told him about the Knocker—a mysterious being that lived deep underground. Then he pushed the idea to the back of his mind. They'd be taking him to the loony-bin next!

So July passed into August. In the woodlands, where the old caves and mine shafts were with secret entrances under-ground, the shadows darkened and grew longer; so did the nights and silences.

So, too, did the shadow of the old Stone that Sam feared so much. At sunset when the black shadows in the woods began to grow and the tired green leaves of August were tipped with silver and gold of the sunset, the shadow of the Stone reached out a little more each day, nearer and nearer, creeping over the fields to Sam's farm.

And Sam, busy on the farm during the holiday, did not dare to go near the Stone: or the woods. But he watched the shadows in the farmyard grow longer each day: even his mother's pots and pans filled with mignonette and nasturtiums had shadows that grew a little each day that passed. And he knew as August passed the shadow of the old magic was reaching out to get him.

Chapter Two

Sam lived a long way out of Lambton in his lonely farm and all that summer holiday he felt more than usually shut off from friends. All around him he could see warning signs of coming disaster. Yet nobody wanted to listen to him. His father complained daily of pain and 'rheumatiz' in his leg. They never even thought for one moment that it could be the curse of the Stone. Only Sam suspected the old magic was working again.

And his father found work increasingly harder. Sam had to carry all the heavy water buckets to the fields for the animals and clean out the cows, hens, and pigs. Then there was his mother. 'My eggs and butter aren't selling down there in Lambton any more—perhaps folks are short of money. I don't know.' Sam knew, but he did not say anything, she would only turn on him if he mentioned the Stone.

It was late August now. The shadows were much longer, the nights longer, the danger growing more and more each day. Sam sat in the kitchen, one evening around this time, eating his supper of bread and butter—plenty of butter in the

73

house—and raspberry jam. He said nothing. There was only one thing he wanted to talk about and they would not. The lamp was lit and every now and again a moth or flying beetle would break the silence by flying into the globe with a ringing note. A jar of sweetpeas scented the warm kitchen. His mother broke the silence.

'Go and get some water to drink from the trough, Sam.' She turned to his father. 'There's something wrong with the scullery well, Tom. The water's really mucky and cloudy.'

'There shouldn't be,' said his father, pausing in his eating. 'That's a right deep and old well, it was here before the farm.'

Sam went grimly to the door. He didn't like the sound of that. Was there something deep under the house? He walked slowly over the yard, glad of the lamplight shining out. It was only half-past eight, but the warm sky was already dusted with faint stars overhead, and the bucket on the nail wet with dew. Jesus, it was almost autumn. His mother's voice floated from the kitchen.

' ... Yes, I know your leg troubles you, Tom, and I know you can't work any harder. But the money from Manchester for the milk is for the rent. There's just no money coming in. We shall be in the workhouse and be split up if things don't ... ' Her voice trailed off and Sam knew she was near to tears. He heard a rumbling reply from his father. Then his mother's voice sharp and angry now.

'No. No. I'm not borrowing from your father. Not likely. I wouldn't lower myself.'

Sam lowered the bucket in the trough, scattering the reflected stars. God, his arm hurt. Ever since that day the shadow of the Stone had touched it, it had ached. When he got back into the kitchen there was a silver snuff box that Sam had not seen before gleaming in the lamplight on the scrubbed table. Then he stared. There was something not quite right ...

'My Aunt Martha, me dad's sister, gave it me for a wedding present,' said Sam's father, turning the box in the lamplight. 'She was housekeeper to the old Duke of Blackdon, Lord Blackdon's Grandad. The old Duke gave it her. It's worth a lot. She said if I ever were in any trouble she'd buy it back from me. Look at yon snake, carved in t' silver. It's part of the Blackdon coat of arms—'

'It's the same snake thing that's on the Stone in Grand-father's field and on Dame Trot's candlestick and—' shouted Sam.

'Don't start that,' said his mother angrily. Sam was silent. Those monsters, snakes, worms, they were everywhere, carved in silver, on stone, written in books, the old stories must be true ... wherever he looked. There was no escape.

'Wilt tha take this box to thy great aunt in Taddington, tomorrow, Sam?' his father was asking. 'We need the money, like ... it'll be a change for thee, Sam. Tha's been working hard for us. You'll enjoy the walk to Taddington. You'll have to call up at thy Grandmother's an' ask the way. I'm not sure. Take her some roses. It'll be a holiday for thee Sam. Tomorrow night (he looked at the almanac by the fireplace) it's thy Grandfather's harvest feast. You'll be ready for a good feed when you get back.'

Sam looked at the almanac too: Friday, August 24—St. Bartholomew's Day ... yes he'd go. And he'd ask old Martha a thing or two. If she was Grandfather's sister she must have heard the old tales too and he'd ask her about the serpent on the box. She might know the whole story. He felt quite cheerful. She might help.

'And now up the wooden hill to bed,' said his mother sharply. She hated the idea of borrowing money off relations. 'Get a good sleep. It's a long walk, but you can go by Monsal Dale, I've heard. That'll be nice for you. Say your prayers.'

Sam would pray all right. Pray with his heart and soul that Martha could help. The year was passing fast: Grandfather always had his harvest supper on St. Bartholomew's Day—the end of summer. He prayed hard and long that Martha would help him warn and alert the family to the terrible dangers ahead.

After midnight a melon yellow moon rose, like a half-opened, watching eye, and the Stone cast ink-black shadows that seemed to stretch for miles, so low was the moon in the sky; the shadows seemed to stretch out to the hills over Monsal Dale and Taddington, as though exploring and investigating the way Sam would take on St. Bartholomew's Day.

Sam gave Grandmother the roses the next day. He listened to her instructions on how to get to Taddington.

'I used to know a grand lad Taddington way, he asked me to wed him before I met thee,' said Grandmother loudly to Grandfather. But Grandfather was thrilled and delighted at the plan to get gold from his sister in Taddington.

'She'll help thee!' he said to Sam. 'She's got all me old dad's gold. Aye. Every bit. All his golden guineas and golden shillings. Aye. Every one.'

'Then why does she keep it under the floorboards in our bedroom, I ask mysen?' said Grandmother, amidst her bowls, crocks, pastry boards, all ready for the final preparations for the harvest supper.

'Eh?' said Grandfather.

'I said there's a pair o' crickets under the floorboards in our bedroom. They chirp the night away. Thy snorin' keeps 'em lively.'

Sam turned away in disgust, grown-ups were always thinking about unimportant things. He felt better when he heard Ted was going down in the cart to Lambton, for he had not known how to face the woods. He went out of the hot kitchen to wait in the yard. Back inside Grandmother was putting the first batch of apple pies in the oven. Grandfather watched her, much cheered by the thought of his sister's money and the feast that night.

'Shall I tell young Sam about me dad's old tale about hearing the Devil playing his fiddle in them woods on Fin Cop near Taddington?' said Grandfather.

'Dunna thee dare!' said Grandmother, nearly upsetting the apple pies. 'It'd frighten the lad to death—it frits thee anyhow, I've seen thee shake a time or two after telling it.'

Silence fell in the hot kitchen. Grandmother waved the rolling pin menacingly, just to make sure Grandfather did not try anything. Sam stood alone outside. It was quiet in the yard now the swifts had gone. Every now and again a windfall apple thumped to the ground. They were bigger than the last time he'd looked. Ted came out and they were away:

76

the cart was full of brooms. Ted cut birch twigs, lashed them with twine, and then fastened them to an ash stick and sold them as cheap brooms. He wanted a farm of his own one day.

For a time nobody spoke. Sam was deep in thought about what to say to Martha. There was just the crunch of the wheels and the trotting horse and one robin singing in the vast woods.

'St. Bartholomew's Day,' said Uncle Ted suddenly. 'St. Bartholomew brings the autumn, thy Grandfeyther says. It's a rare day for a walk. Give my love to Aunt Martha an' tell 'er if she wants to buy me a farm I'll not say no.' He laughed. They rumbled over the station bridge. It was the first time Sam had been down to Lambton for a month. When they were going over Lambton Bridge Sam saw his friends bathing in the river. Matt Barker and two others were walking upside-down, their heads in some shallow water.

'Na then, Sam!' yelled Tom. 'Where't going?'

'Taddington!' yelled back Sam.

'Taddington turdy town!' yelled back Tom. Ted laughed. 'We used to shout that to anyone from Taddington,' he said. But Sam did not laugh. He felt jealous. He wanted to go and swim in the river and forget the horrible things he knew.

'See thee tonight,' said Ted, setting him down. 'Work up a big appetite. Thy Grandmother's got beef an' plum pudding and Hartington cheeses for everyone.'

That's not all they'll have, thought Sam, when I tell them what Martha has said. He felt cheerful again. Perhaps she could write a letter and he'd read it out. He said goodbye, and feeling more hopeful called in Saltby's shop for a bottle of pop for the dusty hot road. Will was in the shop and seemed about to say something, then changed his mind: a horse trotted by and Will rushed out, for his father paid him a farthing for every full pail of horse droppings he collected in the holiday. Sam watched him go ... had he seen anything by the well, he wondered?

'And where art tha causing bother today?' said Mr Saltby, giving Sam the bottle. Sam said nothing to that.

He quite enjoyed the first part of the walk to the village of Ashford. The sky was a very deep blue and he could see a chalk-white moon still visible between the trees. It followed him for the journey. When he had passed through Ashford he leaned against the wall and drank the pop. He looked at the cows knee-deep in the river. He looked at the flowers and undergrowth that were beginning to dry out. Not like that day when the train crashed and anything could have hidden in the thick grass and weeds. He kicked the dried weeds with his boots and some red dock seeds fell on his boots. Nothing sinister about this morning. He picked a harebell and stuck it in his cap for luck. He still did not feel totally safe. But there was nothing. Just the moon behind him.

He left the white dusty turnpike road just after he had crossed a humpbacked bridge and turned into the big wood on his left—just as Grandmother said. At once he was plunged into the half-light of the woodland and heard a sound that he did not like or at first understand. He glanced unhappily towards the big butterbur leaves at the edge of the wood where the hot white road could be seen. He stood amidst the trees, listening to a faint threatening humming and the hiss of the wind in the trees. Again he had the feeling that he was surrounded by warnings that things were not right ... and yet ... this wood was a good four miles from the Stone. He was safe surely? Yet he could not convince himself that he was safe.

Then for a moment he felt relief: he realized the humming was no more than a million flies in the sycamore and ash leaves. He saw a wasps' nest suspended in the fork of a tree and that throbbed with sound. He walked on deeper and deeper into the wood, climbing higher and higher. Cold winds began to breathe through the trees and thistle seeds blew past him as though they were escaping at speed from this enchanted wood ... but this wood can't be evil or magic he told himself.

He passed some open mine shafts, open wide and black as though waiting for him. He kept straight ahead. The hiss of wind in the tall thin trees above him increased. He had to pause for breath in a clearing where there was an abandoned lead mine entrance. Gasping for breath he turned round. He looked down on Monsal Dale where people who had no worries went for walks and picnics. He saw some horse-drawn charabancs and ladies looking no bigger than ants, their parasols, tiny white dots. He could see a man with a barrel organ. He wished he was down there, having a good time. Rising above the valley opposite he saw a great hill, so big it seemed a mountain to Sam's eyes, crouching green and smooth under the blue sky. That must be Fin Cop, that Grandmother had told him he would see.

The path became steeper, the wood darker. His head began to ache with the hum of the insects. Then, through the trees came a thin scraping dry music like the whine of an insect's wings or a badly tuned violin. It made Sam's flesh creep with fear and distaste. He felt a bit like he did when his mother's dry wash-day hands scraped on a dry pillow-case she was folding ... except there was something that was threatening in the music. Suddenly, with no warning, his shadow-touched arm of a month ago quivered with pain. Then it stopped. As he was rubbing his arm in pain and fear an old man carrying a black case and dressed in old black rags passed him. He said some strange words to Sam and leered at him.

Sam could stand no more. He threw away the pop bottle and putting his hand on the silver snuff box so it would not fall from his pocket he ran for his life. He did not stop until he had reached the top of the hill and open fields. There he turned back to look. In an inverted triangle of blue sky between the trees, just showing through the smokelike mists of the August day was the Stone. Nearly six miles away, but still there and watching him.

He ran on. Things were closing in on him. The old woman must help, he thought, as he ran down the old track between the limestone walls. He was hot and bothered but safe when he got to the village. Now and again his arm throbbed as though some hidden force were sending messages to his body. Wiping the sweat from his dusty forehead he looked for Martha's cottage. 'It's bigger than the others,' Grandmother had said. 'An' there's a window at either side of the front door. But you'll know her cottage by her washing. She washes every day an' hangs it out careful like. She wunna put Mr Jackson's vest an' long under-drawers next to any of her own under-bits. Says it's not nice.'

Sam found the cottage and saw the washing in the little orchard drying ground to the side, with the washing hung in order. Socks, long pants, vests, shirts, nightshirts, then her own things well away from her lodger's. A crow that had followed Sam from the wood settled on Martha's washing line.

Martha emerged majestically from her dark green, sun blistered door to shoo the crow away and stop it messing her washing. She flapped at the crow and then saw Sam standing in the street. 'Yon crow means there will be a death in the Walton family this year, Samuel Walton. You're like your Grandfeyther were when he were young.'

Sam stared at her. She had swinging jet ear-rings and an enormous bosom that wobbled as she flapped at the crow. She looked just like Grandfather would look if he dressed as an old woman. And it was a good start. If she believed crows meant death, then she probably believed the old stories.

'Come in, lad,' she said, and steered her enormous belly through the front door. A linnet twittered in a brass cage by the door.

'Pretty lady, pretty lady, death is coming,' cooed the old woman to the bird. 'The bird of death has been.'

'Well, that's good that is,' thought Sam. 'Just what I don't want to hear. But I bet she believes in all the old stories.' He had taken an instant dislike to his great aunt, for he did not like people who kept things in cages. He quickly opened the cage door to let the linnet out. But she saw him as she turned to show him into the parlour. She went to the cage.

'Eh, my little birdie wouldna leave her muzzer, would she then?' crooned the old woman slamming the cage door shut. But Sam could see her cross face. He wished he hadn't done that. The old woman had taken a dislike to him.

She gave Sam some cold mutton, a boiled onion, and some potatoes on an old and beautiful blue plate and Sam gave her the silver snuff box and explained his visit. Her face relaxed again. She fingered the box lovingly.

'The old Duke gave me this box when I'd stayed up all night wi' young Lord John, him that's there now. Coughing his guts up, little lad were, till I gave him some of me raspberry syrup. Aye, them were the days. An' now thy dad needs some cash. Aye, I promised him I'd help if he kept t' box.' She seemed pleased.

80

'Grandfather says you've got a lot of money,' said Sam pleasantly. He thought that would please her more so he could start asking her. 'Grandad says you've got a lot of gold guineas.' Her face became like it had earlier when he had let the cage door fall open.

'I've no golden boys!' she snapped. 'Thy Grandfather kept all family gold.' Her bosom rose and fell and her ear-rings wagged with annoyance as she set down a bowl of stewed damsons in front of Sam. Sam, seeing he had said the wrong thing, tried again. He must make friends with her. She must know a lot.

'When I were coming through the woods I heard a sort of music,' said Sam. 'It were all scrapey and horrible.'

Martha dropped a damson from the spoon. She stared at Sam. 'Eh, first a bird of death and now you say that,' said the old woman. She was silent for a moment, letting purple juice drip. Then she said,

Hear the Fiddler of Fin
On Bartholomew's Day
Devil take you in
Do what you may.

There was silence in the room. Then she said, 'An old woman told me that.'

Sam dropped his spoon now. Warnings. Everywhere he went he had warnings. And only he seemed to understand them. They were both silent. Then quickly Sam said, 'It's a bit like them old stories my—my Great Grandfather, your dad, used to tell you and Grandfather, you know, about that old Stone and things ... ' His voice trailed off. He'd said the wrong thing he could see. Her face had gone hard and her mouth a straight line. She began to scrape at the damson stain.

'Nay,' said she. 'My dad weren't right in the head. I'm certain of that. I know it says in the Good Book "Honour thy father and mother" but I never could. He were half-drunk a lot of the time. Oh, I was glad to get away and go and work in the houses of the gentry that knew how to live decent.'

She suddenly swooped on Sam's unfinished dish of damsons. She seemed upset. Sam stared at her and then the purple stains of the damson juice on the fine silver and white damask tablecloth. Then she returned with a silver salt cellar and began spooning salt on to the purple juice stains. Sam could not decide whether it was the mention of the old stories or the stains that had really upset her: her face was like a mask, but the ear-rings trembled. Sam decided to take a risk.

'But you believe in old stories and legends, Great Aunt Martha, because you told me one just now.' His voice shook as he spoke.

'That's different,' said the old woman in a low voice. 'What's happened today are little warnings ... little signs ... from God above ... Your Great Grandfather's were daft ones, said he'd dreamed them, about worms and shadows, horrible things—not for the ears of young boys. I don't want to talk about them today.' Her voice took on the tone of a superior servant in a big house and her ear-rings shook.

Bloody, bloody grown-ups, thought Sam. They know so much and do nothing. And he could see by the big, hard, cold, pale blue, bulging eyes, so like Grandfather's, that he was not going to get anything out of her. He'd seen Grandfather in such a mood. Obstinate pigs. Pigs, pigs, pigs. He watched the old woman vanish upstairs. He felt like letting the linnet go, kicking her striped cat, and crushing a bunch of glass grapes. The serpent on the silver box glittered in a dusty ray of sun. There was just no escape for him. Then the old woman appeared again.

'Take thy breeches off,' said she. Sam stared at her bewildered.

'I want to sew in this little bag of gold sovs for thy dad. I always liked your dad. Very handsome, he was, like your Grandmother. Yes, I liked your dad.'

Meaning you don't like me, you obstinate old pig, thought Sam, sitting on the horsehair sofa in his white pants, with the horsehair scratching his legs. She was certainly not speaking to Sam now. He realized the old stories bothered her as much as they did Grandfather. They bothered him too: most of all he did not like the way the stories all fitted together. They all said that the Devil would take you.

'I want thee to look at thy Great Aunt May's grave,' said Martha as Sam put on his trousers. The last thing Sam wanted to do was to look at gravestones. But he followed her patiently up the village street. Martha explained to Sam that May was Grandfather's and her own youngest sister—she had come to live at Taddington but the winters were too much. She rambled on.

He turned round suddenly; he had the feeling that he was being watched. His arm began to throb with a strange tingling sensation. Behind him, as tall as he was, was a thin finger of weather-beaten stone. Another one! Too thin to be carved on but another of them. Still his arm throbbed. He turned again, for the feeling of being watched was still there. And there, in the folds of the hills, blue with August noonday haze, was the Stone on the hill at Grandfather's. It was thorn sharp, for all it was six miles or more away. Sam felt trapped, caught in a web of ancient magic.

'God rest her little soul,' said Martha. 'Now come back home and I'll give thee some of my cinnamon biscuits to eat on thy way back.'

Sam followed her. He felt the darkness gathering round him, the shadows growing and the web of magic between the old stones. And nobody cared or wanted to. He was quite unprepared for Martha's next move.

'I've a little treasure for thee,' said she. 'I've no money. Thy Grandfather's got all that. It's a treasure for thee. It'll stop them things that are worrying thee at the moment.' She gave him a rose-tinted shining egg of marble, strangely veined with purple and blue. 'It were thy Great Uncle John's. Mine and thy Grandad's brother. He were killed down one of them lead mines—them that aren't used any more in them woods near thy Grandfather's farm. He allus took this little stone egg down with him, for luck, but one day he didn't, and that very day he heard The Knocker and were killed by a fall of rock.'

Sam was too speechless to thank her. She was just like Grandfather. Full of old sayings and fears and superstitions one moment, then saying they were all rubbish and not worth talking about. He could see from her face that it was not worth trying to talk about the old stories. But he had got something from her.

He waved goodbye and took the new turnpike down the dale. It was not such an interesting walk, Grandmother had said, but Sam decided he did not want interest such as he had seen and felt in that wood that day. His hand curled round the cool egg. He wondered how it could help and how to use it.

Martha went round to see her friend Lily Croft. 'I've just had me great nephew round, Samuel Walton, from Bow Cross,' said she. 'Eh, but it's sad. He'll not live the year out, Lily. I can tell thee that for nothing.' They had a pot of tea and spent a happy hour talking about death and the removal of damson stains from damask cloths.

Sam walked on, unaware of Martha's gloomy warnings. The turnpike was comfortably busy. Three carts of stone, a horse charabanc and the Duke of Pemberly's carriage with outriders. It took him half an hour to reach the spot where he had left the turnpike that morning. A robin sang, the barrel organ played at the entrance to Monsal Dale. Sam began to feel better. At least he had the egg, even if he did not know what to do with it.

He went down to the river and ate his biscuits, watching the crumbs fall to the trout. He was hot and dusty. Despite the earlier cold dew and the long dark shadows on the road it was hot. There was a pump in Ashford but he wanted to wash his feet now. He walked a little up river to where the river was shallower and the giant willowherb, meadowsweet, and mint gave him some shade. He pulled off his boots and paddled. The river refreshed him at once.

Higher up the river he could see a waterfall that had been built to dam the river and its sparkling rush of waters looked so inviting. And so cool. He remembered the boys back at Lambton swimming. Why shouldn't he have a swim too? He was tired of being miserable. He looked around him. There was nobody about. He took his clothes off and folded them. His breeches which contained the egg and the gold he carefully hid under a stone.

Then he splashed happily up the river. He found a deep pool and swam and dived. He forgot that last summer he had played with the others in the river at home and taught himself

84

to swim, that this year he had had no time for fun. He just enjoyed himself. Behind him towered the huge shadowed wood where he had walked that morning and from deep underneath it, ice-cold water bubbled up from the lead mines. But Sam could not see the Stone. He was happy. He sat on the slimy moss-covered steps of the waterfall, happily watching the swallows and dragonflies.

He wished he hadn't been so edgy with old Martha. Now he was cool and relaxed he could see all the wrong things he had said. He needed to keep calm and get at the truth behind the old rhymes and riddles and stories. Then he blinked. He must be dreaming. He saw a beautiful butterfly. Sam had one book at home, his only one called *The Young Gentleman's Guide to the Wonders of Creation*. In it was a marvellous coloured page of British butterflies. Sam knew what this was. It was a Purple Emperor. It was a beautiful purple colour, like a lady's dress he had seen in Matlock or the lights in Grandmother's amethyst brooch. Sam stared and stared. The butterfly fluttered to the side of the waterfall.

It fluttered towards a tunnel opening in the bank that was used in times of flood when the river reached flood levels. The tunnel entrance was dark and forbidding but the butterfly flitted towards it. The tunnel had a curved top and a mist of gnats, golden in the sun, gleamed like an eye in the entrance of the tunnel.

Sam, relaxed and cool, could not resist following the rare butterfly. He saw the tunnel was blocked by thick, cruel brambles. Some white flowers still gleamed on the brambles and there were some reddening berries. Over the white flowers of the blossom the butterfly hovered—then vanished in the tunnel. Using a stick, Sam forced aside the thick, cruel, bramble stems, some as thick as his wrist and with cruel thorns on. He wanted to see the butterfly again. The thorns began to tear at him, but he was so interested he did not notice.

Then he forgot the butterfly. For in the tunnel was a pile of stinking, seething, dead bodies. There were small skulls, claws, bones, and much rotting fur. The whole pile was moving and writhing. For one brief moment Sam was reminded of the heaving of the waters in Saltby's well.

85

On the tunnel walls were swirls of moisture, gleaming palely in the greenish light. A whining filled his ears, not unlike the sound he had heard in the wood earlier. The whole tunnel seemed to breathe out a dank cold air, and there was the sound of a faint hiss in the breath as though of far distant snakes.

In the middle of the pile of bodies Sam thought he saw the gleam of an eye. Sam's stomach turned in fear and revulsion and he staggered forwards. The whole pile seemed to heave and reach up to him. In desperation Sam made himself step back. Something clawed at him with a spitting, splitting sound, and he felt sharp claws at his neck.

He fell back with a cry, catching his head a sharp blow on a big iron sluice bar and falling into a willow-shaded deep, black, stagnant pool.

Ripples rocked the reeds and valerian, then subsided. The dragonflies and swallows skimmed back. Then the black water was still.

Back at Bow Cross Farm Grandfather was on edge. He did not feel well. Earlier that day he had gone up to the old Stone where Ted, his eldest son, said some sheep had got foot rot. When he had reached the Stone he was out of breath and he leaned against it. Soon after, a sharp pain had darted down his arm and then an invisible hand seemed to squeeze the back of his throat and chest.

'Lucy could never fry her bacon right,' said the old man aloud to the sheep. 'Not like me old mam. She could fry bacon just right.' He thought he had indigestion.

Clutching his chest in the hope that Grandmother would see him and feel sorry, he tottered back: he did not notice the black Stone, silent in the silver dew, or the sick sheep.

He did not feel as cheerful as he usually did on the day of his harvest feast. He always had it as near to St. Bartholomew's Day as he could. Usually he enjoyed sitting at the end of the long table in the barn with his 'boys' and his labourers, and casual labourers, all eating their fill and drinking the ale. Now it was afternoon and he still had the pain in his arm and throat. It must be Lucy's cooking. He sat down on the mounting block and stared at the apples on the trees, bathed gold in the afternoon sunshine against the rich blue of the late summer skies. He frowned at the thistledown that floated through the trees in the warm air. A cry in the distance made him frown even more.

'Them lads of mine are muckin' about in thistles instead of mowing them,' he growled, watching one large thistle seed float over towards the old Stone. He stared at the Stone, hot and black in the toast-coloured grass of the top pastures. Now he was an old man he remembered his childhood as though it had only happened yesterday. Grandfather remembered a day like this, way back seventy years ago, when he stared up into the apples, looking greedily for the first signs of red. The long shadows, the hot sun, had all been the same.

'Father,' he had said, 'why dost always have the harvest feast on St. Bartholomew's Day?'

'Because,' his father had said, 'today the shadow of yonder Stone lies cold and long in the white dew. An' all manner of things creep an' crawl in that cold dew. So, us Waltons may as well eat, drink, and be merry because one day will come when yon Stone and t' Devil gets us all!' And then he had laughed and gone off to sample again the harvest ale in the brewhouse.

Grandfather felt as upset now as he had seventy years ago. He swished angrily at a cabbage white butterfly, wavering towards the cabbages over the wall. Still he had that pain in his arm. He walked slowly over to the low wall near the dung heap. Up above the plums were ripening fast. It will be an early autumn, thought the old man.

He pulled some straw out of his smock and began to model a strange shape out of it, half-human, half-cross, like his father had taught him to. But he kept remembering other things his father had said as he twisted the corn dolly for the feast, so he did not enjoy making it. The angry barking of the dog made him look up. A gypsy woman had walked into the yard.

'Gerrout!' yelled Grandfather promptly. 'Us've no truck wi' gippoes and the like of thee, so clear out! She's (he jerked his thumb in the direction of the kitchen) got plenty of pegs.'

The gypsy muttered something. The dog barked angrily.

87

'An' I dunna want thy white heather either. Stuff it up thy dusters. I dunna believe in magic and superstition. Gerrout!'

The gypsy stared steadfastly at the old man. 'You've gold aplenty but your eye is cold as the winter sky. And before the birds fetch yon berries, or before, you'll lose something you value though you've never thought about it!'

Grandfather did not like the sound of that one bit: neither did he understand it. 'Gerrout!' he roared. 'Go an' swallow thy crystal ball. Don't thee come fartlin' round my land again!'

Grandmother appeared, carrying a freshly baked loaf. She bent painfully and picked a fragrant bunch of mint and lavender.

'Take this, love,' said she. 'It's our harvest supper tonight. We're busy, like, so us've not got time to stand and chat—at least some of us haven't.' She looked meaningfully at Grand-father.

The gypsy beamed at her. 'You have a warm eye and a warm heart and you'll have a long life,' said she.

Grandmother watched the gypsy go, wiping her floury hands down her apron. 'How dost thou know how many pegs I've got?' she demanded of Grandfather. 'And what did she say to you to upset thee, Abel?'

'Nowt,' said Grandfather promptly. 'If tha gives gypsies money they say you live for ever. 'Er just said I'm going to lose something I value most. She's probably stole me gold. I'll see if it's there.' He moved swiftly into the house.

'I dunna like gypsies' warnings,' said Grandmother. 'I hope our Sam's all right.' She leaned against the garden wall, warm as her fresh bread. Warm scents of bread and roses, lavender and roasting meat filled the air. Hens clucked and broom pods popped. A red admiral butterfly settled on her hair. She smiled. Everything seemed all right. She sighed, half-tired, half-content. But she did not like the warning.

Sam stared up to see two dark eyes, penetrating and keen, staring into his, eyes as dark as the tunnel entrance had been. There was a violent pain in his chest and his arm throbbed with pain. A roaring rushing sound filled his brain, then all was black again.

Sam's father that afternoon was in the top fields near the Stone, where his fields joined with Grandfather's. Here the soil was thin, the rocks showing through the thin soil. He was cutting all the ragwort he could see and the thistles. Thistledown floated all around him. His leg hurt and he leaned on a crutch. It was a slow job, but somebody had to do it.

He rested for a moment, mopping his brow. After a time he glanced to the right of him, towards the west, where the sun was, so he could see the time by the position of the sun. It was getting late. The sun was close by the old Stone.

What happened next was uncertain. He put his hand to his eyes, glanced at the Stone and the sun again as though he were dazzled or unsure. He swayed. He grabbed at the scythe, causing the blade to tilt upwards. Then he fell against the blade, which cut through his corduroys and the string he had tied them with, gashing his leg. He cried out. Then he began to stagger back to the farm. He made it to the kitchen, groaning aloud, making Jack the dog whimper in sympathy. He fell on the fireside chair.

He was alone in the little farmhouse. Sam's mother, together with Pete the farm man, had gone up to Bow Cross Farm to help get ready the feast. They would not be back. Sam's father was supposed to be taking the cart up himself when he had done the milking. He lay on the Windsor chair, slumped over the arm. After a while the mice came out and one ran up Tom Walton's leg—but it darted back when it saw the fresh blood.

The shadow of the Stone grew blacker and longer as the August day reached evening, and deep shadows filled the tousled fields, where the old lead workings had left little hollows in the ground. A cold wind rippled amongst the scabious and faint mists gathered in the dark trees. Outside Sam's farm the dog began to howl as the long shadow of the Stone reached out over the fields.

Grandmother was surrounded by newly baked loaves, pork pies gleaming hot with gravy, golden, crusted beef and potato pies, apple pies and jam tarts. Meat roasted and spat in the ovens; in the wash-house copper, there were apple dumplings, plum puddings, and blackberry dumplings, all wrapped in muslin bags and bobbing merrily in the simmering water. The steam from the jostling jumping puddings mingled with the thistle seeds and blue sky. Grandmother looked on it all with weary satisfaction. Just a few more things to see to. She wished the gypsy had not said what she had. Grandmother automatically thought something was going to happen to somebody she loved.

Grandfather thought something was going to happen to his gold. He pushed by her table of pies.

'Mind your mucky backside on them pork pies,' she said. 'There's cow muck all up that smock. Get it changed.' But Grandfather was too busy looking for something he was going to lose but did not yet know the value of. He wanted to check all his little hoards of gold and silver he had not seen for a time.

He leaned over a plate of damson tarts to feel behind the dresser where some sovereigns were hidden in an old boot. Grandmother rattled the poker in the fire, stirring the coal to get the ovens hotter still. She pulled it out, red and glowing, and waved it at Grandfather's backside.

'Dunna step back when tha finds thy gold's gone,' said she. 'I'm right behind thee with a red hot poker.'

Grandfather slowly straightened up; the gold was there—but he still had the pain. He shivered. There had been a cold dew that morning, there were a few fallen shrivelled leaves underneath the sycamore. It must be the coming fall of the leaf that was making him feel badly.

'Will you take that cow-muck clarted smock off?' shouted Grandmother. Grandfather was very much in the way, just when she had a few last minute jobs to finish. She didn't want to have him around in the kitchen.

'I think I'll have a bath in front of the fire, mother,' said Grandfather. 'And get all togged up for tonight, like.' But it was the pain in his arm he wanted to soothe away.

'Eh, Mester Walton,' said Grandmother. 'What a grand idea. A right grand idea. To have a bath in front of all my ovens full of meat and grub and tatties so I shall have to step over thee to see to my ovens. Oh aye, it's a grand idea to have a bath in front of the fire.'

Grandfather, worried about the pain, missed the threat in her voice and the poison in her words. He heaved out a bath from a cupboard under the stairs.

'I'll use this little bath, Lucy. It'll save hot water. I know tha needs it for weshing up after the feast.'

'Eh, Abel, tha's a rate considerate soul,' said Grandmother, cutting runner beans, her hand trembling with rage at the old man.

Grandfather filled the bath from the gleaming brass tap near the ovens, then emptied a pail of cold water into the bath. Grandmother had put the pail ready to put the runner beans in while she was waiting to cook them.

'By gum, mother, me arm hurts,' said Grandfather in a loud voice, but Grandmother was so irritated with him she did not hear him. He took all his clothes off then sank down into the bath in front of the fiercely blazing fire. Grandmother muttered to herself as he sank into the bath.

'Eh?' said Grandfather.

'I said these runner beans are rate withered,' said she. Then she rushed out to look at the plum puddings. Then she came back and stretched over the bath and Grandfather to put potatoes out of a big earthenware jar round the roasting meat. She bent over the old man, stretching with difficulty.

'Am I in thy way, Lucy?' said Grandfather.

'Eh, Mester Walton, whatever makes thee think that?' said Grandmother, nearly falling headlong into the fire, as she closed the ovens again.

Grandfather kept dipping a square of red flannel into the hot water and putting it on his aching arm. Normally, Grandmother would have noticed that, but now she was cross and harassed. She began to roll out dough for teacakes.

'Top us up with hot water, Lucy,' asked Grandfather.

Grandmother obediently left the teacakes and topped up the bath from the kettle.

'Pour it down me arm, Lucy. It hurts,' said the old man helplessly.

'I know where I'd like to pour it,' said Grandmother through gritted teeth.

'This were the old Duchess of Pemberly's hip bath,' said Grandfather.

'Gerraway,' said Grandmother, kneading dough with fury. Finding the hot bath and fire did not ease his pain as much as he had hoped, Grandfather decided to get out of the bath. But his arm hurt so much he could not.

'Help us out, Lucy. Me arm's bad,' said the old man.

'Just let me open a window first, Abel. I'm in a muck sweat.' She opened the window and at once several wasps that had been loitering by the smell of cooking, skimmed into the kitchen.

'Help us out, Lucy,' said Grandfather.

'Just let me grease them tins for teacakes,' said Grandmother, bustling about and swatting the wasps.

The door opened and Sam's mother walked in. 'Pete and me are here, mother. Tom's scything thistles. He won't be here yet. He'll come after he's milked. His leg were hurting but he wanted us to come, so I left him scything thistles, or trying to. He's not steady on that leg yet, but he's that obstinate. Sam's on his way back, or should be. I could hear our dog howling when we came through your gate. I hope nothing's wrong back home.'

'You dunna feed that dog right,' said Grandfather from the bath and hot shadows. Sam's mother looked startled to see her father-in-law in the bath by the fire.

'Go an' get us some more scarlet beans and some mint, Bella love,' said Grandmother. 'Thy father-in-law's having a little bath. It's grand to have time to bath in front of the fire an' tittify thysen before a feast.'

Puzzled, Sam's mother went to get the beans.

'Help us out, Lucy, me arm's bad,' said Grandfather.

'Just let us boil up a drop more salt water for some beans,' said Grandmother.

'Pull me out o' this danged bath, mother!' roared Grandfather. Then the door opened, and Mrs Barker, Mrs Broomhead, and Mrs Turner stood there: they were paid to come and help each Feast Day.

'I'm glad to see thee,' said Grandmother. 'Thee, Annie, go to wesh-house and tend puddings ('Me bum's wedged in this piddlin' little bath,' roared Grandfather from the fireside shadows) and thee, May, go to the dairy where you'll see scotch hands all ready for thee. (A rich deep gurgle was heard as Grandfather rose a little in the bath, only to fall back with a fat splash and a ripe word.) And I'll come with thee, Meg, and show thee how I want the tables.' She left the old man roaring loudly.

The three women spent the next fortnight spreading the word round Lambton that the Waltons were mad, particularly old man Walton. 'There he were,' they gossipped, 'as naked as a baby in a bath in front of the fire. No shame.'

'Pull us out, Lucy,' said the old man when Grandmother returned.

'Just bide thy time, Abel, while I see to this batter,' said Grandmother busily.

'There's a wasp stinging us,' roared the old man.

'The tatties, Abel. Just let me tend the tatties,' said Grandmother, flicking expertly at the wasp. Then Jack came in with a small churn of fresh milk.

'I'm rate glad to see thee, our Jack,' said Grandmother calmly. 'I think thy father's stuck in t' bath.'

Jack clucked his tongue. 'Tha chooses a right time to have a bath, father, in the middle of all this, as if me mother hasn't enough to do.'

'Thee mind thy business and I'll mind mine,' said Grandfather, who had always disliked his third son's ready tongue.

Jack heaved the old man out of the bath. Grandfather roared with pain.

'I've just been trying to see what's the matter down at our Tom's place,' said Jack to Grandmother. 'The dog's howling, but I canna see owt wrong.' Grandmother was not listening: she was handing Grandfather a clean smock and towel.

'What's up with thy arm, anyhow?' she asked the old man.

'Our Jack's wrenched it when he were dragging us from bath,' said Grandfather peevishly. 'He's a cruel bugger is our Jack.'

The dark eyes looking closely into Sam's eyes belonged to a smartly dressed man in tweeds. He was looking closely into Sam's eyes, smacking his face and shaking him. It was Lord Blackdon, Lady Selina's nephew and sender of John Mellor to Manchester. He had been having a peaceful afternoon of trout fishing in his river. He had seen Sam climb the wall and

93

then take off his clothes and begin to walk upstream. He had not said anything, for he did not want to disturb the trout. He had sworn and cursed under his breath. His water bailiff should have spotted Sam and sent him off. This was his river. It was private. Then he had seen Sam go to the weir and topple back. Cursing, dropping his rod and line, shouting to his coachman, bailiff, and footman he had run to the weir.

'Damnation and hell to these local boys,' he muttered as he ran. 'They build schools for 'em and then give 'em blasted holidays to tomfool around in. I'll see that fool Middlemas. This boy is ruining m' fishing.'

The bailiff, who had been sorting the day's catch, stripped off, and brought Sam up. When his lordship saw Sam was not dead, he exploded with fury.

'I cannot fish my own rivers in August without the rag tag an' bobtail an' every Lambton urchin gettin' in m' way. I pay you, Roberts, £40 a year to guard m' rivers. See to it, man, in the future.'

Lord Blackdon strode away to leave the sweating river keeper to mop Sam up. The man was shaking. He had feared the loss of his job. He was mopping at a deep and bloody cut on Sam's face that was in the shape of the crescent moon.

'There, in there ... I saw ... ' Sam kept shuddering and pointing. He'd been saying it since he came round.

'The boy is hysterical,' Lord Blackdon had barked over his shoulder as he had strode away. 'He keeps babbling on about bones and bodies. He's seen an otter's den, or kingfisher's or rat's or some such thing and thinks he's seen a charnel house. My brandy flask's in the coach. Fetch it.'

'Yes, my lord,' said the footman, running for it.

They got Sam on the road, out of the sight of Lord Blackdon who went on fishing, and put him down on the dusty roadside amongst the white dusted silverweed and bleached white grass. Sam lay there a while: he saw the men were not interested in him. They were still scared of Lord Blackdon. They were only too glad when he retrieved his clothes and went on his way.

The valley was in shadow now. Only the high hills were touched with sun, and long shadows stretched over the landscape. He was glad to stop in the village of Ashford and

94

wash his face again in a horse trough. As the water stilled he glimpsed his reflection. Framed in the sweetpeas and holly-hocks that tumbled over the garden wall above the trough Sam saw a crescent-shape cut on his face. But his shocked mind could not remember where he had seen that before. He trudged on, his mind full of his own reflection. Then his thoughts would turn to the tunnel by the waterfall ... and try as he might he could not stop himself from thinking of something shadowy, living deep in that tunnel, and creeping, shadow-like, and taking lambs ... and him.

A carter, carting a load of second crop hay, offered him a lift to Hayton Station, a station a mile from Lambton that had really been built for the Duke of Pemberly to use. But it was a lift nearer home. As they came out from the thick trees Sam saw the Stone on the hill and felt a quiver of pain in his cheek and arm. The egg in his pocket comforted him a moment. But he knew it was only a matter of time. The danger to him was growing. Any day, or any night now ...

Thanking the carter, he took a short cut over the fields to Grandfather's farm, using a way he had not taken before, looking fearfully left and right and over his shoulder as he walked slowly up the hill. Over a wall he saw his own farm, a wisp of smoke curling up from the chimney and the dog howling. He thought no more about it. And he could not think what the shape of the cut on his face reminded him of.

The candles were lit for dinner in the dining hall of Blackdon Hall. The table shimmered with silver and cut glass and the air was fragrant with the scent of white roses and sweetpeas. Lord Blackdon was sitting down for dinner with his aunt, Lady Selina. He sipped some ice-cold champagne then frowned at his aunt.

'Not only are the poor boys of Lambton drunk, my dear aunt,' said he, putting the glass down and raising a heavy silver soup spoon to his oiled black moustaches, 'like that dreadful boy Mellor I had sent to Manchester, they are also mad. I pulled some boy from the water today gibbering about monsters, devils, and other gibberish. If I see him again I shall have him sent to the County madhouse.'

'Hush, my dear,' said Lady Selina. 'Do not mention the Devil so lightly. He is around us all the time.' She crumbled a bread roll and began to quote from the Bible.

' "And he laid hold on the dragon, that old serpent, which is the Devil and Satan and bound him a thousand years".' She sipped her champagne. 'I read that today, my dear, in the Bible. Frightening, don't you think?'

Lord Blackdon's face went black: he found his aunt a bore: he ordered the butler to fetch more champagne.

'I shall pray for that poor, dear, mad boy you found, dear John,' said Lady Selina.

The sun had gone, leaving an orange haze as a reminder of the perfect August weather. Lavender-coloured mists crept out from the trees and woods between Blackdon Hall and Bow Cross Farm. It was deathly silent in that woodland with no birds singing. The Stone, on its hill looking down on all, faded into the darkening east. And Grandfather's Feast was ready to begin. Neither Sam nor his father were there.

Grandfather, flushed red with harvest ale, banged the trestle table for silence. He always did this, as his own father had before him, and said a little rhyme as his father had. His son Ted, Sam's uncle, was sitting next to him, wearing some oats in his jacket. He was King of the Feast. Grandfather spoke,

> Let no tree grow
> Let no leaf blow
> 'Twixt us and All Saints' spire,
> Lest we be dragged
> Dead or wick
> To gold and the Devil below.

Nobody understood what it meant and nobody cared. It had always been said. Then Ted, as King of the Feast, banged the table three times and people began to eat.

'And what does that old rhyme mean?' said Sam's mother. Her eyes kept seeking Sam. He should be here by now. Dusk was falling. So should Sam's father. She couldn't think what had kept them.

'Some daft old rhyme,' said Albert, another of Sam's

96

uncles. He was cutting up big chunks of beef and forking them in his mouth at some speed. He grinned at Sam's mother, feeding meat chunks through his black beard. 'You know, like one of them daft old stories me father tells on winter's nights about the Devil and serpents and frits nobody but himself!' He took a long drink of the special ale. 'He always said his old dad said he must never let any trees block the view of the church spire or a bogey-man'd gerrus all.' Jack admired a juicy succulent crisp chunk of beef fat, then ate it. He laughed. 'Old stories or not, he's let that wood grow up an' we canna see the spire any more! Me father knows he'll get a good price for those ash poles next year. He only believes them old tales when there's no money to be lost!' He grinned at his sister-in-law, his white teeth shining in the light of the lambing lanterns that were hung round the barn.

'Or when he's frightening our Sam to death,' said Sam's mother. 'He really believes all that heathen nonsense ... He should be here now, my Sam.'

'Where's our Tom?' said Albert.

'He's coming up after milking. But his leg's so bad he's slow. And Gloria, our best milker, was sickening this morning. He may be with her.'

'There's a lot of sickness in the animals this year,' said Albert half to himself.

Sam's mother could not touch the food on her plate. Albert shovelled in beef and potatoes. She sniffed. Folks were a heathen lot on these hill farms, she thought. Although she had left many a year, a wave of homesickness for her father's farm overwhelmed her. There, near the river and the elms, all would be cosy and safe, the horses stabled, her mother making the first plum jam. But here ... money was short ... life a struggle. And her Sam had been acting strange this year, listening to old heathen tales ... almost as if he were going out of his mind. Then Sam appeared. But Grandfather spotted him first.

'Well, lad,' said Grandfather, 'how didst get on? Did she give thee any gold? And did her old cat give thee that claw scratch on thy face or did she?'

'She gave me five sovereigns and—' said Sam. Then he stopped. What was the use? Grandfather was now drunk on the ale. He gave the coins to his mother.

'Mean old cow!' bellowed Grandfather. 'Our Martha wants rollin' in pig muck and then 'er gold rammed up 'er—'

'Abel!' snapped Grandmother. 'Such talk. About your own sister. And in front of folks. You look pale, Sam. That's a nasty scratch on thy cheek. Been black-berrying?' But she was not really concerned. She was watching to see that Grandfather did not creep away, tickle the back of his throat with a straw, make himself sick in the dung heap, then come back and eat and drink as much as he'd sicked up. So Sam kept silent and ate and drank. It was some kind of comfort.

'Where's my father?' Sam asked his mother between mouthfuls; she told him she thought he had been held up by the sick cow.

All the meat was eaten, the pies and puddings and tarts and the Hartington cheese as big as a small millwheel lay in ruins. Grandfather swayed to his feet. The harvest feast always ended with a game of chase. Ted, as King of the Feast, was chased. If anybody caught him they kept the lucky corn dolly and bunch of oats that Ted had been wearing.

Grandfather shouted, 'What have ye?' and Ted, also swaying, shouted, 'I have the golden crown,' and he held the oats high so they shone gold in the tobacco smoke and lamplight. Then he ran off into the late summer darkness.

'Then get him, boys, by the hair of his head!' shouted Grandfather, and at once all Sam's uncles and the younger labourers gave chase with loud whoops. Out of habit Sam followed the crowd of men, putting his jacket on the bench and quickly seeing the marble egg was safe in his jacket pocket. Then he followed the men to the Top Pasture where Ted had run.

Sam's mother began to clear away some of the pots and plates: her mouth was a thin line of annoyance. Heathen goings on, she thought. 'Now we live in a modern age,' she thought, 'they ought to stop it.' She did not usually mind when her husband was with her but tonight she was irritated. She wanted to take Sam home and settle down by the fire with Sam's father for a nice restful cup of cocoa.

Sam slipped on the ice-cold dew by the Stone. There were a crowd of men all pushing and shoving, trying to get hold of

Ted. Sam was on the outside of the rabble, rolling in the cold dew. Somebody put their wet, ice-cold hand on his shoulder and squeezed hard. He turned round to protest but there was nobody there. The men were now half the field away.

No. There was somebody. Then with a shock he realized it was the Stone, black, ugly, and sullen against the glow of the barn lanterns. Again Sam felt the invisible hand, then he staggered, dizzy, and in pain, and slipped down on the cold dew.

In the woods along the old lane up to Bow Cross the owls were making a fearful racket, as though something was disturbing them. The panic and wild calling of the owls seemed to spread to the owls in the churchyard, particularly those in the lime trees close by Saltby's and Dame Trot's. Old Lil and Old Liz were eating bread by the fire: they were dipping fingers of bread into the tin of condensed milk they had opened—a new invention which they had just discovered.

'Listen to them ullets screeching, now nights are drawin' in: meks you think of all them stories we used to hear when us were little lasses, you know, about them things in churchyard and up on Walton Pastures,' said Liz.

The door opened and Mrs Broomhead, a relative of Liz's, came to see her. 'I've just been up to them Walton's harvest feast to help out, like I always do. Mad as hatters they are. The old man in a bath in front of fire and them grown men playing tiggy in fields! They've all got bats in the belfry, all got a tile missing, them Waltons.'

'I telled thee!' said Lizzy with relish, dipping a strip of bread into the thick yellow milk and sucking it. She licked her fingers. 'There'll be trouble up there before I'm much older,' she said. Then she told them the tale of the mad farmer who had lived up there when she was a girl, in a farm now in ruins near the Waltons: he had been carted away to the madhouse because he said the Devil was putting a curse on him.

Sam managed to get back to the barn: he held his shoulder where the icy grip had been.

'Look at you!' said his mother angrily. 'Wet through and cold. Have you fallen? You manage to walk twelve miles and yet as soon as you get back here you get all mucked up. Your uncles should never have given you all that harvest ale. And fancy turning up for the feast with a scratched face. Come on. We're going. I shall have to get your father his supper, being as he did not come. Go and say thank you to your Grandfather.'

Then, clutching a parcel of food from Grandmother for Sam's father, they set off home. His mother's voice bounced off the walls of the narrow lane. 'You're worn out, Samuel. You should not have ale at your age. I don't hold with it. Did you see your Uncle Jack asleep on the floor, he'd drunk so much? And that young hussy Marion Church trying to give him some more ale? If I were your Grandmother I wouldn't let her near my dairy ...'

Sam heard not one word of his mother's bouncing, echoing, rattling voice in the dark. All he could think of was that he was caught in a web of devilish horror. He could still see those bodies in the tunnel, feel the invisible hand on his shoulder by the Stone. He walked silently by his mother's side under the velvet sky of black and a dusting of misty stars.

Then his mother's voice stopped. She had seen there was no light in the farm below. She began to run, pulling and wrenching Sam's painful arm. They ran in the darkness, stumbling, kicking the loose stones of the road that nobody used any more. Above the rattle of stones they heard Gloria the cow calling in pain. Nobody had been to look after her. A sudden flash of sheet lightning behind them showed them the patient forms of the cows round the gateway waiting to be milked. Again came a flash of silent lightning from behind them and they saw the cows' breath silver in the lightning flash. Still dragging Sam and pulling him, Sam's mother dragged Sam into the kitchen.

She lit a candle, then cried out at what she saw. Sam's father was still in the chair and there was blood on the flagstones. Sam stood at the door too shocked to move. It was all coming true now. As the shadow lengthened, death, evil, and the power of the Devil were growing. Had there—he pushed the thought away but it would not go—had there been something in the house?

100

'For God's sake, Samuel, do something,' screamed his mother, fumbling with the lamp. The glass chimney slid from her hands and shattered on the floor. 'Get me a towel, see to the cows ... oh Tom ... oh Tom ... '

But Sam just could not move. The hand that had squeezed his shoulder had killed his father.

'God knows where the money will come from,' shouted his mother, 'you'll have to fetch Doctor Jones.'

'I dursn't ... ' whispered Sam. 'It'll get me ... like it's got him ... the Stone.'

His mother slapped his face hard. 'How could you, Sam, when your father is dying or dead ... just go, for God's sake ... are you going mad?'

Sam clutched at her wildly. 'Why won't you listen? There's a curse don't you see? I know, I can feel it, I've read about it and today—oh God, why won't you listen?' But his mother had reached for a small handbrush she used for the hearth. She was beating Sam with it. She threw him out of the door and followed him, beating him. She too was wild and hysterical. Again, from behind the Stone on the hill a flash of sheet lightning lit up the yard.

'It's working against us all the time,' shouted Sam, his hands over his head. But his mother was pushing him into the lane. She was calling him names, telling him he was mad, telling him it was the usual summer lightning ripening the corn. Tearing himself away, Sam began to run from her, to run the long way round for the doctor. His mother's shouting grew faint and he ran and ran. His father ... the Stone ... his mind was full of wild thoughts ... he expected to be killed at any time ... the lightning ... the owls ... a drunken tramp in the ditch reaching out at him ... his banging heart ... the lightning ... and finally sipping a glass of water in the doctor's hall while the doctor and his housekeeper tried to understand his story.

Then they jumped in the doctor's trap and were climbing the old way. The dark woods were filled with the sheet lightning shadows. Just as at Matlock Sam felt his arm quiver with pain at every lightning flicker ... they heard singing as they passed Bow Cross Farm.

With ice-cold water from the trough Sam's mother had

101

revived his father. When they got there Sam was sent to milk the cows, with a look as black as the Stone from his mother. So exhausted and frightened was Sam that he was almost sleep walking as he milked the cows: Pete, the farm man, had been given the evening off and was still singing at the feast.

'Tom'll be all right,' the doctor was saying. 'He's lost a lot of blood and it's the leg that was crushed last June, but he'll live ... Rest and good food will see him through ... You are having more than your share of bad luck in 1883, Bella?' said the doctor. He patted her arm comfortingly.

'God's will be done,' said Sam's mother quietly.

'Yes,' said Doctor Jones, watching her blow out the extra candles she had lit. 'It's your Samuel I'm worried about. He was almost delirious in my trap on the way up, talking about evil and stones and the Devil and curses—all he missed out was a wicked witch!'

Bella Walton gave the doctor a tight-lipped smile. 'Oh, I'm that sorry. His Grandfather is always filling his head with daft stories and then his uncles gave him some ale to drink at the feast and he's been a long walk today.'

'Ah,' said the doctor. 'That explains it.' But he left a green bottle of tincture of opium for Sam. 'Give him a good dose of that tonight. Give him a good night's sleep.'

But the doctor was thoughtful as his pony found its way under the stars and the lightning of a far distant storm. Samuel Walton's eyes had darted and rolled with fear. One arm had hung loosely. The doctor had a keen eye for details like that. And when he got in and his housekeeper had brought him hot chocolate and a glass of brandy he lit his lamp and went to his surgery. He pulled out of a drawer a dirty linen-covered book. He took it back to his study and finding a magnifying glass began to read. It was the notebook of old Doctor Benjamin who had been the doctor before him for fifty years. The doctor read the book. Yes. He had been right. There had been madness in the Walton family.

I have long suspected madness and lunacy on Walton Pastures. Many have come to me with hallucinations and painful and trembling limbs. In 1823 Isaiah Mosely tried to hang himself in the barn of his farm. He said the

Devil walked in his fields. I had him taken to the Derby Madhouse. His farm got water from Walton Pastures. The water from the troughs and wells bubbles up from deep wells and lead mines and contains sugars and salts of lead that softens brains and causes madness. And in 1840 young Jacob Walton, Abel Walton's brother, hanged himself, saying the Devil came to him by night. His mother died afterwards of a broken heart. Yet Abel Walton is a giant of a man and he can lift a sheep and shows no fear of Devils. He is not mad.

No, thought Doctor Jones. Old man Walton is not mad and has never mentioned anything about devils to me. And the Walton family have kept very quiet, naturally, about the dead brother. I doubt if anyone else in Lambton knows about it now. The doctor poked his fire.

'I'll keep an eye on young Samuel Walton,' he said aloud to the room. 'It could be he's had the madness passed on to him.'

'Well, is thy arm better?' snapped Grandmother as she and Grandfather got ready for bed.

'Aye. I mean no,' said Grandfather drunkenly, 'Jack pulled it. He likes to hurt his poor old dad.' Grandfather had forgotten the pain had begun that morning. Grandmother snorted and climbed wearily into the big soft bed. But Grandfather suddenly felt off-colour again, none of his usual satisfaction that he usually felt on Feast Night. He felt jumpy, on edge like he did when the winds of winter howled round the farm, or the thunder crashed. Something somewhere was wrong.

He unlaced his boots very slowly. He was very very tired and drunk and sleepy. He turned to look at Grandmother who appeared to be fast asleep.

'Aye,' whispered the old man. He took his boot in his hand and aimed at the candle on the chest of drawers. He could not be bothered to walk across and blow it out.

'Aye,' he whispered and raised the boot high.

'Dunna thee dare chuck thy boot at candle,' came Grandmother's voice from the bed.

'Eh, Lucy, I were only aiming it at yon flying buzzbeetle

103

mankin' round the flame,' said Grandfather. 'I didna want yon beetle a nipping thee in night.' Suddenly the old man burst into tears. 'I missed our Edgar at the Feast tonight. It's only two months since he were killed in yon quarry under t' owd Stone!'

'Gerrin that bed, Abel,' said Grandmother. Then she padded over to the candle and blew it out. 'I canna see no flying buzzbeetles,' she muttered. She shivered as she got into bed. It had been a strange day . . . she did not like the gypsy's warning for one thing. She gave the old man a kiss on his wrinkled cheek, then put her arms round him. The old man sobbed like a frightened child.

Outside, in the thin moonlight, from a moon like a watchful eye, the Stone was still and watchful in the cold August dew.

Exhausted as he was Sam felt he must hide his treasure of the marble egg; he was also unsure of how to use it. But he wanted it for himself. He did not want his mother to take it and put it on the mantelshelf—for it was an attractive thing. He relit his candle with stealth and lifted the loose floorboard where he kept a secret notebook, a broken pen, a penny bottle of ink, a silver button, and a wishbone. To this collection he added his egg. He could not help noticing how much better he felt. It must be the medicine.

'It's damn strange,' he heard his father say in the next room. 'I was blacked out all that time, four till nine, but I remember seeing Sam by the door as you lit the candle. Then when you made him fetch Doctor Jones I blacked out again. Then when he came back I were all right again. Right strange, that.'

Sam carefully put the little treasure, as Martha had called it, under his floor. Then, overcome with Doctor Jones' opium, the long walk, and fearful happenings, he fell promptly asleep.

So August 1883 faded into September. The sunset shadow of the Stone lengthened more and more. Now it was five fields long and more than half-way to Sam's house. And nobody would listen. His mother's face told him he must not even discuss the events of the Harvest Feast Day let alone mention curses and evil forces.

Sam found himself wanting to get back to school; Mellor might have returned. Will might have seen something in the well. Even Jessie might help. He was glad when it was the night before school began again.

Will Saltby was not glad it was school the next day.

'Go down to the old well in the bottom cellar, Will, and bring us some water from there to wesh thy hair ready for school. It's lovely water, brings thy hair up a treat.'

'Oh, mam,' moaned Will. 'Me hair's right clean, I've no dicks crawling in it like—'

His mother raised her finger. 'Don't start. I've had a long day in that shop. I've told you—go on.'

Will went down whistling. He had not been down there since that night his mother had wanted water to cool the cream for the strawberries. Neither, as far as he knew, had anybody else. He had a shock. The water had been over the rim of the well. Water was on the walls. He held his candle up to see. There was a crack in the wall and strange marks. He lowered the bucket and several big bubbles burst. The water was dirty.

'I've never seen owt like it,' said his mother. She threw the water out to swill the yard. A smell of poisoned water filled their nostrils.

Will was very thoughtful while his mother rubbed his hair with red carbolic soap.

'And what's up with thee?' said his mother, towelling his hair with vigour. 'You're not sickening for summat now school's starting? Have I got to put up with thee for longer?'

'I was just thinking,' said Will. 'Do you think some blood's leaked down to well from graveyard?'

'You'll leak blood in a minute, our Will, if you don't get up them stairs and get to sleep ready for school in t'morning. Now go on.'

Will lay awake a long time thinking. And it was not about school.

105

Chapter Three

Sam got up early the morning that school began: he felt cheerful and optimistic even though it was school. Perhaps there was still time to do something. He looked at the almanac hanging by the fireplace as he ate his bread and butter for breakfast ... there was not as much food on the Waltons' table as there used to be. He saw there were three weeks to the end of September and then the whole of the month of October before Hallowe'en itself. He glanced at his father: he was still in pain with his leg, but nothing else had happened.

At school, Sam thought, he would see Mellor: Tom and Will would be in a sober mood now that weeks of school stretched ahead into the autumn. Once they had listened, then they could all tell the grown-ups. Grown-up people would not listen to Sam on his own; he knew that from bitter experience.

His mother gave him some of her own cheese and wrapped it in an oatcake for his dinner. Then Sam took an apple from the tree at the bottom of the yard. Then he was off, whistling for once, along the new turnpike road.

He had worked all the holiday on the farm—except that terrible day at Taddington. Now, to be walking along the road in the morning sun seemed like a holiday. And best of all there would be somebody his own age to talk to. He turned his face away from the Stone on the hill and felt the first warm rays of the sun that had not been risen long over the hills behind Pemberly House. He deliberately looked at the dew-dusted cobwebs in the hedgerow and the pheasants pecking and running in the fields. Today will be a new start, he thought.

Even his mother had seemed on his side that morning. He had offered to go down with the milk (not alone of course, for Pete the farm man would have been there) to the milk-train at half-past six.

'You've been doing a man's work,' said his mother. 'Don't do too much. It's lesson time now. You mustn't burn the candle at both ends. The doctor said I was to keep an eye on you.'

Sam was pleased. Perhaps they would listen soon. He'd tried to make the doctor listen. Sam did not know whether he had listened or not.

But it was a hard task to keep cheerful. He tried not to look at the bunches of red hawthorn berries, the scarlet clusters of mountain ash berries, or the little drifts of dead leaves in the turnpike's gutter. If you did not look at these things you could still pretend it was summer ...

A pheasant exploded out of the roadside with a rattle of wings. Sam found himself sweating; he was still very jumpy. Soon the pheasants would be killed ... and me? What will happen to me?

The school-yard was half-full when he reached it, swept clean, full of long cool shadows. So different from the hot dust of July when he had seen it last. And there was Will! Sam ran over to him.

'Hey up, Will,' said Sam, suddenly shy.

'Now then, Sam,' said Will.

'Where's John Mellor?' Sam asked hopefully.

'He's still in t' loony-bin at Manchester,' said Will. 'He's daft.'

That was a blow. But he had to keep trying.

'Will, you know that afternoon Mellor said there were summat in your well? I think there was. You know that owd Stone near me Grandfeyther's. It's gorra picture on it of what Mellor could have seen, and one day in the holiday I were by the river—'

'Tha's a barm-pot, thee,' said Will. 'Rate barmy. Tha's got bats in the belfry. A tile loose. Thy screws are falling out. Tha's as daft as Mellor.' And he walked slowly away.

Sam was so disappointed he failed to notice three things. Will had not interrupted him straightaway. He had stared at Sam thoughtfully. And he did not sound at all convinced when he called Sam a barm-pot. Sam just stared after Will, longing to talk to somebody. Then Frank Turner bounded up to Sam.

'Let's play *Just Like Me*,' said Frank.

'Go on, then,' said Sam. He needed friends badly.

'I went up a hill on my way home,' said Frank.

'Just like me,' said Sam.

'I saw a tree,' said Frank, his white and waxen face shining in the low sunlight.

'Just like me,' replied Sam obediently.

'I saw a lad whose Granny were a witch,' sniggered Frank.

'Just like me,' said Sam, falling into the trap: he was still looking in Will's direction.

'They're all barmy on Walton Pastures,' said Frank. 'An' us saw thy uncle carrying a load of witches' brooms over Lambton Bridge in t' holidays. Thee were in t' cart.'

Lil Gosling and Lizzy Gomershall, Mrs Broomhead, and Mrs Turner had spread the gossip well. Tom Wilson strolled up next, with six conkers he had threaded on a bootlace so he could harden them up.

'Canst get us any magic conkers, Sam? Canst put these conkers by t' magic stone of thine in Walton Pastures an' mek these conkers as hard as stone? Hast got a magic wand in thy breeches, Sam?' He slapped Sam on the back and went away laughing.

'You wait. You just all wait,' thought Sam, desperately miserable. At that moment he would have been glad if the creatures of the deep had come into the yard . . . He moved to the long shadows and little drifts of leaves where the girls were playing. Fanny Gibbs had organized a skipping game and her mane of blonde hair bobbed on her finely starched pinafore. Then she saw Jessie smile at Sam. She saw Sam's face break into a hopeful and wonderful smile back. Fanny hated any boy who smiled at a girl—unless it was herself. Fanny at once began to lash the rope on the yard, causing a few fallen leaves to rise up and float away. Her face ugly with hatred for Jessie, she chanted a skipping rhyme.

> *As I were going down Coalpit Lane*
> *I thought I smelled some kippers.*
> *I asked a lady what it were*
> *She says, 'It's Jessie's knickers.'*

Her fine hair shone in the sunshine and she laughed. But Jessie was used to ill treatment both at home and at school. She just thought about Sam. Poor Sam. His big blue eyes were so miserable. She felt so sorry for him.

'When I were in Derby I got chickenpox,' whispered Jessie, in a determined bid to cheer Sam up. 'I picked at me scabs on me bum. It's covered in scab marks. I'll show thee if tha wants.' Jessie could not have offered more.

'Look at them two,' shouted the spiteful Fanny. 'They're a rate pair o' nutters together.'

Sam was so busy scowling at Fanny he had not noticed Will. Will was staring at Sam, sucking a lollipop thoughtfully. Then he came up to them. But at that moment Middlemas snapped the gold case of his gold hunter watch and his whistle cut into the fragrant cool September morning.

Miss White, refreshed by the holiday and carefully muffled up in her winter brown dress, bustled through the long morning. Long division on slates, handwriting, and reading round the class. It was during this reading lesson that Jacob Appleby sent round a note that read

GRANNY WALTON IS A WITCH   BY JACOB APPLEBY

He had written it at home, for it was written on a torn-off bit of a blue sugar bag. On the other side was a drawing of a witch on a broomstick and the words

WALTON'S BROOMS IS BEST

'Harvest is coming,' said Miss White, unaware of the fast

moving note. 'We must practise our harvest hymns for Harvest Festival. We will sing now,' said she. The note paused in its travels, for Miss White's piano technique fascinated the class. She played the piano in a reverse position, her hands on the keyboard but her eyes rolling, snapping, and glaring. Her neck could turn a full half-circle. But while she was opening the piano and blowing off the dust, Jacob gave Sam the note.

> Fair waved the golden corn
> In Canaan's pleasant land,

sang the class obediently. Sam read the note under the desk. He went very red.

> When full of joy, some shining morn
> Went forth the reaper band.

A fat smack filled the dusty sunlit room. Sam had thumped Jacob Appleby. Miss White forgot her good temper.

'I am try-ing to tell you of the joys of waving corn in songs of praise to God. But you, Samuel Walton, are more interested in fighting. Very well. The harvest corn will not wave in this room but my cane will. Come out.'

And Sam was caned. Jessie could see and feel Sam's misery. She knew he was frightened of some old stone or something; but she could not really understand that. She lived in an overcrowded slum, in a row of cottages, and slept four to a bed at night. Loneliness was unknown to her. But she wanted to help Sam—make him happy again. Miss White bent down next to Jessie to help Frank Turner divide £100 between various and confusing numbers of workmen.

'Remember, child, that $\frac{23}{91}$ of a penny will count as a farthing,' she said, bending over Frank, her brown-dressed bottom waving with excitement close to Jessie. Miss White became very excited over parts of pennies. Her bottom vibrated closer and closer to Jessie as she did tiny figures on Frank's slate.

As the bottom loomed nearer, Jessie held her nose. That would make Sam laugh. Middlemas, coming in with a register, saw her.

'You crude-minded cheap child, girl of the gutter,' he hissed. 'Stand on your bench till noon.'

So Jessie, with a shaft of hot sun on her neck and aching legs, had to stand on her bench. Wasps, plum drunk from the orchards of Lambton, whined about her as she stood high above the class. She looked longingly outside where the silver and gold September air was full of floating seeds and thistledown, like drifting fireflies. And she could feel Sam's misery, beating up to her in waves, and her eyes filled with tears. Poor old Sam, she thought, he looks proper poorly. 'He looks as though he's going potty or summat,' she whispered to herself, for every now and then Sam's face would be twisted with fear. She noticed too that one side of his body seemed to be leaning and twisted.

Things were no better in the afternoon—Will was late as he had had to help in the shop. The boys were threading baskets (which were undone at the end of each lesson) and the girls were stitching aprons.

Jessie was determined to help Sam. Something. Anything. She looked at him and thought to herself that he looked as though he were being squeezed by a giant's hand, he was so huddled up and twisted. To her dying day Jessie was never quite sure why she did what she did. It was just something to do and something had to be done. Perhaps she wanted to share Sam's misery.

She swallowed a pin. She put her hand up.

'Please, Miss White, ma'am, if you please, I've sucked in and swallowed me pin.'

'What do you mean, child, you've tucked in and borrowed a pin?' said Miss White testily, her own thin lips bristling with pins like a discontented hedgehog. 'What drivel are you mouthing now, child?'

There was a brief silence broken by Fanny's low, rich giggle of delight.

'Please, Miss White, ma'am, I took a pin out o' me bellyband o' t'apron and swallowed it.'

Miss White opened and shut her mouth, the thin pink lips shining, like a fish in a murky pond. Then she uttered a little tight scream and ran for the headmaster.

'I told thee all, her and Sam Walton were nutters,' said Fanny Gibbs in her clear voice, contentedly biting off a thread from her own exquisite feather stitching. Then Middlemas roared in like an autumn gale.

'Stand on your HEAD, child, now,' he cried. 'We must, at

111

ALL COSTS, get the pin back. The inspectors always examine my store of bodkins and have even counted my pins and needles. They know how many I have to the last pinhead. They will know one is missing. And I cannot say the missing pin is in Jessie Smith's ab-do-men. Cough child, and fast!'

Jessie had to cough on her head. Nothing came.

'Exhale, child, briskly,' said Middlemas in a growing panic. 'Pretend you are blowing out your nightly candle.' Jessie pretended but nothing came.

'You will come to the doctor now.' He marched her savagely through Lambton, propelling her through the market day crowds.

'You're driving them all crazy, Middlemas!' roared the doctor, who had been enjoying the sunshine and his chrysanthemums. 'First Walton, now this one.'

Middlemas was furious. 'I must have the pin, doctor. It is no joke. The inspectors are punctilious over pinheads.'

'Well,' replied the doctor. 'If you want to go down the sewers and privies of New Street tomorrow morning when Jessie's done her business you may find it. No guarantee, sir, ha! And it'll be a sticky business!' He laughed loudly. 'Leave young Jessie with me,' he said.

Middlemas returned to school in a black rage: what a vulgar man the doctor was to be sure. And he had had a gross of pins, complete with heads and now there were only 143.

Doctor Jones handed Jessie over to his housekeeper who was instructed to give her a large quantity of fine white bread, thickly buttered. 'Bread'll stop the pin sticking to your insides, the butter'll grease it out!' said the doctor. Jessie ate and ate hungrily. Three-quarters of a loaf vanished fast.

Back at school Sam should have been surprised when Will asked him to go apple scrumping that evening. He was so upset about the note about his Grandmother that he did not notice how Will kept staring at him thoughtfully. At playtime Will kept coming up to Sam as though he were going to ask a question, then he would stop. Sam decided to go apple stealing. He half-expected things to begin happening in Lambton soon and he wanted to be there to explain.

Sam ran home, the long way, did his jobs and puzzled over his father who seemed to limp outside and yet be all right when he was in the house.

'No mischief, mind,' his mother said. She looked tired and worn out and did not ask any more questions. So he ran the long way to Lambton. It was only six o'clock but the town was in shadow and a faint smell of autumn and woodsmoke hung in the air.

He found Will on the big bridge, making a little pile of dead leaves with his boot. He seemed thoughtful. Then Peter, Tom, and Frank joined them.

'Us'll go and scrump Doctor Jones' plums, first,' said Tom. They went along the river towards the walled orchard of Doctor Jones. Will kept close to Sam as though he was going to ask something any minute. The stone walls of the orchard were still sun-warmed and wasps, bees, and hoverflies floated in the quiet air. Butterflies flitted over the tall Michaelmas daisies under the trees.

The doctor stood contentedly at the glass door to his garden, enjoying the last warm scents of his flowers. He had lit a cigar and he smiled as he watched the boys make the Michaelmas daisies wobble as they crept under them, thinking they had not been seen. The doctor stepped back into the shadows, only his cigar glowing like a ruby. He whistled softly and took his eyes away from the rocking Michaelmas daisies and looked at the sky: a plump cheese-coloured half-moon hung low in it. Soon that moon would silver and brighten with frost. The doctor shivered. He had never known such a cool September. A sort of cold seemed to hang over Lambton—he'd signed three death certificates today. Many of his patients had died that year ... one of those things he supposed ... he hoped the frost would not kill his fragrant tobacco plants under his study window ... he chuckled softly ... he could see young Walton and young Saltby sitting side by side on the Victoria plum tree branch, stuffing down the ripe rich plums. Young Wilson and young Turner were in his greengages doing the same. The doctor was fond of the greengages himself. His eyes narrowed. Young Walton looks ill, he thought, withered and crooked as he sat on the branch.

'Art tha still frit o' that Stone?' asked Will, plum juice streaming down his chin. Sam now thought that Will was

113

going to make fun. But Will had never been so serious in his life. He leaned over to Sam, peeling the skin off a plum and revealing its netted gold flesh.

'You know our well,' said Will, 'where big fat Mellor said he saw a monster?'

The question was never answered. A loud roar sent the blackbirds chinking in fear and anger.

'I can see you, damn you, Walton . . . Saltby . . . Wilson . . .' bellowed the doctor. 'Every damn one of you scoundrels and scallywags . . . no, blast ye, don't run . . . one step out of this garden and I'll have Middlemas tan your backsides, your fathers whip ye, Constable Gratton arrest ye . . . stay where ye are . . . I'll deal with ye!'

The boys came, boot-nails rattling, scraping the old golden flagstones of the doctor's garden path.

'Go round to the side door—and wait,' said the doctor curtly. They went.

'Step inside, young gentlemen,' said the doctor grimly. He led them to his dispensary where huge brown jars and blue and green bottles shone in the light of the candle.

'My plums,' said the doctor, 'rot your guts when eaten raw. If I don't give you some medicine you'll be bent double in your privies for a week, roaring aloud with bellyache. I'll mix the medicine now.'

Silently, not daring to move, they watched while he mixed greasy castor oil with a sharp smelling, white peppermint stuff that looked like ice cream but most certainly was not. Then he added bicarbonate of soda and shook in several bitter powders. He added no syrup of fruit that he usually did to his bitter medicines. He poured the oily, brown, streaky potion into medicine glasses and watched the boys drink the oily stinking mess to the last drop. Except Sam. He did not give Sam a glass.

'You come with me, young Walton,' said he. Then he turned on the others swiftly.

'You saw me pound my crystals to powder just then? Yes? Good. Because if I catch you round my plums and pippins again I will personally see to it that Mr Middlemas pounds your arses to powder too!'

Brown, blue, pale blue, and dark brown eyes stared at the

doctor's strong language, round-eyed that he should threaten them with such bad language.

'Now you,' he said to Sam. 'Come with me.' Worried and upset Sam followed him. He did hope that the doctor was not going to cause bother at home. He could tell by his mother's and father's faces they were worried over money. The doctor took Sam into his study. It was beginning to get dark but a fire crackled in the grate. The doctor lit two candles and rang for his housekeeper.

'Keep my dinner waiting,' said he. Then he poured two large glasses of port and gave Sam one.

'Drink it,' he said. Sam dared do no other. He drank the sweet wine and nibbled the thin biscuit the doctor thrust in his hand. Sam began to sink in the deep leather chair, his head in shadow, resting on the greasy circle where the doctor's head usually rested. The ash logs blazed away, filling the room with golden light. Above the fireplace was a picture of a road with big trees and cows going down it. There was a rug in front of the fire. A vase of chrysanthemums scented the air with their bitterness. It was so different from his own house . . . the wine was nice . . . would the doctor help?

'Now, Sam,' said the doctor. 'Tell me everything that's troubling you. Every worry. Every ache. Every pain. Every weakness. I'm ready, boy.'

And Sam did. Beginning with the thunderstorm of 1882 when he had first seen the Stone, he went through all his suspicions. He told the doctor about the book of Annie Dale and the shadow monsters deep in the mines. He told him of the power of the Devil, the Stone's growing shadow and the pains in his arm and head. He told him of the strange tingling feelings and the painful grip of the invisible hand on the night of the harvest supper. And last, but not least, he told him about the train accident, the ever increasing bad luck to the family beginning with the death of his uncle. He left nothing out.

'I'll get some real help now,' he thought from the firelit nest in the chair.

The fire hissed and crackled and the room was full of gentle and comforting light and shadow. Outside a robin sang in the twilight. The doctor was silent. He fetched a small hammer

115

from his surgery and tapped Sam's elbows, wrists, knees. He felt carefully at Sam's arms and legs, turning and pulling them gently. Then he took one of the candles and held the flame close to Sam's eyes and looked long and hard. He tapped Sam's forehead many times.

He put the candle down. He stood lost in thought for several minutes and a distant chiming clock silvered the air with bell music and eight notes. Then the doctor did everything again. He held the candle near Sam's eyes and did things to them with a magnifying glass. Then he sat down.

'Now listen, Samuel,' said he. 'Forget those strange old stories your Grandfather tells. Forget, too, old Mrs Trotter's book. There are no such things as ghosts and certainly not monsters. The powers of evil do not exist. I have ridden, alone, Samuel, down the darkest lanes in this parish, often at midnight, in thunder, howling winds, snowstorms. And seen and felt—nothing, Samuel. There is nothing. Believe me, my boy, there's nothing to worry about. And as for an old standing stone causing death and evil—well, it's all in your imagination. Forget it, Samuel, help your mother. I'll give you some more medicine, my boy!'

Sam looked into the flames. Nobody ever helped. Nobody. He heard the doctor in the next room, mixing medicine and muttering ... 'laudanum to make him sleep ... a mild laxative ... nothing like opening your bowels daily ... a little salt of copper and iron as a tonic ... it'll help him for a bit ... not for long, though.'

'What does he mean?' thought Sam.

For not one minute did the doctor think the medicine would help. It might help for a time ... The doctor had lied to Sam.

'Now off home, Samuel. Straight off. Take a spoonful of this every night and we'll soon have you as right as nine-pence!' lied the doctor. Then the doctor went back inside for his meal. He felt so upset he went down to his cellar and opened a bottle of claret. He drank this with an excellent rabbit and game pie given him by a patient too poor to pay his bills. The doctor sipped his wine thoughtfully.

When he had been a young student, long long ago, in Edinburgh, he had been shown a boy of about Sam's age with

116

a cancer growing in his brain. The dullness of one of Sam's eyes, as he had held the candle to it, the weakness down one side of his body were the same. And the boy was talking madly. He was going insane. Samuel Walton would go mad and then die. It was nothing to do with the water as he had thought earlier.

Poor Mrs Walton, thought the doctor. Her husband badly injured, her brother-in-law dies and now her son Samuel ... poor lad. He'd leave him alone as long as he could but the boy would get worse. He'd have to be locked away in the end. He would have to be taken to the County Lunatic Asylum near Derby.

The doctor began to demolish a damson pie. It was very sad. Samuel Walton might just live to the end of October.

Will waited for Sam in the street. He waited and waited for ages, so it seemed. Will sucked a striped bull's eye humbug, three lemon drops, a liquorice pipe, and a sherbet dab and still Sam did not come and still the taste of the medicine stayed in his throat and mouth. Tom had said it was pig tiddle. Then Will saw his mother on the warpath heading his way.

'And just what have you been up to? That Tom Wilson says you've been in the doctor's garden. I'll doctor's-garden you. Just wait till I get thee home, young man. And your father wants a word with you as well. Have you been in that cellar, splashing water? He says there's water all up the walls and if it wasn't you, who was it? A right mess. You've got it coming to you—'

'Gerroff, mam,' wailed Will. 'You're hurting me!'

'I will hurt you,' rejoined Mrs Saltby.

'Boys will be boys!' said the Lambton lamplighter, who had thoroughly enjoyed the drama. He touched a gaslamp with his pole and the lamp glowed warmly on the mother and son, making the twilight a darker richer blue.

'Just you wait. Just you wait,' Mrs Saltby kept repeating as they walked under the golden radiance of the gaslamps through the square.

'Oh, mam!' said Will, as he was marched away.

117

Sam ran the long way home in the September moonlight. His mind pounded with the thoughts, nobody helps, nobody believes ... and high on the hill, like a thorn in the silver moonlight waited the Stone. And it was so still. It was as if moon-silvered walls, trees, fields, and hills held their breath. It was all very beautiful and evil.

Mrs Walton pounced with as much gusto as Mrs Saltby had. 'Where've you been? We needed you here. Your father has had to go to bed. He was working in that top field and his leg began to bleed again.'

She spat on the hot iron she lifted from the fire, to test its heat. Sam could see her eyes bright with tears as she trimmed the lamp with her other hand. She sniffed.

'And don't you dare tell me it's that Stone ...' She pressed the iron down with unnecessary force on Sam's shirt. Sam began to eat the supper of bread and plum jam and the golden butter of late summer. Then his mother turned on him.

'I don't know what we're going to do, Samuel. We've no money coming in. Just the milk money from Manchester. And that's not quite enough to pay the rent at Michaelmas in a fortnight's time. We've had to use that money from the silver snuff box to order hay. Ours were that thin this year and late. What's the matter with your arm?'

'It's that Stone—'

'Don't start. Get off to bed. I'm doing my best to make ends meet and I can't get a grain of sense nor reason from you. All you've got is growing pains and the strain of carrying heavy buckets day in and day out. You must change hands and sides. You've been doing the work of a man.' She did not carry out her threat to send him up. Her mind was so concerned with money.

'Why don't you ask Grandfather?' said Sam, mixing the plum jam and butter on his bread into a sunset of red and gold.

'Oh no. Oh no. If he can't see what a mess we're in, I'm not asking. No, Samuel. You and me tomorrow—you'll have to miss school—we'll go to the workhouse and see if they'll give us some relief money ... I never thought it would come to this.' She was near to tears again.

118

'I don't care,' thought Sam. 'It's a waste of time anyway. It would not be so bad if I could talk to Will.' He said nothing.

His mother poked the fire and raked the ashes out. The clock struck half-past nine. Sam locked the door. His mother turned out the lamp and they went upstairs to bed. Sam took the bottle of medicine and hid it under the floorboards. He dared not tell his mother about the visit. He looked at the marble egg. It *was* a treasure. It looked beautiful in the candlelight. Then he took a swallow of the medicine.

He took the egg in his hands and felt it, feeling the medicine warm and relax his whole body.

'I'm feeling a bit better, Bella,' Sam heard his father say. 'I allus does when I get up here. It's walking them steep fields up by my father's fields that does me in. I'm all right when I lay down. I must be getting old.'

'Not thee,' Sam heard his mother say, and he heard the tears in her voice again.

The medicine was making Sam feel drowsy and he almost dropped the egg, glistening with a wet look to it in the shine of the candle. Six weeks to Hallowe'en, he thought as he drifted off to sleep ... and nobody cares.

The first real mist of autumn swirled about Sam and his mother as they climbed the old lane to Bow Cross on their way to the workhouse the next morning. Sam felt numb. His arm tingled. He knew it was the Stone at work. He half-hoped something horrible would crawl out of an old mine shaft and show his mother, who was walking along, head held high and trusting, she had told Sam earlier, in God. Then they met Jack in the lane carrying a pail.

'Yo' two are up with the birds,' said he. 'There's summat up with our well. Water's right cloudy. Me father says there's a devil at t'bottom stirring it up! Me mother says the only devil within a dozen miles around is him! They're going at each other hammer an' tongs. I've had to go to owd trough in woods to get this to drink.' He grinned at them both, his face brown and healthy from the summer sun.

'We've got to go to workhouse because we've got no money left, all because of that—' said Sam listlessly.

'Just you start all that twaddle, young man,' said his mother furiously and cuffed his ears. 'Well, you should listen to me,' thought Sam, rubbing his ear. He knew his mother was ashamed of having to go and beg at the workhouse. This was one way he could punish her for not listening. And things were happening deep in the earth. He was glad he opened his mouth, for his mother would not have told her brother-in-law.

'We're a bit short, Jack, for the rent and winter feed. I don't want to bother Tom.' His mother spoke coldly.

'I've a bit put by in a tin in me bedroom,' began Jack, but Sam's mother stopped him.

'No, Jack, thank you. It's good of you all the same. Come along you,' she said, and grabbed Sam and marched away. When they were in the mist-filled woods she rounded on Sam.

'You little trouble-maker, you,' said she, and she shook Sam vigorously. Sam clutched at an elder bush and that began to shake as well, tiny droplets flying in the mist. Her boots dislodged some small stones that went rattling down the path. They seemed to dislodge more stones below and the misty trees echoed eerily for some time with the sound. Then his mother yanked at him and they continued on their way down the lonely abandoned road. Sam shook free and walked a little way behind her. He saw she had a sticky burdock seed ball stuck below her bottom. He did not tell her. He was close to hating her this morning.

The woods dripped. Out of one old mine shaft the mist seemed to be moving like breath. Again Sam heard that strange rattle of stones. Bumps and rustles made him jump. Now and again an early falling leaf spun slowly down. But nothing was said until the great iron gates of the workhouse, neatly beaded with drops of moisture, swung open and they were in.

It's better than school, thought Sam. Nobody wants to talk to me there.

But he was wrong. Somebody did want to speak to Sam.

'Where's Sam Walton?' asked Will in the school-yard, hitting out at a conker with his own ninetysixer and smashing the other into fragments.

120

'How am I supposed to know?' said Tom Wilson angrily, looking irritably round at the white pulp particles that had been his conker. 'Why? Dost want a spell off him to get thee a girlfriend?'

'I just want to ask him summat, that's all,' said Will, putting a liquorice pipe in his mouth. His face had a closed look on it.

But Will got every one of his long division sums wrong that morning. Something was bothering him.

'There's a long queue for parish relief,' said the old man on the door to Sam's mother, but he showed her where to go. 'Half of them won't get anything,' said the old man after her. 'It's cheaper for them to get you in this place.' He pulled at Sam.

'You're not allowed before the Board. Thee mun wait here.' So his mother went off and Sam waited.

Ten o'clock clanged dismally from the Spike clock in the tower above. Eleven o'clock. He heard a man screaming somewhere. His arm ached.

Twelve o'clock struck. Still Sam sat on the bench with the smell of stew and yellow soap floating round him: a curious sadness in the air seemed to waft round him too. Then just as the muffled strokes of twelve had died away he saw Doctor Jones (who was the workhouse doctor) walking down the corridor with the master and the matron of the workhouse and a man with a silk top-hat in his hands and amazing lengths of gold watch chain. They were discussing inmates loudly and cheerfully.

'You agree, then, doctor, that Thomas Dryfield is mad and you'll have him locked away at Derby Asylum? He needs locking away,' said the matron in her loud manly voice. 'Full moon nights are the worst. He screams and roars and points to the hills over Walton Pastures. He is exceedingly violent. He used to have the little farm on the edge of Pemberly Park, not all that far from Walton Pastures. He cannot POSSIBLY be left here.'

'Certainly, matron,' said the tall man. 'Anything to reduce the number of paupers in the workhouse.'

121

Doctor Jones saw Sam and nodded. 'Taking your medicine, young fellow?' he asked. Sam nodded sulkily. Then the group passed through a door to the side of Sam and it closed firmly. Not long afterwards, Sam saw girls and boys in long aprons, not much older than himself, carrying steaming hot dishes into the room. The door stood open for a while.

'And then,' boomed matron's voice, 'there's Joshua White. He's a tramp that came knocking at the gates, would you believe it, one morning in July. He thinks something or somebody is after him! Of course, it's the demon drink that has rotted his brain—'

The door shut again. Sam was very thoughtful on his bench. Inside, under a huge picture of the Duke of Pemberly who had given the land for the workhouse, the master and the matron and the doctors began to eat a roast beef dinner. A watery sun gleamed on the chrysanthemums as golden as the picture-frame of the duke's portrait. The sun shone on the shining floor, polished daily by a pauper boy. Somebody had left the door open a crack. Sam heard every word and smelled every delicious meat smell. He was hungry, stiff, and cold.

'Of course I could not possibly suggest we give relief to Bella Walton. I see she's waiting to see us after luncheon.' There was a pause while the doctor slopped horse-radish sauce on his meat. 'They have a farm, a guinea a week from milk sent to Manchester, and they make their own butter and cheese. She must see the Duke of Pemberly. It's his estate. No. That's the boy outside. Very sad. I examined him last night. He shows every sign of growing madness. Says he is going to be attacked by stones and creatures from under the earth. I am uncertain whether he has a growth of cancer in his brain or whether the drinking water on Walton Pastures is full of salts and sugars of lead that have softened his brain. I have said long enough that the water for Lambton wells should not be taken from those ancient flooded mines. Well, Samuel Walton is mad from—'

Sam could stand it no longer. He burst in from the cold stone corridor with its smell of misery and into the sunlit room, fragrant with roast beef, polish, and wood-smoke.

'Get out! This is PRIVATE!' screamed the enraged matron, swelling dangerously in her black dress.

'I'm not mad! I'm not mad! You see. You see. You wait until somebody else is killed. I'm not mad. By Hallowe'en—'

The matron put a firm, cruel, expert, Pears soap-scented hand over Sam's mouth. It was surprisingly strong and boney. But it was very effective.

Sam kicked backwards then sank his teeth into her pink finger above a wide gold ring.

'You young blackguard!' she yelled and smacked his face hard. The master rang a brass bell hidden behind the golden chrysanthemums and two maids appeared.

'Fetch John and Percy NOW,' commanded the master.

'I did not know his insanity had progressed as far as this, Daniel,' said Doctor Jones standing up and wiping the gravy from his lips on a white napkin.

Matron slapped Sam so hard he fell to the floor. She was obviously an expert in this form of control. 'Until the poor people of this country obey authority and realize their place in God's world this country will never be truly great,' said she.

Two big men came in. 'I think he'd better go to a cell, Percy,' said Doctor Jones. 'We'll examine him after luncheon.'

He reached for the mustard and sat down. 'There's two doctors present, matron. We can keep him all day if necessary—or longer.'

'Aren't tha playing at football, lad?' Tom Wilson asked Will just before school began in the afternoon.

'Nay. I'm waiting to see Sam Walton. I thought he might be here this afternoon. I wanted to show him summat down our well,' Will continued, looking out of the school gate. Tom ran off, not interested, to where the girls were.

'Gi' us a kiss, Fanny,' said Tom. 'Or I'll tek one!'

'Thee an' whose army?' said Fanny calmly, sucking in a liquorice bootlace as a frog sucks in a worm. Dolly Cresswell, her friend, giggled and they huddled together and made sheep's eyes at Tom.

'I wouldna kiss thee if tha were the last lad on earth,' said Fanny, striking languidly at a passing wasp that was interested in her hair. She saw Jessie staring at her in admiration.

'No,' added Fanny, the bootlace almost gone. 'I'm a liar, I am. I'd kiss thee before I kissed mad Sam Walton.' She raised her voice loud enough for Jessie to hear. 'He's horrible, Sam Walton.' Then she stuck out her liquorice-black tongue at Jessie.

But Will wanted Sam badly. He crunched humbugs, one a minute. Where was Sam Walton? He wanted to talk to him. It would not wait.

Sam was thrown into a cell-like room. It had walls and floor made of a sort of tent canvas. He kicked against this and shouted and called, for he had heard the key turn in the lock. The cell stank vilely of sick and he saw yellow stains on the floor. There was a high window with bars on it. Sam knew he was a helpless prisoner.

After plum pie and a glass of port Doctor Jones found Sam's mother and talked to her quietly and gently. He lied to her. He said Sam was suffering from a fever of the brain. He said it was caused by over-tiredness after his summer of hard work on the farm. He said Sam's mother must not listen to the rubbish he was talking about stones and other strange fantasies. He said he had seen Sam last night and given him some medicine. The fever, he said, had weakened one side of Sam's body. He told his mother he was just going to have a little look at Sam now with another doctor who was an authority on brain fever.

She believed every word. The doctor did not tell her that in his opinion Sam would die before October was out. He thought that was a kindness.

A crunch of wheels and a galloping horse for a time made the swallows on the workhouse roof forget their excited twitterings about leaving for Africa. The swallows wanted to leave, now the darker nights and cold shadows were here.

Grandmother climbed down from the cart without being helped by Grandfather. He was very red in the face. Grandmother was very white, her mouth a thin line. She clasped her umbrella, now forty years old; it had an ivory goose head for its handle. She made her way to the main door.

'You canna go in there, mam,' said a frail and papery old man, weeding the steps that led to the great front door of the workhouse.

'Can't I?' said Grandmother and went. She reappeared three minutes later into the pale sunshine clasping Sam's mother who was weeping bitterly.

'Eh, my dear lass, I never knew things were that bad,' said Grandmother, pulling Sam's mother down on to the steps of the workhouse. 'You should have said, lass, you should have said ...' Both women clutched each other and began to cry together.

'You shouldna have gone in there, Lucy. It's private,' said Grandfather from the cart. The weeping continued. 'It says private,' said Grandfather again.

'Shut up thee,' said Grandmother loudly. Her dark eyes shone with tears and rage. Grandfather's eyes rounded palely at his wife's rude reply.

'We'm having a good roar,' said Grandmother. 'A good cry does you good.' She dabbed at her eyes and turned on the old man who had been weeding.

'Hast thou seen enough or dost want a picture painting?' she said to the wispy old man who had not seen a woman of Grandmother's calibre for years. In amazement he watched them finish their crying and begin to talk in low voices so that Grandfather could not hear them. Then both women dried their eyes. Grandmother helped Sam's mother into the cart and then pulled at Grandfather's sleeve, nearly overturning him in the gravel.

'You're coming in to get thy grandson out,' said Grandmother. Sam's mother sat up very straight in the cart and tried to get the better of her crying. Grandmother, with a reluctant Grandfather in tow, marched into the mirror-polished hall of the workhouse just in time to see matron, the master, Doctor Jones and Doctor Nolan on their way to see Sam. Doctor Jones was murmuring something about madness. He saw Grandmother and began to tell her in calm tones that he was going to keep Sam in the Workhouse Hospital for a time.

'Fiddlesticks!' said Grandmother. 'Mad? All Waltons are mad. I should know. I married one and lived with him nigh on fifty year!' She gave Grandfather a withering stare and pulled his sleeve.

'Grand place you keep here,' said Grandfather politely. But matron was swelling up again.

'You have no right in this entrance. It is for staff only and certainly no right to talk to doctors like this. It is against the rules. We shall keep your grandson in as long as he is a danger to the parish with his mad ways.'

To hear her grandson so described brought Grandmother to the boil. 'And who art thou, tha great puffed-up, ugly toad? We've got one at home like thee at the bottom of a mucky well. Us poked it with a stick.' She raised the umbrella to demonstrate.

'I am the MATRON,' hissed the matron, almost speechless.

'Oh aye. I know thee now,' said Grandmother. 'I've heard of thee. Boiled bones and soup for them as is forced to come here, an' fine sides of prime beef for thee an' master. Get that lad out. NOW!'

Matron lifted her ever-ready hand to slap but saw the ivory goose head on the umbrella with its bead eye rising up to meet her hand, so she thought better of it.

'That's right love,' said Grandmother. 'I've not pulled another woman's hair out since Prince Regent died. I was just thinking I was going to get another chance afore I died.'

'I am Doctor Daniel Nolan, MA and Fellow of the Royal College of Physicians. Your grandson—' began the other doctor hopefully.

'Aye!' said Grandmother. 'An' I'm Queen Victoria just rolled in on a muck cart. I want our Sam out—NOW!'

'Pleased to meet thee,' said Grandfather. His hand was smacked back and the goose head rose high. Matron, sighing, muttering about the gutter-breed of the lower orders (but not too loudly) brought Sam.

He was comforted and petted by Grandmother. But

nobody wanted to listen to him. They climbed in the cart. Grandfather clucked his tongue to the horse.

'Grand place that workhouse,' said Grandfather. 'They treat them paupers too well, letting them live in a girt place as big as that. No wonder the poor rate is so high. I can hardly find gold to pay it this year.'

The goose head handle rose up in the autumn sun.

'Careful with that Lucy,' said Grandfather ducking. 'Them fine gents were frit on that umbyrella.'

'I thought I saw a horse-fly settle on thy little head, my love an' I were going to bat it off with me umbrella,' said Grandmother, in a voice as sour as unsugared damsons.

Nobody talked to Sam, pale and trembling.

By teatime all of Lambton had heard the story. Judgement was passed. The Waltons were mad. Young Samuel had had to be locked up for a time.

'Mam,' said Will, after school, for he had run straight home for once, 'can I go up an' play with Sammy Walton for a bit?'

'That you canna,' said Will's father. 'From what I've heard in this shop today they're all bleeding mad. And it's getting dark earlier.'

Will did not argue. He knew it would make things harder. But he must see Sam soon. There was so much to talk about. He would see Sam tomorrow at school.

Grandmother seethed with rage. She trembled with it. Sam's mother was still ashamed that the family had got to know. But it was a relief to know she'd get help to pay the Michaelmas rent. Sam could see nobody wanted to talk to him. They all walked silently behind the cart as it climbed the steep old road through the woods.

'Why didn't you tell me about the doctor giving you the medicine, Samuel?' said his mother suddenly. Trust her, thought Sam, to be thinking about that.

'I didn't want to worry you,' he said softly. His mother looked at him with alarm. He did not seem to be walking properly. Perhaps they should have listened to the doctors. Her mother-in-law should not have been so hasty.

127

Grandmother, who had been poking for blackberries as she walked, brushed a red elder leaf from her hair and stared too. But she was still angry with Grandfather.

'Dost want a blackberry pie, Abel my love?' she said sweetly to confuse the old man even more.

'Nay. I dunna fancy one,' said Grandfather. 'I've had this pain, like, it's like a cruel hand squeezing me arm and throat. I've had it since our Jack pulled me out o' me bath before I were ready to get out.'

Now it was Sam's turn to stare hard. A hand squeezing ... an invisible hand ... the hand of the Devil ...

Grandmother had made a fine stew. She wanted Sam and his mother to stay and eat. All Grandfather's eggs and cheese and butter went to big houses or to Chesterfield. Money was still coming in.

'Where's the money coming from to give to Bella and our Tom to pay their rent?' asked Grandfather suddenly.

'I'll tell thee,' said Grandmother. The ladle she was ladling soup with on to the blue willow-pattern dishes shook with rage and scattered drops of gravy on to the scrubbed wood of the table.

'I'll tell thee. It can come from thy little baccy tin three bricks up in the parlour chimbley where there's fifty half-sovereigns if there's one. Or under that tenth stair where boards creak an' tha keeps some o' thy father's golden shillings. Worth a tidy sum, they must be, Abel. Or there's that little tin tha bought in Coronation Year full o' sovs at the bottom of that sack of fine corn in t' pantry. If there's not enough there I should—'

'Aye. I were forgetting,' said Grandfather, crumbling bread at a fast rate into his stew.

Sam watched his uncles nudge each other and grin. If only they would take me seriously. If only I'd never read that book. If only ... thought Sam with every spoonful of stew. Even through the thick walls of the farm he could feel the power of the Stone pulling him, dragging him ...

'Sit up to the table properly, Samuel, and mind your manners,' said his mother.

'Do you want any of us to come down to your house and give thee a hand?' said Grandmother to his mother.

128

'No thanks,' said she. 'Our Sam'll have to take time off school the next few weeks. I don't like him missing school. By the end of October we should be pulling through.'

'Oh God,' groaned Sam as he mopped up the stew. But he cheered up a bit. He would be able to stay at home. Nobody wanted him at school. He did not care if he never went there again. Was there a chance he might escape if he stayed at home?

'We're that short of wood and coal,' he heard his mother saying. 'Tom just hasn't got the strength to chop wood and Sam and Pete have so much to do. Buying some coal is impossible. Buying corn and hay comes first.'

After dinner Grandfather hurriedly left the table and the others followed him into the yard. Grandfather seemed to want to keep them away from his coal house where fifty tons of best coal were waiting for winter.

'There's a big pile o' coal in t' Station Yard if tha's short,' he said cheerfully to Sam and his mother. 'It's only bits and slack but they'll let thee have it at threepence a load if tha fetches it thysen.'

Grandmother was unable to speak: both women could see through the door of the coal shed the dark piles of coal, enough for two winters at Bow Cross Farm.

'Station Yard coal'll do nicely for us,' Sam's mother said angrily. 'Poor quality coal. It'll do for our Tom to get better by. I'll fetch some now. Get that barrow, Sam. I'll borrow that handcart.' She was red with anger. So was Sam. What fools they were. And that doctor had called him mad. They were mad. Grandfather was mad. There was that Stone on the hill one field away and they were arguing over coal.

Grandmother stared at Grandfather. Two of the red elder leaves spun gently to the ground as she stared. A wasp had time to burrow deep into a plum as she looked at him. Then she grabbed her old, rusty, iron pram with its iron wheels. A pile of rusty old machinery fell as she dragged it out, making the pheasants in the wood call in alarm.

'I'm going with them,' said Grandmother to Grandfather. 'They need help.' Sam did not even look round. He hated Grandfather. He knew the old stories and did nothing to help. It would serve the old man right if he were killed. He should have done something instead of being so mean.

Grandfather sat on a wall. He looked to the Stone where silvery gleams in the cloud made it blacker and blacker.

'If I die when tha's gone tha'll be sorry tha looked at me like that,' he called after Grandmother. As he shouted it that invisible hand seemed to squeeze inside his chest and throat again. The old man suddenly felt a great wave of fear and panic wash over his body. Something was going to happen. Grandmother pretended not to hear; Sam was too far down the old road to hear.

'Nobody listens to me,' said Grandfather to Tissy the farm cat. 'Never mind. Walk'll do 'em good. They all ate too much stew. But they should listen to me.' He stroked the cat and for a moment his other arm hung down like Sam's. But Tissy was restless. She kept walking round Grandfather in circles as he stroked her. He stroked behind her ear. As he did so the plum-drunk wasp fell from the tree on to the cat and stung her. Tissy howled and hissed.

'By gum, Tissy,' said Grandfather. 'Tha's been stung. Aye. I've been stung by my Lucy's tongue and thee by a wasp. My Lucy's got a sting like a wasp. She talks too much. She should listen to me.'

The sun filtered weakly through the plum tree and Grandfather narrowed his eyes and looked at the Stone. Again that invisible hand squeezed him. Again the panic gripped him. He stared at the Stone, remembering old far-off things and tales. 'All a load o' muck,' he whispered. 'But they should listen ... mebbee ... I dunna know ...' He was grey with fear and pain, alone on the low wall under the plum tree.

Grandmother had the pram full of coal. Sam's mother, a handcart. Sam, the barrow. It was warm work. They seemed to be the only living, moving things in the deep and silent woods. The ground seemed to shake silently like a deep organ note. Sam, mopping his forehead, looked up. There was the Stone, framed in a gap between some yellow leaves on an elm branch. It seemed to him to take a step towards them. All down the side of his body he was full of pain.

Grandmother suddenly called out, 'Bella! Bella!' Sam's

130

mother left her cart and caught her in time. 'Indigestion, or summat ... I dunno.' She sat down on the first of the fallen sycamore leaves, her back against the tree. Sam could see her small, neat, black buttoned boots. 'Eh, I do feel badly,' said the old lady. 'Go ... an' get Ted or Jack to get this coal ... an' help us back,' she said feebly. Sam's mother ran ahead.

A shaft of brighter sunshine seemed to fill the woods with yellow light and long shadows. Again the earth seemed to shudder gently. 'It's that Stone,' said Sam softly and hopelessly. His eyes were full of tears. He liked his Grandmother. 'They should listen ...' he whispered through his tears. Sam himself was grey with fear and pain as he stood on the thin carpet of first fallen leaves.

Sam's mother helped the old lady to bed. She turned down the quilt. 'I've a pain like what I've never had before,' gasped Grandmother. Slowly she got in bed.

'So have I,' said Grandfather hovering by the bedroom door. 'Our Jack gave me my pain when he pulled me out o' t' bath before I were ready.' Grandmother, in the deep feather-bed, replied by shutting her eyes. Sam's mother tiptoed out.

'Best call the doctor,' she whispered to Grandfather. 'She's never had a pain like that before—'

'I have,' said Grandfather promptly. 'It's all down ...' But Sam's mother had turned and gone in disgust.

'Nobody listens to me,' said Grandfather to himself. 'They'll be sorry soon.'

Slowly the pale candle flame of the September sun moved in the calm sky towards the hills to the west of Lambton. In Grandmother's bedroom it made a four-square pattern of gold on the floorboards and rug; the squares became parallelograms and moved up the wall.

The grandfather clock struck three o'clock. Then four o'clock. The only movement in Grandmother's room was a wasp that vanished into a vase with TO A DEAR WIFE AND MOTHER A PRESENT FROM BUXTON written in gold on it. The wasp was a long time gone. Then it came out and hovered

131

round an embroidered picture which said DEATH WHERE IS THY STING? GRAVE THY VICTORY? The old lady lay very still, her arms folded. A thistle seed came in and floated to the floorboards. There was no movement from the bed.

When the grandfather clock struck five o'clock Grandfather was still muttering, 'Lucy's got a bit of pain. Aye, 'er has. It's nowt much. I've had a pain since Bartholomewtide. Aye. I have. She mun rest while I get the tea.' Getting the tea ready eased the old man's anxiety—he thought he was doing something very clever. He cut monumental slices of ham, centimetres thick. He cut a slice of bread that Jack said looked like Aunty Nellie's doorstep. Then he cut his thumb. He began to wail and shout, putting the geese and cockerel in uproar outside.

'I've gorra bleeding thumb. Can you hear me, mother? Are you there?' Grandfather stood at the bottom of the stairs calling up to Grandmother. But all was still in the room; except for the thistledown which moved along the floor.

'Can you hear us, Lucy? I'm down 'ere with a bleeding thumb,' called Grandfather again. But all was still.

Jo and Jack tiptoed upstairs and stared at their mother and then tiptoed down again, very subdued.

'Stop mekkin' all that row with thy feet, our Jack,' said Grandfather. 'Your mother's not feeling too good. She needs a bit of hush and quiet!' He retired to the fireside.

Jo and Jack went outside to finish their work. They were overcome with the strangeness of it all. The last time they had seen their mother in bed was when Edgar, their youngest brother, was born ...

And Edgar was dead, killed last summer ... Long cold shadows filled the farmyard. Their mother in bed during daylight ... It seemed like the end of a world they had thought would last for ever.

'Go down t'cellar and get some real cold water to stand this milk in,' said Mrs Saltby to Will. Will was hanging about and getting on her nerves, round her feet since he had come in from school.

'I canna. I hurt me leg in football,' lied Will ... his eyes

132

darted nervously. He wasn't going down there. Sighing loudly, his mother snatched up the jug and went.

'WILL! WILL!' she cried to her husband. 'Cellars ankle-deep in black water from t' well. It's all mucky as though summat's stirred it up. There's a right stink and mess. And it's as cold as Christmas.'

'Can I go and see Sam Walton, mam?' said Will when his mother returned with the empty jug. She could not use that water any more.

'Not if your leg's bad. It's a long way. Anyway, your dad's told you. You're not going playing near them Walton Pastures. Tales we've heard in that shop. And no sneaking off. I'm watching.'

At seven o'clock Jack knocked at Sam's back door.

'We canna wake 'er up,' said Jack when Sam's mother asked anxiously about Grandmother. 'Father won't get the doctor. He says he has had a pain like that for weeks and it's not killed him so it won't kill her.'

'I really don't know why you listen to him, I really don't,' said Sam's mother angrily. 'You don't take any notice of him usually.' She was peeling beetroot as though she were peeling Grandfather.

No, thought Sam. Nobody listens at all in this family. That's why things are going wrong.

'There's a sheep in our lane, Tom,' Jack was saying to his father. 'I think it's got thy mark on. Can Sam come and fetch it?'

Sam followed Jack wearily up the dusk-filled lane. What a day it had been. He was exhausted. His eyes ached in the soft amber light of a low moon that shone now and again through pansy-shaped clouds. But he saw the Stone as black as hell. Sam found the sheep in the lane and Jack left him to it.

It was so quiet. Sam could hear the sheep gently tearing at the grass on the side of the old turnpike road. He could even hear the rattle of dock seeds that the sheep kept nudging as it foraged. The docks grew by the old piles of stones that Grandfather said held down evil things when the old road was still used. Then in that deep silence there was a deep rumble as though something had moved deep in the earth.

The sheep stopped pulling the grass and stared at Sam, the moon in its eyes. The whole earth shook. Then again. Sam felt a cold finger on his shoulder and then his neck. He turned round wildly. There was the Stone and the moon was behind it, shining out from the flower-petal clouds. The shadow slid over his body and Sam could feel a terrible weariness and cold.

Again came a deep rumble. Louder this time. Something was coming. Sam's knees turned to water. He had been caught. He trembled so much that his legs buckled under him. He fell in the cold dew. The Stone's shadow grew stronger and blacker as the moon swam out of a cloud like a round, clear eye watching Sam. It shone with brilliance now from a patch of clear, royal blue sky.

'Oh God what a fool I was to come here,' thought Sam. His legs and whole body were too weak to move. The sheep stared and trotted away.

At half-past seven a deep and low rumble was felt and heard all over Lambton.

' 'Tis the Old Man moving deep below,' said the old lead miners. A feeling of unease rippled through the moonlit town where the gaslamps made shimmering moving pools of gold.

Archdeacon Ball, the vicar of Lambton, was praying in the church as he usually did before dinner at eight o'clock. Greatly alarmed by the rumble, the Archdeacon got up. Moonlight poured in through the stained glass windows—it seemed so peaceful, yet the Archdeacon felt suddenly afraid. He shouted to the verger for a candle. The verger rushed from the vestry where he had been tidying and sweeping and brushing the Archdeacon's second-best gown.

Again the church shuddered. A marble statue of one of the first Dukes of Blackdon, a huge white knight in armour, crashed to the floor of the church with a noise like a bomb exploding.

'We'd best get ourselves out of church, Doctor Ball,' said the verger. Both men strode like flapping black ravens through the moonlight patterns of windows that made a quick pattern on them as they passed. The verger held the large studded South Door wide to let Doctor Ball flap through. They were out into the moonlight.

'See that Stone on yonder hill?' said the verger. 'My old grandfather used to say that old Stone was older than the church and one day it would destroy this church. And there's been some right strange tales going round Lambton about the folk up there this year.' The verger cast an anxious stare over his shoulder at the church looming behind him. 'The old man used to tell me,' he went on darkly, 'that Stone could charm devils and darkness and great worms that would swallow up this church whole!' Again the verger looked back at the massive church.

'How very remarkable,' said the Archdeacon, who had spent many years in Oxford and considered himself very clever. 'How very remarkable that your grandfather should know one of the oldest legends of history, the legend of the Cockatrice. The Cockatrice,' he lectured in the moonlight, 'was a mythical serpent that crawled out of the ground and ate rocks and all before it. Remarkable *your* grandfather knowing that.'

The Archdeacon flicked a speck of fallen plaster from his cloak. He looked loftily at Herbert Green, his verger.

'Alas, Green, your strange tale is not true. Thank God!' He raised his eyes to the moonlit clouds to congratulate God. 'No, Green. There is a much more serious explanation! Yes indeed! I was talking this very day to the Duke of Blackdon's mining agent. He tells me some of the ancient lead mines under the town and church are for some reason fast filling up with water and may collapse. He tells me the new dam that Arkwright is building for that satanic new cotton mill is flooding the old workings. Did you know, Green, that many of the old tunnels under the town are a thousand years or more old? No? I fear that earth tremor we just felt in God's House was a tunnel caving in. I shall expect the Duke of Blackdon to pay for any damage done to All Saints' Church.'

Green, the verger, said nothing. If His Reverence were so clever let him believe in his cock-of-tricks. He remembered the old tales about how the first All Saints' had been destroyed by a giant worm.

They walked on in the moonlight. Doctor Ball began examining the church walls in the light of the moon and the candle he carried.

'Aha, Green!' cried the Archdeacon, 'I spy a crack.' Sure enough by a small priest's door was a crack in the great wall. They walked on in the shadowed graveyard. The owls are silent, thought the verger uneasily. It was deathly still. By the North Door, with its pattern worn away and broken like the archway to Will's well, there was a crack wide enough to put your finger in.

There would be, thought Herbert Green. The old folk always said the Devil came to church through the North Door. A cold wind suddenly blew at the candle and the wind vane high on the spire could be heard creaking. A few dry leaves rustled. But still the owls were silent. The candle flame recovered and flared up, making the diamond in Doctor Ball's ring, probing the crack, glitter.

Then both men stood still. A painful sound, felt rather than heard, began to hurt their ears. A menacing low, ugly, humming sound. They stared at each other. High up, under the creaking vane, in the octagonal bell tower, the eight great bells were shuddering with sound. Something was gently shaking the church. Doctor Ball's candle began to shake little drops of molten wax on to a clump of enchanters nightshade that grew out of the crumbling archway of the North Door of All Saints' Church.

Dame Trot had always feared her mother and her magic. She thought about her wicked old mother now as she lit the silver candlestick on her table. It had a coiling writhing silver serpent crawling up it. One of the young sons of the Duke of Blackdon had given it to her mother, a hundred years ago. Dame Trot hated it but feared to throw it out. It was the same with her old books. They were locked away. But one thing the old woman loved was her mother's crystal ball. Nobody in Lambton knew she had this treasure.

She reached up into her many bloomers, drawers, and knickers and found two drawer knobs. She screwed these on

136

a drawer in a chest. Then out of the drawer she took the huge crystal. She placed it on the windowsill. It gave the old woman much pleasure to look at the moon and stars and the gaslight at the end of the alley reflected in it.

But tonight the crystal was as black as ink. Try as she could the old woman could not make it reflect the moon and the stars. Then without warning her whole cottage shook and the wonderful ball rolled and crashed to the floor and smashed into a thousand stars of fiery candlelit glass. Dame Trot hid her face in her hands and wept. Although she was nearly one hundred years old, she recalled her mother's words.

'And when I'm gone, Betsy, don't think you'll be rid of me. I shall still have power. Smash anything of mine, burn it— and the Devil will fetch thee too.'

The old woman rocked and sobbed like a little girl of three.

Sam had staggered home, eventually, terrified by the shaking earth. Grandmother had seemingly recovered next morning and Grandfather had said he knew she would all along. But the days moved on, ever nearer to Hallowe'en. Nearer and nearer to Sam's lonely little farmhouse crept the evening shadow of the Stone. Each sunset saw the dusky shadow darker and longer. And what sunsets they were, those sunsets of 1883. Blood seemed to be smeared across the western skies and the Stone itself shone like dark blood.

And gentle yet menacing earth tremors shook Lambton every day. And Sam, like a toy that is winding down, went slower and slower about his daily tasks on the farm.

September became October. Sam's mother, anxious, fed Sam as best she could, gave him the doctor's medicine, and prayed to God morning and night for Sam and his father who only seemed to be themselves when they were upstairs resting. They seemed so weak and exhausted.

Driving rain and winds came and hid the blood-red sunsets. A cold rose from the ground that stiffened Sam's already aching exhausted body. But even though the Stone had no shadow in the days of rain, time passed. The time the Stone had waited for a thousand years, thought Sam, was close.

137

Lo, a shadow of horror is risen
In Eternity! Unknown, unprolific,
Self-clos'd, all-repelling: what Demon
Hath form'd this abominable void,
This soul shudd'ring vacuum?

William Blake from the *Book of Urizen*, Chapter 1

BOOK TWO
The Curse of the Stone

Chapter One

Sammy Walton must have caught cold, thought Will miserably. For two weeks or more he had waited at the school gate
every morning to tell Sam something that was puzzling and
worrying him. He had been disappointed. Now Will was
staring at the rain that lashed the windows and blurred the
world outside. He shivered. How cold it was. The cold that
had hidden in shadows and caves all summer through was
now rising and creeping through old stone floors and cellars,
through old forgotten tunnels and secret passages.

'Mam?' said Will to his mother, 'did Mrs Mellor say when
John Mellor were coming back home when 'er bought that
candle?'

'Aye,' said his mother, stuffing a sack up to the door, for
the chill October rain was creeping through the gap between
the step and door.

'When?' said Will urgently.

'What's it to thee, our Will,' said his mother, lighting an
extra candle—it seemed so dark. 'I thought tha couldna
stand the sight of big John Mellor. She said he were expected

141

soon. But I didna ask the day, so I don't know, do I?' She shivered as Will had done. She pulled the shop blinds down over the streaming windows.

'I want to talk to him and Sam Walton,' said Will softly.

'You can get thysen ready for bed, never mind talking on a night like this. You look as white as that lump of lard.' His mother busied herself tidying up.

Will didn't tell her what he had thought he had seen in the yard last night, when the wind had blown so hard and the rain rattled so threateningly and the gas lamp in the alley had been blown to a spear of wicked devilish blue flame behind its glass, hissing in rage ... he didn't tell her of that creeping shadow and that shape on the wall by the old apple tree ... He wanted a long talk with Sam and John. He could not get out of his mind those eyes in the corner of the yard by the wash-house and cellar door ... so vivid in the pale blue wind-blown gaslight, reflected in a puddle ... so still and watchful as he watched from behind his wind-rattled window.

On Tuesday, 2 October 1883, with twenty-nine days left to Hallowe'en, Doctor Ball, Archdeacon of Lambton, and Herbert Green, the verger, examined the church. Grinning devilish gargoyles high on the church walls spouted cold water from the church roof. A cold wind ripped the leaves from the churchyard lime trees and blew a drift by the cracked North Door through which the Devil was supposed to get in. And the crack by the North Door had widened.

'I don't want to hear any of your old country tales or poppycock superstitions. Do you hear me Green?' barked the Archdeacon, gripping his silver-topped cane, then skidding in a puddle of slippery wet lime leaves. Doctor Ball marched away to the vicarage. With his mouth turned down he wrote a letter to the Duke of Blackdon ... 'I fear the great and glorious collegiate Church of All Saints', Lambton, will crash to the ground if your estate does not prevent the collapse of any more of the strange and ancient passages that lie beneath the Church ...' scratched Doctor Ball's steel nib. Then he had to stop, for the wind blew smoke down his chimney into his study and he heard

142

the rain claw at the window. In spite of himself he shivered.

Herbert Green shivered in the cottage on Church Alley. He knew in his bones there was more to all this than the collapse of old lead mines. This was the work of the Devil and all his kind.

That night of cold rain and wind all the people of Lambton heard the great tenor bell of All Saints' Church begin to ring. It began as a muffled humming and then grew to an uncertain striking and then it began to toll its booming notes as though for a funeral.

No living person was in the church ringing it. The booming notes were tossed to the cold night wind, the black wind, and the rising cold and darkness. Something deep and mysterious was shaking and vibrating the church, making the bell ring on its own. The sound sent deep shivers up the spine of Herbert Green. He thought of the empty, dark, vast church, filled with the sound of whispering and chuckling rain and the scream of the wind—and the rope swinging by the pew where he usually sat to pull it for funerals: swinging in that darkness as though some invisible devilish hand were pulling at it, sounding a warning to the townsfolk.

On Wednesday, 3 October, Lil Gosling's cat vanished. A pool of rain-smeared blood was seen by the old well in North Street. Will saw the blood-stained amber leaves blowing up Church Alley on his way home from school.

People shook their heads at their pets' behaviour. They seemed bewildered, enchanted. They circled invisible (to human eyes) objects, they walked in circles, they swore, they spat, they chased their tails. Tissy, the cat at Bow Cross, refused to go out for the first time in her life. She deposited a neat heap of dung behind the dresser, again for the first time in her spotless life. It was found close by Grandfather's gold-filled old boot.

'Dirty old bugger,' said Grandfather.

'It teks one to know one,' said Grandmother.

'Eh?' said Grandfather.

'I said Tissy's been no trouble to no one,' said Grandmother, trying to push Tissy out of the door. But nothing would make the cat go out.

On Thursday, 4 October, Minnie Adams ('three sheets to the wind, poor lass,' as Lambton people said about her, meaning the poor girl had a serious brain handicap) went nutting in the woods, a day of cold rain and drizzle. She was struck dumb. Minnie never spoke again from that day onwards. Nobody knew what had happened. One of the Duke of Blackdon's wood cutters had heard a hissing and a falling of stones ... Minnie had come home with a foaming mouth, muddy, white, and hysterical.

Will asked his mother that Wednesday night if he could go and see Sam the next Saturday. He said he could get some nuts. But Mrs Saltby gave a stern refusal. 'Not after Minnie Adams. You don't know who's in them woods. Tramps, runaway soldiers, wild dogs ... you just don't know. Go and chop some sticks and clean thy father's boots.'

Will had a gnawing and growing suspicion what was in the woods. It was none of the things his mother said.

On Friday, 5 October, the cold rain cleared and an even colder, hard blue sky appeared. Herbert Green, sweeping up the remains of a fallen devilish gargoyle glanced eastwards and saw that old Stone on Walton Pastures needle clear. He remembered his mother saying that when the sun rose behind the Stone on Walton Pastures at the end of October then witches were at work. He shaded his eyes to look at it.

'Come along, Green, not still thinking about the Cockatrice are we?' It was the Archdeacon, bustling by in a cloud of eau-de-Cologne and black silk gown. 'You will rejoice with God and myself to hear the Duke of Blackdon will pay for all the repairs to the church. Of course he agrees with me it is the collapse of old workings that is causing these mysterious events.'

'Church clock's stopped, Your Reverence,' said Herbert. 'John Clay says it's because t'spire is leaning a bit, like ...'

144

'Stuff and nonsense!' rapped out the Archdeacon.

But the streets of Lambton were oddly quiet in the thin sunshine and shining, wet, fallen leaves, without the bells sounding the quarter hours. Leaves fell silently through the air. Everywhere water gushed out from wells, pipes, and drains as though some force were pushing it out.

Grandfather was much shaken by not hearing the distant chime on the hill at Bow Cross. 'Me old dad used to say when you couldna hear t' bell of church tha'd be dead,' said he.

'Well of course you couldna see or hear if tha were dead!' said Jack irritably, legging deep in autumn mud and leaves, pulling a young heifer on a rope.

Grandfather spent the whole of the day pacing about, his smock flapping in the cold wind, cupping his ear in vain to hear the church bell. He was still there when the sky seemed to fill with blood and fire at half-past four. Streamers of fire, pools of blood, and slabs of rock tipped with fire filled the western sky. The old man was reminded of huge fire-tipped tombstones. He stared at this awful sunset. It was a warning. He stared at the red and orange, the tumbled woolly, blood-red fleecy clouds, the streamers, the pools. It was the end of the world, he thought. He stared and stared until a thin, silver, curved slit of moon rode out from behind a bruised and blood-red cloud tuft. The slit of moon watched him.

End of the world or not, the new moon brought Grandfather to his senses fast. He ran indoors to fetch a stocking full of gold to turn over in front of the new moon to bring good luck.

'Gi' us thy stocking of gold, Abel, I want to make a wish,' said Grandmother standing by Grandfather's side. She smiled at him sweetly. She had come to get some apples from the tree for baking for tea. She turned the stocking, looking the old man in the eye.

'I dunna believe in't,' said Grandfather. 'I'm not superstitious. I dunna believe in all these old tales and moon magic.'

'I'm right glad,' said Grandmother, 'after what I've just wished on thee.' She plucked three of the big, cold, smooth-pointed cooking apples from the tree.

Then both old people turned round quickly. Both felt they had been touched by a hand. Grandfather began to shiver. 'Come on in, Lucy. Making me stand about an' gape at moon. I've too much to do.' The old man went quickly inside. He felt as if he had been touched by a hand of ice.

'Mam,' pleaded Will, as the thin, curved, clawlike moon glittered behind the spire with its silent clock. '*Can* I go and get some wood for bonfire night from woods?'

'And creep off an' see Sam Walton?' said his mother. 'I've told thee till I'm sick of telling thee you're not going in them woods near Walton Pastures. You can clear up all that muck and sludge by our wash-house door. I can't think what made it.'

Like Grandfather, two miles away on Walton Pastures, Will found himself shivering. Why, why, he thought, hadn't he listened to Sam! He had been his best friend after all.

And a little later that same night Ted went up to the Top Pasture to check the sheep. They had been restless all day and one or two were limping. It was cold and still now with the chill of winter ice in the air. Now and again a wet leaf fell and touched his face. The moon on its back was lurking behind a wood on the western hills, thin and sharp and watchful, about to set. Ted kicked irritably at the masses of dark toadstools with his boot. Ugly, black toadstools with thin wormlike stalks, stretching away up the bank in the dim moonlight and after-glow of the sunset. The sheep were restless: they were silent, not bleating. Far away to the south Ted heard the bloodhound pack at Blackdon Hall begin a long, dismal howling. A ripple of movement ran along the sheep and they huddled together, stamping their feet, their breath clouding the cold air.

Then, nearer, like a threatening echo, all the dogs of Lambton began to howl. Their howling echoed up through the woods and Ted heard a rattle of falling stones. Ted, who had never been scared in his life, felt the hair at the back of his neck rise. Behind the sheep and on

146

the edge of the wildwood was a maple that was golden yellow by day. Ted found himself staring at it. It appeared to be shining with a light of its own. Again Ted heard a rattle of stones in the woods. Then Ted sniffed the air. He could smell something, above the wet leaf and mud smell and toadstools.

Fire!

The maple tree had been reflecting the glow of fire in its own golden leaves. Ted turned swiftly round. It must have been a trick of the light, for at first there seemed to be a vast shadowy form over the farm with an eye of gold, curved like the moon, yet flickering, like the fronds of the gold autumn bracken. He blinked in disbelief, then his eye saw it as a tongue of fire alive and dancing through a gap in the tiles on the old barn that was next to the farmhouse.

Then Ted was running to the house, slipping and falling. Fire! Christ! They'd all be ruined. Or worse.

Sam had got up that day as usual at six o'clock in the morning. He was sleeping better now—but whether it was from exhaustion, the medicine of Doctor Jones, or some creeping magic from the Stone he could not tell. It was strange, he thought, how much better he felt at night in his room. But not during the day. And not on this day.

His first job had been to take water to the hens; then he had to go and get some mushrooms for breakfast. He had gone into the field, cold and frosted with dew. He gave his usual look at the Stone. He staggered back. His dream was coming true. A long, dark shadow reached out to him over the fields, even though it was morning. As he stood there transfixed, he slowly realized it was hundreds and hundreds of tiny black worm-stemmed toadstools. After the shock of that he had found a few mushrooms. Seeing a large mushroom in the middle of a dense patch of toadstools he accidentally touched one of the slimy things.

It was as if a switch had been pressed. Pain flooded through his body. A blue fire seemed to hover over the deadly toadstools. The air seemed filled with a strange high-pitched whining, not unlike the strange insect whine he had heard in the wood on his way to Taddington. Invisible throbbing

147

wires seemed to vibrate and throb around him. The air was filled with invisible power. Dimly, Sam realized this was indeed the beginning of the end.

He got back to the house. His mother, pleased with the mushrooms, smiled at him. 'You've spider silk and gossamer all over you,' she said, pulling away the cold wet strands. 'You're caught up in a right big web.'

Sam thought of the web of magic he had felt that day in Taddington. His mother began to fry the mushrooms.

Sam went out. At once the throbbing, invisible, ugly music was all around him. He was violently sick. A creeping cold spread over his body.

'Beds are for being born in, sleeping in, and dying in,' his mother usually said. But she sent him up to bed now. He was not usually allowed upstairs in the daytime. Yet the sickness passed upstairs. An hour later he took up his floorboard and examined his treasures. He held the egg in his hand while he swallowed some medicine. He felt better. Looking out and seeing his father limping and struggling with the calves he went down. As he stepped outside the cold was on him, the sickness and the whining, invisible evil music. Worse, he felt as if he were covered in crawling threads and strands like cold worms. His scalp felt as if claws were scratching at it.

His mother had gone down to Lambton to fetch the necessary yeast and candles and get some more medicine for Sam. 'Give him it as often as he needs it,' the doctor had said. He did not tell Sam's mother he thought that it would soon be of little use to Sam. He did not expect Sam to live for much longer.

Sam meanwhile found he could not see properly out of one eye ... the one the shadow had touched. Again he went upstairs and felt better after a while. So Sam spent that nightmarish day battling with the growing fear and gathering shadows.

He watched the blood-coloured sunset, sipping milk and brown sugar on his bed. It was like his dream. The shadow reaching out ... then he must have dozed a little with his marble egg in his hand. Then came panic and voices.

'Sam ... Sam ... SAM! ... Thy Grandfeyther's farm's afire.' Staring out through his window he seemed to see a serpent of flame round the farm on the hill. Crouching by it was the Stone and the curved claw of the setting moon.

Then they were running up the lane ... Sam, his mother, Pete, but his father was too lame ... and in the air was that music, the ugly whining, and as they ran to the farm, they all heard the crackle of the greedy fire. Streams and gusts of sparks soared to the troubled skies where a few cold silent stars shone as well. Sam, shaking his head to free it of sickness and headache, saw a column of smoke and fire—and was at once reminded of that fearful thundercloud that had grown over Lambton and reached out to him that day at Matlock. He shook his head again: for a moment at one of the barn windows he thought he saw two fiery eyes.

Grandfather was quite beside himself. Like all hill farmers he dreaded fire.

'Calm down, Abel. Tha'll do thysen a mischief!' warned Grandmother. Grandfather blundered about, his eyes as wild as Sam's. He kept getting in everybody's way. Grandmother followed him. She seemed more concerned about Grandfather than the barn or the house. His four sons had made a chain of buckets and were passing them to each other.

'Let it burn—just watch the house,' implored Grandmother as Grandfather staggered dangerously near the blaze. 'Tha can buy ten hundred ton o' new hay with all thy gold ... mind thysen, Abel.' She was near to tears. Grandfather's face was ashen. His lips looked blue. He kept clutching his chest.

On the hill the Stone glowed red and triumphant in the fire-glow. Sam, his mother, and Pete joined the human chain. Ted and Jack had to soak sacks in the water troughs to cover their heads and shoulders, for the heat was so great.

'Eh dear me. Eh dear me. Eh dearie me,' moaned Grandfather. Then he shouted to Jack, pulling Grandmother and himself dangerously near the blaze.

'Run a pipe down to river, Jack,' Grandfather shouted.

'Aye, I will, father,' shouted Jack. Sweat poured down his face. 'It's only two miles away. When I've taken a pipe to it, I'll tie a broom to my arse an' sweep away t'snow, for it'll be January then.'

'Our Jack allus were an uncaring bugger,' said Grandfather, pulling poor Grandmother ever nearer to the inferno.

As Sam passed his first bucket, a gust of angry wind seemed to blow down at the fire from the Stone. It fanned the blazing hay white-hot through the barn windows and with a roar of thunder the roof fell in. The blaze was covered by tons of tiles.

'We can save the farmhouse now,' gasped Jack, stepping back, his face black and shining with sweat and soot. Nobody saw Sam step back. The wind from the Stone had blown a strand of burning hay into his hair. He shouted in pain, but another gust of wind blew the hay under the tiles to white heat again, and the air was full of the sound of cracking and exploding roof tiles.

Grandmother saw him. She left Grandfather dangerously near the leaning walls and pushed Sam head-first into a water trough. Then she pushed him into her smoke-filled kitchen to wrap a wet towel round the burn. Sam sat in the kitchen, his whole body crawling with invisible tentacles of pain that seemed to crawl to the rhythm of the flames outside. And there he was left until the smouldering heap was finally drenched with water from the pumps of the Lambton Fire Engine that four horses had dragged up the hill from the town.

'I've just put it out,' Grandfather told them as they turned in the farm drive. But it was two hours later when Sam's uncles, his mother, and grandparents came in, exhausted and black with smoke. They collapsed on the chairs and settle and drank mug after mug of ale that Grandmother fetched from the brewhouse. Suddenly Grandfather shouted wildly from his chair.

'There's a curse on us Waltons! My old dad said t'Devil'd get us one day. I know. I can tell.' He was almost in tears. 'Them sunsets ... canna hear church bells ...' His face was still the colour of ash. He had a burn near his eye.

'God Almighty, father,' said Jack. 'Don't start going on about all that superstitious muck.' His eyes were bloodshot and his corduroys almost scorched black.

'Aye,' said Grandmother, sipping her ale. 'Maybe there is ...' She talked softly sipping her ale. 'Us'll talk about it later.' She talked softly, gently. Sam turned his head. Part of his hair had been singed away. He looked at Grandmother's wondering eyes. Were they ... were they going to start listening to him ... at last? Three weeks to go? They were ready at last to listen? There was still time to save himself and them. He waited for the next move.

'Wilt mek us a blackberry pie, mother?' said Grandfather. Grandmother's look of puzzled wonder left her eyes and anger flared.

'When I asked thee back in September just afore I were taken badly you said no.'

'Aye ... er no ... yes,' said Grandfather. 'But now me best hay's gone I shall be short o' gold. Pick us some blackberries, Lucy!' He drank deeply. 'They cost nowt!'

Grandmother, tired and angry, forgot her language in front of Sam. 'But tha allus telled me t' Devil pisses o'er blackberries in October.'

'Just one of me old dad's daft tales. Thee make a pie, Lucy.' And he drank long and deep. Nothing like a drink to make you forget the evil old tales and pretend nothing was wrong.

'Aye. I'll make thee a pie,' said Grandmother gently. And Sam could not tell whether she was angry or sad.

Three weeks to go and they argued over blackberry pies.

Of course it was no good talking to his mother on the way home. And he had no real fear for his father: he knew himself to be the victim. He was utterly miserable as he crunched the curled fallen sycamore leaves under his boots and breathed quickly the air tainted with poisonous fungi.

He turned sharply to look in the direction of the Stone. At once he saw the flash of magic fire and his head throbbed with the ringing devilish music. A pain stabbed his head. And then he knew, just as he had known months ago there was something wrong, he knew that tomorrow was going to be the last day. It was as though some deep voice from the earth itself filled his mind.

'Don't drag your feet, and look where you're going,' nagged his mother wearily. 'There's no money left to repair your boots if they wear out.'

'And whose fault is that?' thought Sam to himself. If only, he thought for the ten thousandth time, somebody listened or cared ... Will ... Grandmother ... Nobody cared.

'Tomorrow ... tomorrow ...' sighed the wind in the laneside sycamores. And nobody cared.

Down in Lambton the fire had been seen. But this time there were no jokes, gossip or tittle-tattle. Heads were shaken. Something was very much wrong. They remembered the earth tremors, the bell that rang itself, and the silent church clock.

'Mam, can I go and see Auntie Bertha in Pillerton tomorrow? It's Saturday,' Will coaxed. Sam's farm was on the old unused lane to Pillerton. Will would go the old way. He waited breathlessly for the answer. He had not been able to sleep and had crept down for a cup of water. There was a pause ...

'Aye,' said his mother. 'An' call and see how Sam Walton is if tha goes the old road. But mind! Keep to the road through the woods. No going for nuts and conkers. Hast heard? See if thy aunt has been bothered by all these rum happenings.'

Will drank the water. At last! He did not in the least want to see the old aunt. She was enormously fat and smelly and demanded frequent wet kisses. But he wanted to see Sam. There was a lot to talk about and things to do.

Grandmother, unknown to Sam, had been thinking. She had thought a great deal. And on that Saturday morning she was up at five o'clock. She would go and get Grandfather the blackberries—she knew the very spot. There was an old deep quarry close by a ruined chimney and a lead mine shaft. In fact there were a great many deep shafts there, but Grandmother was confident she knew the paths well. It was a shady, shadowy place but the blackberries came late. Few people went there—there were tales about the place. But Grandmother had her mind on other things than blackberries. Ever since that gypsy had warned Grandfather in August, she had been uneasy. Now she knew what she would do. She would go and see her friend, Old Winny, in Crowley, the next village down the path. Winny was a Wise Woman.

152

She could read your palm, make you medicine and see your future by staring into a bowl of water. They were the same age and had played together as girls. Grandmother would have gone to see Dame Trot but the old woman, it was said, was afraid to see anyone these days.

Grandmother was now certain something was wrong. What, she did not know. She needed to talk that over with someone who knew about these things. Now she had been busy making the beef and potato pies for the men's dinner. She put a cloth on the end of the table and put out her own pickled cabbage, her own tomato chutney and horse-radish relish, all in big pot jars: she put out the pork pies and apple pies she had made yesterday and a big plum cake. She covered it all with another cloth and then cooked breakfast.

'I'm going out for t'day,' she said to Grandfather, who looked white and pale in the early light.

'But what'll us eat, Lucy?' he said, clutching his chest. 'A poor owd man like me shouldna be left to starve.'

'Thy grub's under yon white cloth an' thy breakfast's staring thee full in the face. Call the lads from the yard.' She struggled to get into her heavy cloak. She was getting old and stiff. She struggled to get it on. Grandfather stared at her and Grandmother muttered.

'I'd help thee with thy lamming-gown, Lucy, but me arm's still right badly since our Jack pulled me from that bath.'

'Aye, an' thy bum's not much better t'way it's been stuck to that chair since six o'clock,' said Grandmother, as she adjusted her bonnet by the tin mirror over the sink. She glared at the old man and went.

It was a wild morning, but warm. Big clouds hid the distant hills and every now and then the woods were filled with patterings, as large raindrops and nuts fell. A rainbow, its red, orange, and yellow as bright as the autumn woods, leaped out from a dark cloud.

'Rainbow in the morning is God's warning,' said Grandmother to herself. She shivered suddenly despite the warmth and made her way to the old shafts. She soon saw through the thinning trees the big chimney that had once been a ventilating shaft to a deep mine. The old chimney was coated in ivy and full of rustlings. Grandmother heard thunder as she

153

approached. As she drew near she thought she heard the rattle of falling stones in the chimney. For a moment she was sure she saw eyes watching her. She blinked the warm rain from her eyes. It must have been the gleam of black glossy elderberries tangled in the ivy. The old woman walked away quickly. Something was not right here either, she thought. She suddenly felt afraid. She would talk to Wise Winny first ... maybe there would still be some blackberries lower down the path.

Once again she heard falling stones in the shaft. She turned round. This time there was no mistaking it. A pair of eyes watched her. Big cat's eyes, very wide apart, unless there were three wild cats ... she could not make it out.

She walked quickly away. Her flesh was crawling with fear. They were probably only cats ... she walked away into the falling leaves.

The woods seemed to be swallowing up the fragile figure in its black cloak. A gust of wind moaned round the chimney. Grandmother had been mistaken. There were only two eyes. They moved in the ivy as she went. They watched her go. They settled to watch for her return and there were no more falling stones in the old deep tunnel.

For a woman of nearly one hundred years to want her mother, whom she'd never really liked, it was strange: strange or not, Dame Trot wanted her mother that Saturday morning. Since the night of the earth tremor when her crystal ball had smashed, she had been like a frightened child. She knew the Devil was at work—and her herbs and simple charms were useless against that evil shadowy power.

And last night, Friday, she had double-locked the door, piled coal half-way up the chimney, removed five dirty shawls that almost stood up by themselves with filth, and fumbled long and hard down her bosom. After much heaving she brought forth a brass key. Then she went to the corner cupboard and fetched her mother's books. Books backed in linen and leather, the colour of the leaves blowing in the alley outside. She lit a fine wax penny candle bought from Saltby's. She fetched a magnifying glass and a pair of glasses Lil

154

Gosling had given her ('As good as new, Betsy. They fit thee a treat') and she began to look in the old witch's books. She never had looked before. She had always thought if she had she would have become an evil witch like her mother and the Devil would fetch her. But she did not look in the big brown book Sam had seen back in July. That was pushed right to the back.

As she read, the magnifying glass began to shake and then her head. The room was full of shadows, her trembling one and the candle and fire shadows blowing in wafts of air. Dame Trot became a mumbling, nodding, old, old, terrified woman. Her shadow loomed large in the shadowy room, hooknosed and fluid, witchlike. It was as if her mother's shadow was watching—not her own.

She had read far into the night. Now it was Saturday morning. She must go to Walton Pastures and Bow Cross Farm and see young Lucy Walton and tell her. (Grandmother had been born on Dame Trot's thirty-fifth birthday.) She must tell and warn of all the evil and magic her mother had placed in the woods and round the Stone, the curses, the wickedness. But she, Dame Trot, never wanted to go near the woods or Bow Cross again ... not after what she had read about how the Devil was more than at home up there on the high hills ... But she must tell young Lucy Walton ... she had been the midwife when she was born ...

The old woman got ready to go out. But she was shaking so much that she could not fasten the clothes peg round her shawls.

Sam felt cold, cold as the cold shadows outside that Saturday morning.

'I want thee to go up to Top Field, Sam,' said his father. 'I canna walk that far with me bad leg. All the walls are down up by t'owd Stone, just where thy Grandfather's fields start. It'll be them tremors and wind, I've no doubt. You're good at walling, Sam. See what tha can do. Perhaps I'll get up later.'

Sam said nothing. He knew why the walls had fallen up there. Slowly, his shoulders bowed, Sam made his way up the steep fields. When he dared to look up he saw those blue

155

flickerings and flashes of silent blue fire. The rising wind stung his face with rain and the wildwood roared with a wintry sound. He heard the cockerel back at home crowing three times. Then a long growl of thunder shook the hills. And he knew he was now in the centre of the web of magic, for it was in thundery weather that the Stone did its evil. He knew that now. He could feel the thin webs of ice creeping and crawling over his flesh as he walked.

He walked up the hill to his fate.

If courage could be measured that Saturday morning then Jessie's courage was worth ten of the bravest soldiers fighting for Queen Victoria that moment in Afghanistan.

She'd seen the fire flickering on Friday night. She had seen the Stone, dark and evil. She remembered Sam telling her about it on that not-never-to-be-forgotten day in July on the school trip. His face that day, the pain, the fear, had become fixed in the picture book of her mind. She looked at it time and time again. She must help him. She must.

The last three Saturdays since she had seen him had been cold with drenching rain. Jessie had no proper boots or shawl or coat. If she had gone out in that weather she would have caught her death of cold. And that would not have helped her mam or Sam. Although Jessie found difficulty in doing Miss White's sums about the cost of twenty-three and a half yards of elastic at 1¼d. a yard, she had much common sense.

But today there were gleams of lemon-yellow sunlight on the grey-gold cobbles of the narrow street. She'd go and see him.

She was scared stiff. There were tales that Walton Pastures and Manor Wood were filled with boggarts, devils, great wild cats, evil spirits. Hadn't daft Minnie been struck dumb? Then there had been the tales she had heard of giant worms, that crawled round you and in you and pulled you down into the deep old mines so you never saw the light of day again. The children had stories of shadows that turned into witches ... killer dogs ... tramps with knives ... a giant wild cat. The gossip had grown from children and adults alike. Some of the worst tales she had heard late at night after her Great Aunt

156

Lily Gosling had had a glass or two of gin and was telling her mother and father.

Jessie looked out like a robin in spring. A shower of heavy rain made the roof tops gleam. Smoke blew down the street. Jessie was used to the crowded slum. She did not like the idea of the lonely hills and woods.

She picked the smuts off her mother's none-too-clean washing.

'Mam. Mam? I'm going into woods to see if I can gerrus some sticks and chestnuts for tonight, mam, for a Saturday treat.'

'You're a right good lass, our Jessie,' said her mother, wiping her red hands down the sack tied round her waist. 'Be careful, duck. I canna manage without thee. There's been some rate tales about them woods o' lately. But a few chestnuts round a blaze of sticks an' some tatties'd be a grand treat for a Saturday night.' So her mother let her go.

Jessie got as far as the bridge where she stood hugging a green gas lamp-post. She was shivering. Down river a couple of blackbirds were scolding something long and black and shining, that was moving in the calm lake of the mill pond to the Marble Works. Jessie needed glasses. She screwed up her eyes to see, but all she saw was a lake of gold, for there were fallen lime leaves in the water, and the movement of something black. She heard a rumble of angry thunder.

She let go of the rain-wet friendly gas lamp-post and marched resolutely up Station Road. Soon after, that brave little figure was lost to sight in the wind-torn wet wildwoods.

It was not long after that Will ran over Lambton Bridge. He had a brown paper parcel containing Aunty Bertha's cake. He was glad to be going and seeing Sam. He wanted to talk to Sam about the strange sounds from their flooded cellar. He wanted to talk of the strange blackness and shadow shapes by the gaslight at the end of the alley. He wanted to talk about the strange cracks in the church and the rotten, evil, creeping smell from the graveyard. And he wanted to tell Sam about the eyes that he had seen after midnight in the deep black by the wash-house door.

157

Will did not go straight into the woods on the old road. He stood for a time looking over his shoulder. Then like Jessie he went in.

John Mellor was in the woods. He had arrived home by train from Manchester the evening before. He had had meat to eat every day, military style P.T., cold baths, drill, and much hard work in the stables. It had been decided that when he left school at Christmas he would go to Blackdon Hall as a stable lad.

'Eh, our John, tha'll be stable lad, then afore us knows it, tha'll be coachman to Duke of Blackdon,' his mother crowed. She thought her problems were over.

John's fear had gone. Manchester smoke, gaslight, and exhaustion from hard work had destroyed his sensitivity. His fear was forgotten. Nearly six feet tall in his new boots and breeches, he walked down from Lambton Station, his old clothes in a red spotted cloth over his shoulder.

The first thing he had seen was Tom Wilson building a bonfire for Guy Fawkes, in Blackdown Craft, a bit of waste ground at the end of Jessie's street.

'Call that a bonfire, Wilson?' roared Mellor. 'I could pee on it from here an' put it out.' His voice was as loud as ever.

'Say that again, Mellor,' said Tom menacingly.

Mellor did. Wilson raised his fist and advanced like a side-stepping tom cat. The next thing he knew he was face down in the orange and red pulp of horse chestnut leaves with Mellor's well-blacked boot on his back. Mellor then swaggered off.

'I like thy hair, John,' mocked Tom Wilson. 'I wish I could go to a loony-bin prison in Manchester an' have my hair cut round a basin like thine. Eh, John, were there any monsters in prison, like tha saw in t' well?' Tom had not been worried by all the strange stories—one reason why Will had not talked to him.

A few seconds later Tom Wilson was sprawled over his bonfire and Mellor was lighting it.

Fanny Gibbs and Dolly Cresswell had paused in their skipping to admire John Mellor.

'Eh, he looks all right, Fan,' said Dolly, greatly impressed by Mellor's tough approach.

158

'Gerroff. He's mine,' snapped Fanny, and resumed her skipping, her rope lashing the wet leaves on the ground and her eye on John Mellor.

Bonfire night, the stars are bright,
Every little angel's dressed in white, chanted Fanny.

Now, the next day, this Saturday morning, Mellor grinned to himself as he went in the woods. He'd get the biggest branches he could. He'd show them what a bonfire should be. He ignored the rumble of thunder.

And Marmaduke Middlemas had come to the woods as well that Saturday and had entered them at eleven o'clock precisely. He stood now in a golden glade of horse-chestnut leaves, his stick held high, listening.

Surely—that was a child's cry for help? There it was again. It sounded like a child in great distress. He had come to the woods to do a little scientific research. Since he had been headmaster at Lambton he had noticed, particularly on nights when the moon was long past full and rising late in the night, a stump of stone on a hilltop. Very likely a Saxon Preaching Cross. And yet ... he had heard stories in shops and from children. Once or twice he had had the most foolish idea that stump was watching him. How absurd! And yet ... And the old legends ...

So he had come, as an educated man, to see for himself. He would find facts. None of the ridiculous superstitions would fill his mind. He would collect FACTS. It was quite disgraceful all this talk of devils and monsters, bad luck and so on. He had had a college education in London. A silk gown hung on a peg to prove it. He was the man to find where the stories came from. Yes, indeed he was.

There was the cry again. He had set off with his gold pencil and *Gentleman's Pocket Notebook* (bound in finest morocco leather). He had written, in his perfect copperplate writing ...

Hot sunshine.
Lightning over old stone on hill—interesting optical
*   illusion.*

159

Thunder all round—no point or centre of a storm seen.
Cold air from old mine shafts blows in face.
Much rustling. A large cat's eye gleaming in foliage.
Dark shadows.

The cry again. This was no foolery. He could ignore that no longer. He climbed upwards. He hated woods. All these squashed wet leaves and rotting berries. Surely it was getting darker? Thunder rumbled nearer. Why had he ever left London? It was evil here in these woods—evil.

Again the cry—desperate.

He began to pray to God. He was scared. His top hat fell in a badger's hole. He hacked through golden and red bracken as he tried to reach the voice. Sweating profusely he began to chant Psalm Fifty-five.

Fearfulness and trembling are come upon men, and
horror hath overwhelmed me.
And I said, Oh that I had wings like a dove! For then
would I fly away, and be at rest.

The cry of help became one of pain.

Grandfather had fidgeted ever since Grandmother had left. There was thunder in the air. He remembered the old stories about the thunder. He wished Lucy had not gone in the woods alone. He had walked over to the little ash wood. The wind was blowing the leaves off. Last night had been clear and frosty. And he remembered clearly talking to his father as though it were yesterday.

'Dunna let them young ash poles hide Lambton Spire from thy view,' his father had said.

'Why?' he had asked.

Keep thy eye on t' spire, thy ear on t'bell
An tha'll see or hear nowt on t'devil or hell.

Now he could neither see the spire, for he had let the trees grow for the fine ash wood, and the bell was silent. Grandfather began to bellow for one of his sons—his usual way out of difficulties. Albert came.

'Help us make a pile of these ash leaves, our Albert. They're spoiling grass. They'll fill t' cows wi' gas if they eat 'em.'

160

Then to Albert's amazement he began to shake the young trees to get the leaves off. He wanted to see the spire below. When he could, he made a big pile of the green ash leaves. He sent Albert for the matches. The leaves had been loosened on the tree until last night's frost and were still falling.

'Them'll not burn, father,' said Albert.

'I'll mek the buggers burn,' said Grandfather.

'He's going off his rocker,' said Albert to his brother Jack who passed by with some corn for the sheep.

Grandfather began to mutter, then he fetched the big brown pot bottle of lamp oil and uncorked it with a pop while scowling at Albert. He emptied it on the green leaves. Then he lit it. Clouds of smoke from the wet leaves billowed up. The old man stepped back in satisfaction. He'd got the leaves off the trees. A gust of wind blew at the smoke, turning it into a darting dragon of oily smoke with a life of its own: it blew to the west of Grandfather and hid the church spire in the valley ... Pain gripped at the old man like a squeezing devilish hand. He cried out suddenly.

Like a pathetic echo, the old man's cry was answered by the terrified cry of someone in the woods below.

Grandmother felt 'right glad' to be out of the wood. She had found some late blackberries in the lane and found Winny's cottage in Crowley. She knocked at the door.

'Lucy Walton!' said Winny. 'Thee must step inside.'

They chatted of the old days until a strong gust of wind blew rain and leaves against the cottage window. Then Grandmother changed the subject.

'I need thy help, Winny. Things are wrong at our house. My owd man's going daft. My youngest lad were killed at Midsummer. My grandson looks as if he's in a decline, though he's no cough. And I'm riddled wi' strange twinges an' aches an' rheumatiz.'

Winny looked at Grandmother. She took her hands in hers. The wind boomed in the chimney and distant thunder echoed. Winny got up and filled a brass bowl of water and put it by her side. Then she took Grandmother's hand again. She stared in the water for a long time.

161

'There's summat or something or somebody causing thee and thine some bother. I see suffering and pain. And there'll be a death to thee and thine unless this thing, which I canna see proper, is carted away to rest in t' churchyard ... What it is I canna see ... just a solid lump that needs taking and carting off to churchyard ... a big lump ...'

'Tha must mean my Abel,' said Grandmother drily.

'Nay, now Lucy,' said Winny sorrowfully. 'You loved that man of yours. They called him the Giant of the Peak in Prince Regent's day. I wouldna have said no if he'd asked me to wed him, Lucy, nor many another lass. Thee were lucky to marry him.'

Both women were silent as they remembered the big fair-haired giant of a man that Grandfather had been when he was young.

'Dunna let anyone eat them blackberries in thy basket,' said Winny suddenly.

'He wants a pie,' said Grandmother simply.

'It'll be his last then,' advised Winny. Grandmother struggled into her cloak.

'I've not been much help,' said Winny. 'Just told thee what tha knows already.' She gave Grandmother a bottle of the water from a spring in the woods, water that was orange with iron. She told Grandmother to drink a little each day.

'I'll come over mysen and see if I can help,' said Winny. 'Just let us know.'

Walking back, deep in thought about what Winny had said and the meaning of it, Grandmother saw a flicker of silent lightning dance eerily round the old chimney in the trees. She heard no sound but the drifting yellow birch leaves blowing in the wind. Then she heard a cry of great terror that chilled her heart and set it racing. It sounded like their Sam. The wind rocked the trees. Part of the loose stonework of the chimney fell to the ground as the earth shivered. Clutching wildly at branches Grandmother began to stumble home towards Bow Cross Farm and the direction of the cry.

Now the wind was roaring through the October woods. It stripped the poplars and silver birches in minutes. It hissed in

162

the gold of the beeches and brown oaks like an angry sea. The big fanlike leaves of the horse-chestnut span through the air and past Will as though they were escaping from this enchantment. He clutched at the parcel and squashed the cake.

He had to admit it. There could be monsters in this wood. He watched a branch fall on the woodland floor. Then he too heard a cry for help. The cry of another boy. The wind took the cry just as it took the birch leaves. Like the yellow leaves the cry was lost high in the darkening tumbled clouds.

A fall of stone by a deep bramble-hidden stream made Will turn quickly. Then the wind pushed at him, pushing him towards the cry and the danger, and he could not resist.

Will did not know it, but Jessie was struggling round the next corner. She was crying and sobbing, the wind drowning her sobbing. Chestnuts and acorns fell around her, but she did not pause to pick any up. The rain and wind had made her hair hang in thin rat's tails round her white face. Oh, why, why, why had she come? She could not go back. The wind was too strong.

Then she heard the cry of Samuel Walton. Biting her lips to stop them shaking, clenching her teeth to stop them chattering, she pushed through the rain-wet red bracken; brambles tore her dirty, patched, thin, cheap stockings to shreds.

She must help Sam.

Will heard the cry again. He knew that voice. It wasn't Sam's.

Then he saw a dark shape in the trees moving towards him, rhythmic in the gusts of wind with a slow devilish dance. It darted and turned through the darkening woods as though searching for something. It was still a great distance from Will. He stared at it wide-eyed.

It was coming for him.

Somewhere in the belly of the moving shadow came the cry again. A flash of lightning was followed by thunder. Will felt the earth move under him. His feet were as heavy as lead. This must be a nightmare.

He turned and ran into the angry wind, running away. Running for his life.

The stay in Manchester had removed all fear from John Mellor. He marched up to the black opening of a cave that led to ancient air shafts and mines deep below. He did not even turn his head when he heard the rattle of falling stones. His cheeks were brown with health and fitness, glowing in the wind. His eye was clear and bright with health. He did not see other eyes watching him.

He wanted a big, thick, black branch half-buried in grass and gleaming orange bracken. The branch seemed to be growing out of the cave. Just right for the centre pole of the biggest and best bonfire in Lambton. He kicked away some black toadstools.

He bent to the branch and flexed his muscles in pride, though there was nobody to see. He did not see the crescent shape and gleam of wicked eyes. Then he cried out in agony and terror.

Dame Trot had never felt so poorly in her life. She puffed and wheezed up the old lane to Bow Cross, pulling dirty shawls round her, remembering the times she had walked to Chesterfield along it when it was a busy road. But now ... all had changed. The road was abandoned to evil ... she remembered things she had tried to forget about the woods. Things her mother had said she had seen and done ... The wind took a shawl and blew it high in an ash tree where to the old woman's dim eyes it flapped and waved to her like a thin witch, like her mother had been. And she remembered her mother's words.

'The Devil rides out in cold air and evil vapours along the lightning path and will take you for his own in Manor Woods.' She had read that last night. The old woman began sobbing and was deaf and blind to everything around her until she reached the back door of Bow Cross. She banged loudly.

Inside the kitchen Jack and Albert were trying to work out the value of the hay lost in the fire. They had left Grandfather outside with his fire, listening for the bell. He had ignored the

164

cry for help. When he heard more cries he was suddenly filled with a fear that was like Sam's and he had run into the kitchen where his sons were sitting at the table.

'What's up, father?' asked Jack. 'I've not seen thee so nimble since our Ted said he'd lost a sovereign in the yard last Martinmas.'

Then there was a banging at the door, and Dame Trot fell in and staggered over to Grandfather on the settle. 'I've come to warn thy missis of dark and devilish things around here,' she croaked. 'Aye, thee may well blink thy eyes at me, Abel Walton. There's dark things in thy fields and woods.' She pulled up her dress and gave her leg a good scratch. Grandfather looked the other way. He could not stand any more of the old stories.

Grandfather looked towards the table and saw his son Jack grin at Albert. Jack was lighting a candle and his eyes gleamed with laughter as he held the taper to the candle. It was getting dark, though only a little after dinnertime: the wind roared in the chimney and thunder rumbled. The kitchen was grey and gold with shadow and firelight. Then Grandfather began to shout. He could not bear being laughed at by his sons. He shouted at Dame Trot.

'Nobody invited thee to come an' rant at my fireside like a Methody preacher an' tell old tales!'

'Tha's told many an old tale thysen in thy time, father,' said Albert quietly, licking the stub of a pencil and making his tongue purple. He was counting on his fingers, with great skill working out the cost of hay.

'Thee hold thy tongue, our Albert,' said Grandfather. 'Tha knows I never believe them old wives' tales. I heard too many from me own father!'

'Thy Lucy'll listen,' said Dame Trot, scratching at cat flea-bites round her bony ankle, with broken, rasping fingernails.

'She wunna,' blustered Grandfather. 'My Lucy does as I tells her.' Albert and Jack smirked at each other.

'She'll listen,' said Dame Trot, feeling deep in her bosom to check her keys and drawer knobs were all there. 'And tha'll listen, Abel Walton, when I tell about the Devil's store of gold and treasure my mam said's hidden deep in thy fields!' She cackled with glee.

165

'Eh?' said Grandfather, cupping his ear anxiously.

Ted came in at that moment. 'I'm sure I've heard our Sam shouting. I've looked but I canna see him. He were walling a bit ago and finding it hard going. He looked half-dead.' Ted shook his head and went to the pump to wash his hands. Grandfather shook from head to toe as he put on more coal. He jumped and so did Dame Trot when a vicious flash of lightning tore open the grey sky.

Middlemas pushed his way to the voice. It seemed to be getting fainter, as though the caller were being dragged under the ground. His heartbeats shook his body. His fine leather boots kept tripping over tussocks of straw-coloured summer grass. The wind took him for a time. Then something grabbed his throat. It was a grip of ice and iron. Middlemas tried to shout but could not. The ice-cold grip held him for a minute. Then he was hurled forwards with violent force at the same time as lightning and thunder split the sky together. He lost all sense of control or direction. He lost his balance, fell, slid at gathering speed on his backside down a steep and greasy bank of clay under an overhanging tent of yellow horse-chestnut leaves. He hit the conker tree with some force at the bottom and was promptly showered with large spined conker cases.

'Our Lord Jesus Christ save me,' he groaned, using words almost the same as he had told Mellor off for using in July. He bounced off and hit a wall. The wall partly collapsed, being of a great age, and Middlemas heard the rattle of falling stones as they fell. He found himself able to peer over the crumbling wall. There was nothing. He was staring into the sickening emptiness of a black pit, an ancient shaft to a deep mine.

Behind him he plainly heard the sound of snapping branches and falling stones. And it suddenly entered Middlemas's brain that he was going to be pushed into the seemingly bottomless pit. Spitting and coughing blood, Marmaduke Middlemas ran through the dark roaring pattering wood, his black trouser bottoms caked with brown mud like chocolate icing on a cake.

Behind him, something followed.

166

Sam had walked to the Top Pasture, his body tingling, his eyes full of the magic blue fire. As he walked up the wind blew harder. When he finally reached the top he made some attempt to lift the big blocks of gritstone that had fallen off the drystone walls. Whole sections of the wall had fallen. Stones were scattered everywhere.

The Stone was black and dominating against the rising storm. It seemed to be pulling the strength and energy out of his body. He failed several times to lift even a small stone and so begin the repair. Then Sam heard the cry. A cry to be answered. He left the fallen walls and dragged his body towards it. He kept the Stone at a field's distance.

To his bewilderment he found Jessie Smith at the top of the old road into the woods. Her hair was in wet strands over her face. She grabbed Sam's hand and together they struggled towards the cries that now seemed to be getting fainter. The sky darkened. Hail and rain lashed the woods.

'Oh God,' thought Sam. He knew very well what this kind of weather brought into these woods. And he could not feel Jessie's hand in his. His body was numb, as though he had been frozen. Pain hammered in his head. He saw blue fire filling the woods like a rising sea. He could faintly hear Jessie begin screaming as she dragged him along.

Then they both saw John Mellor half-dragged into a cave, his legs sprawled out on the dim gold of the bracken. But Sam found he had not strength to help. Jessie was underfed and weak. Sam could not see properly. Dark shadows seemed to have fixed themselves on his eyes. Something seemed to be pulling John Mellor back into the cave. As they pulled, they felt him being pulled back. Their shouts and screams echoed down the tunnel and were mingled with a low hissing, which was heard outside, mixed with the last of the sound of leaves on the trees.

Jessie screamed loudly. There were eyes at the back of the cave. And they pulled and they struggled. John pulled too, clawing and struggling. A large boulder was dislodged and fell with a rattle of stones. An adder, whipping round, sank its venomous fang deep into John's hand. Now they were all frantic. Another adder was seen. By the lightning flash Sam saw that John had a crescent-shape cut pouring blood down his cheek—like the cut by the well.

Then Jessie looked up and began to scream and scream and scream. Sam's eyes were filled with dark and shadow.

Middlemas ran down the Station Road to the town, praying and hoping that whatever it was that had caught him would not follow him. The streets were quiet and deserted, and shining cobbles, wet with rain, reflected the lightning. Middlemas could not get the fear out of his head that whatever it was in the woods that had attacked him would follow him home. Perhaps later tonight. There was a horse and cart outside The Wheatsheaf so Middlemas sidled past that, his muddy bottom to the wall. He decided to go home via Church Alley. He hoped he would be unseen. But he met the Archdeacon.

'Ah, Middlemas!' boomed the Archdeacon. 'Just the fellow I want to talk to!' Middlemas turned his mud-caked bottom to Saltby's shopwindow. 'I want to come into school, Middlemas, and WARN, yes, WARN the children against listening to all this DISGRACEFUL talk of devils and magic and witchcraft that fills the town. They are actually saying in the town now that the Devil and his kind are walking at this very moment in Manor Wood. Ha? Ha! Pah and poppycock, Middlemas. What nonsense! Why, my dear sir, you have a nasty curved cut on your cheek. How came you by that? You must attend to it shortly when I am done. To continue. I will not have the children of my parish listening to fairy tales and superstitious twaddle. We will stamp the stories out, Middlemas. Why, even Green, my trusty verger, talks of giant things underground that will topple my church! We must enlighten these children, Middlemas, go forward with God into the twentieth century. It is our mission. What's the matter, Middlemas? Has the cat got your tongue sir?'

'No, Archdeacon,' murmured Middlemas, his bottom to the wall. But he wasn't sure, the children might be right ... should he say anything? He looked at the Archdeacon and stayed silent.

'Good good good good. We'll quell all this talk on Monday, Middlemas.' The Archdeacon tried to slap Middle-

mas on his back but Middlemas, not wanting his muddy
bottom displayed, moved round. But the Archdeacon felt a
need to give a hearty back slap. The two men circled each
other on the fallen gold of the lime leaves. Finding it
impossible, the Archdeacon said good-day and strode away
shouting, 'And I will come near to you in judgement and I
will be a swift witness against the sorcerers ...' Middlemas
watched him go thankfully. He could not help thinking the
children were wise to listen to the old stories, but he knew he
would lose his job if he opened his mouth.

'Excuse me, Mester Middlemas, but dost tha know thy
backside's clarted up wi' mud an' leaves an' what looks like
cow muck?' said Mr Saltby, coming from his shop.

'I had a little ... er ... sit down in the woods,' said
Middlemas loftily.

'Funny time o' the year to have a bleeding picnic,' said Mr
Saltby, just loud enough for Middlemas to hear.

Middlemas ignored him. Then he saw some of his school-
children. Dodging children and adults down side-streets
Middlemas found himself near the station again. He found a
seat and sat on it. There he would wait till nightfall. And he
would tell nobody of his adventures in case the Archdeacon
found out.

Sam's Uncle Jo found Sam and Jessie and John. He was
returning from Lambton. He saw them crouched in the cave
as though dead. To his horror a huge adder struck at his boot
as he came near to them. He crushed it, staring at it in
distaste. He'd never seen a nedder that size ... and its fangs.
Then Jessie had got up and clung to his hand and sobbing had
pointed to the trees and cried out about eyes and crawling
things. John, who was nearly as tall as Jo, clung to Jo's jacket
like a small child.

Jo was the biggest, roughest, and least talkative of Sam's
uncles.

'What's up then? What's up?' he kept saying, as all three
clung to him whimpering. 'What's up then?' Jo kept repeating, as though to one of his horses, as he managed to get them
back to the farm kitchen.

169

Grandfather had lit two lamps and piled coal on the fire. The old man was very frightened. He knew something was wrong but would not admit it. John collapsed on the rag rug in front of the fire, his face a mass of cuts and blood. Jessie hid in the shadows, her eyes like those of a snared rabbit. Sam stood on the doorstep and was very sick.

'I told thee, cleverclogs Walton!' screamed Dame Trot. 'See thee! See thee! T' Devil's out an' they've seen him!' The old woman was going hysterical with fear and glee at being proved right.

'There's more sense in a load o' steamin' pig muck than that big gabbin' gob of thine,' roared Grandfather. He was shaking all over. His worst imaginings were coming true. Things he hadn't dared think about for seventy years. He shouted and bellowed, hoping all this was not the truth.

'I saw this black thing,' sobbed Jessie. 'It were like a shadder, all dark ... crawlin' ... eyes ...'

'An' all the time I were being dragged into the cave,' croaked John.

'A big buck tom cat!' guffawed Jack. 'That's what it were!'

'It were scratching me an' dragging me in,' said John in a low voice. 'An' there were cold things an' a great snake.'

Sam, sick and ill as he was, felt a wash of relief fill his body. The truth at last was being told.

'It fastened itself on us,' said John Mellor softly. He had the courage to ignore Jack's loud noises and whoops. 'There were this dark shape as big as a man, watchin' at the back of the cave ...'

'An' I saw it in t'hazel bushes,' cried Jessie.

'Gerraway with thee!' said Jack. 'It were Sam's Grandfather looking for a penny he lost twenty year ago!'

Albert who was eating one of Grandmother's pasties choked with laughter and Ted had to bang on his back: he coughed and spluttered and pasty crumbs were sprayed on to John's red hair as he sat by the fire.

'Tha'll be laughing the other side of thy face soon, Jack Walton,' howled Dame Trot, clutching at falling shawls. 'Thee see! Thee see!'

'Thy mother were a witch an' nobody believes owt like that any more—I dunna!' said Grandfather, now scared out of his wits. All his father said was coming true. He put another log on the already blazing fire.

'It wrapped itsen round me face,' said John huskily, ignoring the men's laughter. 'An' darkness dragged me in—'

Albert's laughter drowned his voice. Jessie, seeing the door open, screamed loudly. 'It's Owd Nick hysen come to get us,' cried Dame Trot, burying her face in her thin brown hands.

So Grandmother saw the chaos as she entered the kitchen. As soon as he saw her, Sam began shouting the whole story of the Stone. Grandmother took off her wet cloak and hung it on the nail behind the door. Sam followed, talking almost incoherently. Grandmother covered the shivering John Mellor with a horse rug and gave him a rag and a bowl of warm water to clean his face with. She said nothing but muttered darkly about daft owd men who wouldn't shift their arses to help kids in trouble and grown men she was ashamed to say were her sons. Sam shouted and shouted and shouted so his uncles and Dame Trot began to stare at him. Next, still tight-lipped, Grandmother, still the only person doing anything in the emergency, pushed Jessie on to the settle. She took Jessie's boots off and the tatters and shreds that had once been stockings. Still Sam shouted out the story.

Jo's deep gruff voice suddenly cut into the room.

'Summat ought to be done about yon snake-bit on young John there. I've never seen a nedder as long. It were as long as me arm. There's summat going off down there.' Everybody stared. Jo had made one of the longest speeches in his life. And he had not been laughing with his brothers.

Dame Trot scuttled across the kitchen. 'I'll get some plantain juice for the bite,' said she.

Sam still followed Grandmother. Grandmother gave Jessie a pair of ancient silk stockings bought from a pedlar fifty years ago. Then she gave her a pie to eat. Then she got her big brown mixing-bowl and began to mix flour and fat together for the crust of Grandfather's pie. Sam went everywhere with her, plucking at her sleeve, going on with the story.

'An there were this tall shadow thing near to cave,' half-sobbed Jessie, her mouth full of tasty beef and potato pie.

John Mellor suddenly spoke to Grandmother. 'An' what

171

he's been telling thee, well, I've seen it. It tried to pull me down into cave.'

'I've never really seen anything,' ended Sam, 'but I've always known something was there … watching … waiting … waiting till the end of this month to kill us.'

Silence fell in the kitchen. Just the dry rustle of Grandmother sprinkling sugar on the blackberries, the rain on the window, the spitting of the log on the fire, and Albert's munching.

'I told thee,' said Dame Trot. She was cutting the snakebite with a tiny silver knife she always carried.

Jack belched loudly, somehow putting an expression of great scorn into the sound.

'JACK!' said Grandmother. 'There are childer here.'

'Our Sam's mad,' said Ted. 'T'others have caught it. Just like when hens get hysteria when one thinks it's seen a snake or fox an' runs squawking. It only takes one to set the others off.'

At once the kitchen exploded into a row of grown-ups arguing and shouting, laughing and swearing.

Another silence. Grandfather emptied the rest of the coal on the fire as though he hoped the fire would protect him. He said not a word. If he kept quiet perhaps he might not have to believe … believe what he had dreaded happening since he was a boy.

'I'm only baking thee a blackberry pie,' said Grandmother, shielding her face with her hand against the fierce fire, as she put the pie in the oven. 'I'm not roasting an ox, Abel.' Then she straightened up wearily.

'I believe thee, Sam,' she said clearly. 'Every word, lad.'

Uproar filled the kitchen again.

'Tha's making our Sam worse than what he is. Tha's turning him into a rate wet nelly,' said Ted. He spoke loudly, angrily, scornfully. 'Sam and John are two big lads, mother, frit to go in woods. It's daft at their age. An' if our Sam doesna pull his wits round he'll be no more of a man than his mother.'

Grandmother said not a word. She stared. She stared at her sons till one by one they were all looking at their boots.

'It's all in thy big brown book,' said Sam, turning to Dame Trot. 'It tells thee what to do in there.' There was a hopeful

172

note in his voice. Everybody in the room looked at Dame Trot. But she shook her head.

'I'm not looking in that book, my masters. Not after what I know now. I'll never look in that book. She says it's the Devil's book. Him an' 'er made it together. That's why them medicines were so good. But I'll never look in it again. Devil will fetch me if I look. I know too much already. They'll fetch me.' And she began to weep the dry sobs of great old age.

Another row started. The old woman's nose began to run as she sobbed and she flicked the snot expertly with her knobbly old fingers into the fire.

'Mucky old dame!' shouted Grandfather, speaking at last. 'Gerroff home an' take thy daft stories with thee.'

'Abel Walton, hold thy tongue in company,' said Grandmother, examining the blackberry pie that was bubbling purple at the edges from the hot oven. She fixed them all with her eyes. She began rapping out orders.

'Albert. Wipe that daft gormless grin from thy chops and take these childer back to Lambton and bring us back some pickling spice. I'm right out of it—'

'There's some in that crock in larder on third shelf,' began Jack. 'I saw it—'

'Will you shut up, our Jack? It's you I'm thinking of, all the pickled cabbage you like to stuff yourself with.'

Jack stared at his mother; he didn't believe her. Grandmother went up to Sam.

'Us'll think of something. I believe what tha's said. It all makes sense. I've been to a wise woman today.'

'But,' stammered Sam. 'It's getting us, yon Stone and all the rest. It'll get us before the end of the month—the old brown book said so—'

'Nobody's looking in that book,' shouted Dame Trot.

'Aye. All right, Betsy love, no one will,' said Grandmother soothingly, as the old woman got to her feet.

'But they must, they must, it tells us—' said Sam. They were still not taking things seriously enough: it was not enough to say they believed. They should *do* something.

'I'll take 'em back down, mother,' said Albert irritably. 'Our Jack's best here milking. Are you coming or not?' he demanded roughly to John and Jessie.

173

'I've got to go down to Lambton for some balm for me mam,' lied Sam. He had a plan.

Grandmother wrapped some pies in a clean cloth for Jessie to take home and looked in a little black teapot on the dresser and took out a silver threepence. When she had cleaned up John's face she saw he needed a shave.

'Buy thysen a razor, lad,' said she. 'One o' men in thy yard will show thee what to do.'

'He's growing his whiskers an' he's afraid o' dark an' frit o' shadows,' said Albert sulkily and with scorn.

'How long hast thou had thy little store of silver, Lucy?' asked Grandfather, anxious to talk about anything but the nightmare that he had just seen coming true before his very eyes.

'As long as tha's had that little flowerpot of gold in roof of privy,' said Grandmother calmly.

Jessie was so overcome by the food in the cloth she kissed Grandmother.

'You're welcome, love,' said Grandmother. 'We're not short up here, tho' to listen to some you'd think so.'

'I'm going. I'm not waiting no longer,' growled Albert.

Grandmother threw a shawl over Jessie's shoulders and then the three and Albert were out in the October gale again. They trotted obediently in a scared line behind Albert down the old way. Sam thought quickly. When they were in front of the cave Albert stopped. He picked up a massive boulder. Albert was the neatest and smartest of Sam's uncles and thought a lot about himself. Every year he waxed his moustaches and built up his muscles to win the Strong Man competition at the Wakes. He now began to show off to the children. Jessie, lovingly fingering the hot pie in the napkin, with a frightened eye on the cave, thought he was very handsome. Now Albert hurled the giant boulder into the cave. There was a crash that echoed strangely, followed by a strange rattle and then a faint tap. Sam and John stared into each others eyes with fear.

'See then?' sneered Albert. But while Albert had been showing off, both John and Sam had been staring at the deep marks on the drifts of leaves, crescent-shape marks, the marks of great coils.

174

By the time they were out of the woods and on the railway bridge, Sam and John were exhausted. 'I'm not standing about waiting for thee,' said Albert shortly. His temper boiled up. 'I'd thought tha'd more sense, our Sam. Tha should be helping thy dad instead o' playing wi' girls and listening to old woman's ghost tales. What thy dad'll have to say to all this I don't know.' And he strode off.

'I don't care,' thought Sam. He had Jessie and John who knew. He was no longer alone. He turned to John. The two boys stared at each other for a moment. A strange moment. They had been enemies and hated each other for so long. Yet sometimes we understand our enemies better than our friends. Both had enjoyed hating each other in better times. Meanwhile Jessie leaned on the bridge, warm in her thick shawl and peeping at the pies.

'Have a pipe o' baccy, Sam,' said Mellor. 'It'll calm thee down.' He showed Sam how to light the pipe and draw in the smoke. They might have been friends for years instead of enemies. Leaning on the rain-wet bridge they exchanged stories. What John had seen at the railway accident. Sam told of his fears and dreams, about the book and how the shadow was creeping nearer. Then both John and Jessie told Sam about the shapes, the shadows, the eyes, and the misty figures of darkness in the trees. But it was the eyes, the crescent-shape eyes of evil that both John and Jessie kept telling Sam of.

Jessie shyly touched Sam's shadow-touched arm. Then John in his gruff, grating voice described his nightmares for the first time. Dreams of creeping, underground, evil things, slowly and surely as each dream came, getting closer to him. Sam just stared and stared. John's dreams were worse than anything he had thought of or imagined.

'I'm right frit again,' said Jessie suddenly.

'Us'll look after thee,' said John grandly. 'We need to get that spell book, Sam. Tha said tha had to do something in churchyard?'

'I'm not sure,' said Sam, 'so much has happened and there's so little time left we need to plan—that's why I came down with thee.' He paused with a worried frown deepening. 'We could be attacked or taken tonight.'

175

'Right,' said John. 'The best thing for thee, me, and Jessie to do is to stay in all day tomorrow. It's Sunday anyhow. Let old Trot calm down. Canst come to school on Monday, Sam? If tha can, thee and me and Jessie too could go and see her on Monday night after school. She'll have calmed down by then. We could see what to do.'

John puffed on his pipe. 'Us'll be safe in school Sam. Devil'll not come in classroom. Owd Nelly White's face'd scare breeches off Devil himself!'

They laughed. Despite the great danger they all felt relief that their secret was now a shared secret. Sam had to say goodbye on Lambton Bridge. That was the worst bit. He looked up to the woods roaring and throbbing in the gale. Would he be safe till Monday? His heart beating wildly, looking all around him, he ran the long way home on the new road, his boots soundless on the wet leaves.

But the thought that the Stone would get him before Monday so he could not make plans would not go out of his mind. He made himself look at the Stone. It looked bigger. He stood still, petrified for a moment as he thought of John and Jessie's stories. The tentacles ... the eyes ... the dark shapes gathering round them, closing in, tall shapes, creeping shapes. Unconsciously his boot made snake patterns in a pile of sludge and wet leaves by a drain. He saw the blue fire again.

It's not fair, he thought. Just when I've got help. The evil was playing with him, like a giant, devilish cat would play with a mouse. Just as he'd got help he would be killed. The thought that it was too late would not go away.

None of them had seen Middlemas huddled like a wet crow sitting on his wet, cold, muddy bottom on a rain-beaded cast-iron Midland Railway bench half-way up Station Road. But Middlemas, cowering and crouching in the shadows, had seen them. He'd seen Mellor teach Walton how to smoke. He had seen that forward hussy Jessie Smith come out of the woods with two boys. As they had passed, Middlemas had heard Mellor say that Miss White's face was enough to frighten the Devil away. He'd seen them laugh.

Middlemas was scandalized: God alone knew what the

pupils had been up to in those woods. He knew what boys and girls did in the woods together. He did indeed. He wasn't born yesterday. And they were joking about the Devil. Just let them wait till Monday. He would thrash the living daylights out of all three. In front of the Archdeacon. Middlemas felt warmer and cheered. He would take action in God's name. He felt warmer even to the seat of his sodden backside. He reached for his gold pencil to make a note of what he would say. It had gone. So had the pocket-book. And his gold chain ... and gold watch. Middlemas spoke his thoughts aloud.

'Mellor and Walton have been cavorting and keeping company with tramps in the woods. Has Mellor stolen my watch?' So saying, full of dark thoughts for his revenge on Monday, he sidled home in the twilight. Another spell in prison would do Mellor good.

Sam washed at the pump in the scullery when he got home. Nobody said anything. He heard his father's heavy limping tread go upstairs to rest—the only place where he was free of the nagging pain, he said.

Sam went into the kitchen and blinked in the lamplight. His mother looked at him and sniffed. She could smell a strange tobacco.

'Trust her to smell tobacco and yet not sense the danger all around us,' thought Sam to himself. There was tension in the air. But Sam did not care. He had friends now. He sat down and reached for a stick of celery, sparkling with the cold spring water it had been washed in. He smothered a piece of freshly baked bread in butter. God, his arm hurt, but he was so hungry. And he must keep his strength up for the last battle. Still nothing was said. His mother sniffed again. She went to the oven and gave Sam one of the pointed cooking apples from the tree in the field: she had baked it and now the juice was a froth of apple and sugar. Sam licked at it, his mind on plans for Monday.

His father clomped down the stairs again. He was restless. 'I dunna see tha's done much on them walls, Sam,' said he. The pain made him irritable. 'I need thy help, Sam. I saw thee walk over Top Pasture and down towards the woods. Tha'd

177

not lifted more than three stones, Sam. I need thy help, lad.'

'Are you listening, Sam?' echoed his mother crossly.

Sam's father went on and on about it. Sam noticed how his father's hand shook as he dipped his celery in a little mountain of salt ... His father had been a fine man a year ago ... still he nagged at Sam ... Sam wanted to shout out, 'But I am bloody well helping you! I am trying to save us from death and evil!' But he did not dare. Instead he munched steadily. He noticed too how weak his own hand was.

Sam went to bed early. He would need his energy in the days ahead. He took his medicine and lifted the loose board to get the marble egg. He went down to get a glass of water but really to put his marble egg in his jacket pocket. It might come in useful.

The night wind rattled his window as though trying to get in. The house and Sam's room seemed to be getting colder and colder. Outside a wide crescent moon, nearly half, like an eye slowly opening with fear, raced through the wild skies as though racing with triumph at some event on the earth below. Colder and colder. A dark cold shadow seemed to settle on Sam's house.

Up at Bow Cross Farm Sam's Grandfather jumped as the wind rattled at a loose shutter. He dropped his glasses when a door banged upstairs. For him, every minute that passed threatened to bring the fear of his life into reality. And like Sam, fear gave the old man an enormous appetite. He ate a prodigious pile of cold ham, chewing the cool white fat with relish and eating many thick slices of butter with his bread and mouthful after mouthful of pickled red cabbage. Then he ate half of the blackberry pie.

'I'll leave thee a slice, Jack,' said he. 'I can see tha gawpin' at me. I'll leave thee a morsel. I'm not greedy like thee. I dunna eat much.'

Jack ate a slice of the blackberry pie and said not a word. He was watching how his father's hand was shaking and he saw a bead of purple juice bounce down the corrugated belly folds of his father's waistcoat.

178

'Tha's all of a swale and a dither, father,' said Ted, who had also seen the spillage. 'Art all right?'

Grandmother said nothing. She was deep in thought. She was thinking about Sam and his friends, Wise Winny, and the old stories Grandfather had often told. The door banged again upstairs, more loudly this time. Grandfather let slip his juice and pie-laden spoon.

'It's them boggarts that old woman were telling thee about, father, come to get thee, father,' said Albert. His brothers laughed.

'We'll hear no more about it,' said Grandmother calmly. She fetched a cloth and mopped up the old man with gentle touches. But Grandfather said nothing. He just imagined the worst. But when the wind-tossed widening slit of the moon was setting behind the creaking and clattering branches of the ash trees on the far hill, the old man turned as white as a sheet. Trembling with fear he went out into the yard and splashed about in the dying moonlight, staggering all round. He felt his time to die was coming.

'I told Lucy not to pick blackberries after Michaelmas. The Devil poisons 'em. I told her!' Then the old man was wretchedly sick. Violent stomach pains grabbed him next. He caught sight of the moonlight glimmering on the old Stone and he groaned. It was all coming true. This was the end of the good times: what he had hoped would never happen had done so. Grandfather was now so weak he could not shut the privy door and it banged open and shut as the old man huddled on the bench, a pathetic and miserable sight in the wavering moonlight.

By midnight Grandfather was so ill that Jack and Ted had to carry him from his bed across the rain-filled yard, leaves and rain flying past Grandfather's flapping nightshirt, flickering for a moment in the swing of the lantern.

'Which end dost tha want us to put down first?' chided Jack, who was convinced his father was suffering from simple overeating.

A gold sovereign tumbled from the nightshirt—Grandfather loved to carry gold everywhere he went. It made him feel secure. The coin lay golden in the yellow, wet, lantern-lit birch leaves that drifted into the privy on the October gale.

179

'Yo' two are wicked varmints robbing thy dying old dad,'
said Grandfather weakly.

Back in the kitchen Grandmother waited anxiously. She
had made a jug of meadow-sweet tea to dry up the old man.
But the old man had to keep going back to the privy again
and again. Then Jack had to hold him while he was
very sick again. Jack, still thinking his father was paying
the penalty of being greedy, thumped Grandfather's back
to get up some wind. As he thumped, Grandfather's teeth fell
in the hole.

'Now see what tha's made me do!' said Grandfather.
'Them teeth were real china an' cost us five bob from
Nottingham Goose Fair in '61. He were a real gent
that fitted them. Real clever gent. Not like thee, our Jack.
Fitted 'em real well. I couldna talk for a month after he
fitted 'em.'

'By gum, father,' said Jack promptly. 'I'll get a train to
Nottingham an' get thee another pair tomorrow.'

'Ye'll be sorry soon,' said Grandfather. He knew his time
was short.

'Me teeth have gone, Lucy,' said Grandfather when he
returned to the kitchen again. 'I shan't live much longer now.'

'I'll see thee lives, Abel,' said Grandmother quietly. She
was worried. 'I'll save thee from owt out there.' And she
nodded in the direction of the Stone. She took the old man up
to bed again, soothing him with gentle talk. But the old man
would not be comforted. It was as though an icy shadow had
settled on him. And he knew from the old stories that he was
doomed.

Soon after, the troubled moon set and only a few stars
glimmered in the scudding clouds before being swallowed up
again. As the last tip of moon vanished, the Stone seemed to
swell in size and its shadow spread like dark water in the
feeble starlight.

Sam, cold and still in his cold room, dreamed he was
caught in a web of cold shadowy worms that slowly choked
him to death. The more he struggled the more he choked, the
tighter the web of darkness became. He awoke, his throat

hurting. He had shouted with fear. His mother was bending over him with a candle, its flame jumping and shuddering in invisible cold airs.

'I can smell tobacco on you, Samuel,' said she. 'So that's why you disappeared today. To go and smoke. Oh, Samuel. We're as poor as church mice and the bit of money you spend you get tobacco with. No wonder you're pale and sick. This explains everything. I wonder I've never smelled it on your breath and clothes before. You'll stop it at once, now do you hear? You're too young. Boys do not smoke pipes.'

Sam was silent with resentment. One minute she said he was doing a man's work, the next she called him boy. She blew out the candle and rustled away.

He lay there in the moving darkness of the wind-filled night time. 'Monday. Monday. Please come before it gets too late.'

Sunday was a day of driving rain that stripped the trees of their highest leaves, leaving the cold look of winter on the wet countryside. The Stone seemed to be bigger by the black skeletons of the trees.

Sam was on edge. He brushed his jacket that hung on a nail behind the door ready for school; he had a quick feel at the marble egg and wondered if it was any good. His father stayed down and seemed better. He ate the Sunday pie. They had not had a joint of meat since July.

'Make today go fast,' prayed Sam. Sunday was a day of rest and Sam was glad to sit by the fire and listen to his mother read from the Bible. He watched a sunset of black clouds and blood-coloured sky grow behind the Stone as though its reflected evil were being thrown back to the clouds. 'Just get me through tonight safely,' prayed Sam. 'Then tomorrow we'll find out what has to be done to stop the final curse from working.'

Like Sam, Grandfather was edgy. He was terrified what might happen next. On one of his many trails to the privy he

181

caught sight of Donkey Jack. He was a little bent old man who travelled the old lanes on a donkey. He was one of the last of the pedlars. Grandfather had known him all his life, from the times when the lane outside the farm was a busy way. The old pedlar inquired over Grandfather's health.

'I'm proper poorly,' Grandfather said. 'She gave us a blackberry pie she'd made'—he pointed towards the farm and Grandmother who was digging up some fresh horse-radish to go with the Sunday joint of beef— 'it nearly killed me!'

'What tha needs is a bit of comfrey, mester,' said Donkey Jack. 'There's plenty round them old caves by side of old way. I saw it when I rode up.' He paused, screwing up his eyes, filmy with cataracts. Donkey Jack was half blind. 'Jest pick a leaf an' pour boiling water on it.'

To Donkey Jack's amazement, for he guessed Grand-father's mean ways, Grandfather gave him a whole bucket of corn for his donkey. 'Thee wait here while I go in t'woods an' get a leaf,' said Grandfather. 'Let thy beast eat as much of that corn as it wants. Thee can stand an' see nothing happens to me in them woods—I'm unsteady on me feet these days,' he added, as the pedlar stared at him. 'Let thy beast eat up. Dunna let Lucy see thee. Dunna let Lucy see thee, 'er's got mean in 'er old age. Aye, 'er has. Thee watch me.'

In reality, Grandfather was very scared of going into the woods alone. But he scuttled down the old road and found some dark green, thick leaves growing near the cave where John had been attacked the day before. Grandfather pulled at the plant, roots and all, until it came away from the loose stones and leaf mould. Then he rushed back up the old way. He remembered a story his father had told him about that cave; he was so weak now that two tears of fear and self-pity trickled down his old furrowed cheeks.

Donkey Jack had gone when he returned and so had the corn. Grandfather was unable to show the pedlar whether he had got the right herb. But the old man was certain it was comfrey. He rushed into the kitchen just like John and Sam and Jessie had done yesterday, looking over his shoulder as he came in.

He grabbed the big copper kettle. 'I'm just going to make

182

some mash for them hens,' said Grandfather. 'Our Jack canna make it proper.' He kept the plant that he thought was comfrey behind his back. Even now he was unwilling to admit to himself or to Grandmother just how scared he was. But Grandmother was busy basting the roast beef and putting roast potatoes round the meat and she did not see the ugly plant that Grandfather had picked.

Grandfather, who trusted Donkey Jack totally, went to the brewhouse, made the tea from a leaf in a cup, and hid the plant behind the copper in a big jar. He drank a cup of the leaf tea. After dinner Grandfather, like Sam, was glad to sit by the fire. Like Sam he was afraid of the future. Both were in fear of their lives.

'I don't know about going to school,' said Sam's mother on Monday morning. 'Your father, as soon as he got upstairs last night, were proper poorly.' Sam, who had already taken his jacket from off the nail and was feeling the egg, began to argue.

'But mam, school bobby'll get us. I've been off nearly a month. And I'm forgetting how to do long division,' he added slyly. She believed him. He knew those two arguments together would work.

It was a steely grey morning with a cold and gusty wind. Yet faint in the cold grey he fancied he heard the devilish high whine of the ugly music he had heard on Saturday. He rushed around doing as many jobs for his father as he could. It made him late, but he was glad to run fast down the new turnpike. He got to school just as the wind-blown school bell had finished and Middlemas had seen the children in. But Miss White was reverently opening the register and she did not see him creep in. She loved her register next to her Bible.

John Mellor nodded at him and grinned. In spite of everything Sam felt better. He was no longer alone in the fight. He smiled at Jessie. The warm feeling was short-lived. The handle on the door turned slowly and then Middlemas and the Archdeacon came slowly in, both in black gowns, both carrying a Bible. The class at once scrambled to its feet. The boys bowed. The girls curtsied.

183

Middlemas with a swirl of gown fetched canes from the cupboard. The Archdeacon held up a long white finger to Miss White who also curtsied and tried to smile.

The Archdeacon rocked solemnly backwards and forwards on his polished heels like the poplar trees outside in the rising wind. He stuck his thumbs behind his gown and cleared his throat loudly. But Middlemas stared at Sam. 'What's up with him?' thought Sam. 'Is it because I've been away for so long?' Middlemas stared at Sam for many minutes, fingering his cane. Then he stared at John. Then Jessie. Then back to Sam. All the time he fingered his cane. But the Archdeacon was in full flood.

'I will not permit in my Parish all this talk of devilry, magic, witchcraft, and superstition. From henceforth it will stop. I have spoken.' But he could not resist speaking a little longer. He told them God's anger would rain down on them and they would all go to Hell and burn for ever.

Fanny Gibbs rolled her eyes at John Mellor. He had grown very tall and strong. She could not take her eyes off him. He was right handsome, she thought. Miss White pounced on her.

'Yes, Hell, Fanny Gibbs. That is where you'll surely go, like the Archdeacon says.' She wanted the Archdeacon to see what a good teacher she was.

'Soft old cow,' thought Fanny. 'Yes, Miss White, ma'am,' said Fanny.

But the Archdeacon had become sidetracked with Hell. It seemed to give him pleasure to describe it in detail. 'Wicked souls go to Hell,' he explained, spreading his gown like an expanding crow. 'Devils toss the wicked of this world into the deep fires of Hell where they burn for ever and ever, yea, till the end of time.'

'What will the devils do, Jessie Smith?' hissed Middlemas, stroking his cane in front of her.

'They'll burn for ever and ever, Amen,' whispered Jessie and she began to weep, for she remembered the watching shadow on Saturday ... and the eyes.

'Well may you weep, child,' boomed the Archdeacon, his diamond ring flashing as he waved his hand about. 'God will strike you down if you even THINK of devilry and magic!'

184

Then the Archdeacon read from the Bible and banged about a bit more.

'I, the Reverend Doctor Ball, will deliver Lambton from hundreds of years of superstition and shadow. I will deliver the children of Lambton into the hands of God—now!' And he thumped the blackboard. Jessie jumped in her seat.

Then there was silence as they were delivered save for the rustle of a few leaves that were blowing in the cloakroom. Then Middlemas began. 'Alas, Archdeacon, I have in this school, boys who laugh and joke about these things. Boys who take girls in yonder evil woodland and ... smoke.' He paused. He fingered the cheap brass watch chain he had to wear. Then he handed a cane to Miss White.

'Come out, Mellor ... come out, Walton ... and you, Jessie Smith. Miss White will cane you. You are wanton and wayward.' Then Middlemas caned witchcraft and smoking out of Sam and John, and Miss White caned witchcraft and wantonness out of Jessie, with biting and bruising strokes.

John took the worst caning he had ever had without flinching. He had had good food and hard work and he was healthy that October morning—confident he was going to be able to help Sam and overcome his own fears and dreams.

'I'm not going to cry,' thought Sam. But the strain of the last year had weakened him and the tears stung his eyes as the pain burned his hand.

The Archdeacon and Middlemas made their exit with a swish of silk gowns.

'A good morning's work for God,' said the Archdeacon, very pleased with himself.

Miss White was left with the class, staring at them behind her desk. She had a chill on the bladder, for it had been a cold damp October; the excitement of the Archdeacon's little sermon had made her want to spend a penny again.

'Sit down children and be SIL-ENT,' said she. 'Do not talk. THINK about what the good Doctor Ball has spoken. I have a message to deliver.' Then, glaring at the class, her finger to her thin lips, she tiptoed out of the room.

Will stood on his bench. He had long been the unofficial lavatory watcher. 'She's in,' said he to the class, as he saw her shut the door.

185

At once Sam was aware of a sea of whispering and giggling. Faces turned in his direction. He heard fragments of whispering like a menacing, approaching sea.

'He's been caned because his Granny Walton's a witch ... They're all doing magic up on them Walton Pastures ... 'er puts toadstools in t'milk ... 'er chases Sam Walton's Grandad wi' a broomstick round a fire in their fields, I've seen 'em ... they eat spider stew up on them hill farms ...'

'Granny Walton's a withered old hag bag,' said Fanny Gibbs and giggled, her blue eyes radiant on John Mellor.

'What didst say, Fanny?' said John Mellor in his rasping voice. He stood up. He was wearing his new corduroys and boots from Manchester, bought with Lady Selina's gold sovereign sent to Manchester to 'dress God's poor little boy of Lambton.' He was also wearing one of Sam's Uncle Edgar's shirts which Grandmother had sent down: Uncle Edgar had been killed close by the Stone in June. He also had a waistcoat on, again from Grandmother. And he'd grown very tall. Fanny smiled at him. She liked the look of him more than ever.

'Granny Walton's a fly-be-night,' said Fanny clearly and sweetly, tossing her fine blonde ringlets at John and then giggling behind her hand with Dolly her friend.

'Aye. We all know Granny Walton's a real witch!' shouted Tom Wilson.

'Shut your face, Tom Wilson, or I'll put thy face where thy arse is and send thy teeth down to chatter in't. And thee shut thy big red gob, Fanny-Gob-Almighty Gibbs or I'll shoot thy kneecaps off with me catapult.' He pulled out his catapult and twanged it in the direction of Fanny's knees. Fanny smoothed down her spotless pinafore in horror. What had she said wrong?

'I beg your pardon? I BEG your pardon, John Mellor?' said the returning Miss White, her penny spent.

'I were just teaching Fanny Gibbs her two times table,' said John insolently. ''ers not very bright, our Fanny these days. I were learning her a thing or two about witches—'er still believes in witches. I've always wanted to be a teacher like thee, Miss White, ma'am.'

Miss White wisely did not reply. Boys who were leaving

school at twelve were a problem. They could be very naughty. At playtime no football was played. No hopscotch. No skipping. No late conkers. The children just gazed to see John and Sam, once the biggest enemies in the school, talking together. Will dared not go near: Mellor's fists were bigger than ever.

But it was Fanny who stared and stared and stared. Dirty, smelly, mucky, Jessie Smith, wearing daft old women's stockings that wrinkled at the knee and wearing a shawl too big for her, was talking to John Mellor. And he was smiling at her. And once when she looked troubled he put his arm round her. Fanny chewed her liquorice root faster and faster. And when she saw John smile at Jessie again she savagely pinched her friend Dolly Cresswell.

But Sam and John were making plans. For when school was over they must go and get the old brown book. And they knew every moment lost was dangerous to them—and others.

John and Sam raced to Dame Trot's cottage as soon as they were released from school. Tom and Will watched them run off in amazement. They knocked on the door and she called them in. She was sitting by the fire and chewing apple cores. She kept in a good store of apple cores, some a month old.

'Please, Mrs Trotter, could we see in your brown book so we know what to do with Stone and magic?' pleaded Sam.

'We'll read it. You've no need to look. Us'll take the risk o' Devil coming,' added John Mellor cleverly.

'Nay, masters,' said Dame Trot. 'Devil an' me mam'll fetch me if I let folk see her book she an' Devil wrote together.' She began to panic and play for time. 'Let's see if beetles can tell us owt,' said she. 'Blackclocks know a lot.' She opened a cupboard and stared at the immobile black beetles on the wall.

'Beetles is no good, Mrs Trotter,' said John politely and firmly.

But the old woman, like Grandfather, could not squarely face up to the problem. She still hoped it would go away. She played for time again. She lit the candle in the great silver candlestick with its writhing serpent and took the candle to her oven and took a pie out. The boys watched her helplessly.

'Tha's done well to make thysen a pie, Betsy,' said Dame Trot, who like many old people talked incessantly to herself. 'Th'art a rate good girl, Betsy.' She patted the pie with a dirty hand.

'Oh, hell,' groaned John. 'It's useless, Sam. What'll us do?'

As if in reply there was a violent crash in the cellar as though something was bursting through. John, Sam, and Dame Trot clung to each other in terror. They were all very much on edge with fear. A light tap came on the window. Dame Trot's dirty nails dug in Sam's hand, she was so scared.

'Hey up, missus,' came Tom Wilson's voice. 'Thy cat's just dropped dead in the cellar.' He had dropped a big stone down the coal hole into Dame Trot's cellar.

'Varmints!' screamed the old woman, grabbed her stick, and was gone.

'That cupboard—quick,' said Sam. They rushed over to it with the candle, but it was locked.

'Hell,' said John again. 'Sam, what'll us do?' As if to answer him the cottage shook gently. They felt some movement deep in the earth. Sam heard the strange whining in his ears again, felt the numb pain growing in his head. They heard the tenor bell in the belfry softly ring through the grey light, and Sam heard the sound of the bell and the ugly high music become one threatening sound, vibrating through the nearly leafless lime trees behind the cottage.

Dame Trot came gasping hurriedly back. 'That bell's tolled by Devil for me,' whimpered Dame Trot.

'Then let's see in your book what to do,' shouted Sam. Wouldn't anybody do anything? But they could not get any sense out of the old woman; so they left her.

'I'll come with thee part of the way,' said John and they trudged along the new turnpike. 'There's more chance of thee being caught than me—at least for a day or two. I just canna get the idea out of my head that something's going to come up through the churchyard.' John stopped by the big stone gateposts of the lawyer's house and beckoned Sam into the thick shrubbery that surrounded the house. They sheltered under the thick tent of a spotted laurel bush that kept out the

188

rain. John gave Sam a penny clay pipe. They smoked solemnly, deep in thought as rain patterned on the laurel leaves and the wind blew orange beech leaves into the shelter.

'I'll ask me Gran again,' said Sam. But as he ran into the deepening grey beyond the last of the gaslamps that was spluttering and bubbling in the wind, he heard the sound that he had come to dread the most. Thunder. A long low rumble of it. The signal for the final attack, he was sure.

It was a three-mile run back home for Sam. Once the dark clouds parted and the last of the blood-red sky and sun could be seen, the blood-coloured sun that had become so noticeable during that autumn of 1883. The sky turned the Stone to the colour of blood.

Sam, on the turnpike, did not see one thing. The sinking blood-red sun made the Stone cast a shadow, long and faint like a trembling insect feeler, a shadow that had at last reached Sam's little farmhouse.

Sam rushed in with the lie ready that the corn merchant had seen him and he had to take a message up to Bow Cross Farm. He saw his father stretched out on the rag rug in front of the golden glow of the kitchen fire.

His mother told Sam he had been ill all day. She was not interested enough in Sam at that moment to detect the lie. So Sam, his hand in his jacket pocket clasped round the egg— why, he was uncertain, except that he just liked the feel of it—raced up the darkening lane where the bracken eerily seemed to be glowing with the light of the vanished sunset on its rain-wet fronds. His shadow-touched arm prickled and throbbed as he ran.

He found Grandmother in the cool dairy with a candle perched on a three-legged stool, lighting her work of making cream cheese. Shadows swayed in the cold stone room and an oak leaf rustled on the floor in the draught. For a moment Sam thought he saw a flicker of blue lightning through the wild tangle of rose hips that crowded through the little window of the dairy. A window that faced north to the Stone.

189

Grandmother listened to Sam, but said nothing to him. Then she took him through to the candlelit kitchen. Grandfather was staring into the usual gigantic fire as though seeking help from it. Grandmother poured Sam a glass of elderberry wine, added a drop of brandy and then some of her raspberry syrup to it and gave it to Sam to drink.

'Drink that quick,' Grandmother said to him. 'Then get home before the owls are about. I'll watch thee down the lane.'

'But—' said Sam.

'Go on,' said Grandmother.

'But what are you going to do?'

'I've a bit of an idea, lad,' was all that she would say.

'Art all right my little love?' said she to Grandfather by the fire. This time she sounded as if she meant it. The old man put his hand to his face and did not reply. An old cup stood on the table by his side with water and a bit of leaf in it. He was still drinking what he thought was his comfrey tea.

Grandmother said one final word. 'Keep thy eyes skinned tomorrow, Sam. Just keep watching for me.' And that was all.

Sam ran for his life back home. The sky seemed a mass of darting blue sparks. Once the wind took his weakened body and blew him into a thorn bush, so that the damp berries fell round him. He heard the faint, evil whining again.

His mother started on him as soon as he got in. 'Running about on other folk's business when your place is here with your father, and his leg worse than it's been since Midsummer.'

Yes, thought Sam, it would be. And it'll get worse. But he kept quiet. Usually too she told him it was his Christian duty to help others. He kept quiet. Then she began sniffing. 'You stink of tobacco, Samuel. Oh, Samuel. If God had meant little boys to smoke they would have been born with a chimney. And no gentleman smokes a clay pipe, Samuel. I've tried to bring you up decent in this God-forsaken spot...'

Sam stopped listening. Had Grandmother got a plan? What could she do? He could feel the evil closing in on them all.

'And what would Mr Middlemas do if he saw you with a

190

clay pipe?' he heard his mother saying. She was really wound up with worry and irritation.

'Can I have a smoke?' said Sam, who was thinking of Grandmother.

His mother smacked her hand over his ear with a smart slap.

'Leave the lad alone, Bella,' said his father, rising up on one elbow from the hearthrug. He felt better now Sam was back. 'I was eight when I had a clay pipe. It won't hurt him. Let him go and help Pete with the milking.'

Sam went out. He had hardly heard a word or felt a smack. Outside he saw a fragment of sky behind the Stone, glowing like a red-hot coal: the Stone was black and waiting against the red. He heard the faint whine of the devilish music of the air. To the left of the Stone the lamp of Bow Cross Farm shone out like a beckoning star.

If only he knew what Grandmother was planning and if it would work.

But Grandmother had already started on her plan. She had got the tea. She had washed up. Then she started.

'I want the horse and trap out.' There was a silence. Grandmother sniffed. 'I'm going visiting.' Again there was silence. Grandmother began to tense. 'I can drive mysen if one of you wunna tek me. It wunna be the first time I've taken horse out at night, so take that sick dog look off thy face, Jack Walton.'

Albert got the horse ready. Jo got the trap and trimmed the lamp. Jack fetched the whip and rugs.

'I'll drive thee,' said Jack sulkily. 'It's a dark night to be out on thy own.' They drove off into the night, down to Lambton. Grandmother went straight to Dame Trot's. She was inside the cottage for an hour while Jack stood by the horse's head, clapping his hands and stamping his feet and swearing with impatience.

When they came out, Dame Trot carried a big cloth bag. Grandmother helped her into the trap. Dame Trot was very nervous. She clung to Jack in the moonlit woods like a scared child and held his hand. Jack was unable to get out

191

to ease the horse's burden up the steep old road. It was a slow journey.

By the cave the moonlight was sharp and cold and clear. Dame Trot's eyes stared in horror. 'See thee, see thee,' she whispered, her voice just audible above the autumn whisperings of the woods. 'Look! That's deadly nightshade that's started to grow by yon cave where the childer saw the Devil. That's the Devil's own herb, Lucy. Where he goes, deadly nightshade allus follows ... and it's late in the year ... but it's come.'

Grandmother looked for a moment on the thick ugly leaves, a dull silver in the moonlight. Then the moon went behind a sharp-edged cloud and the woods and cave were lost to the night.

Grandmother sat Dame Trot in front of Grandfather's enormous fire.

'Sit there, Betsy,' said she, and lit a candle and went out again.

'What's in thy cup o' water, Abel Walton?' asked Dame Trot. She had a professional interest in teas and medicines.

'Comfrey,' said Grandfather dully. The old woman wanted to look, but Grandfather snatched the cup away.

'Comfrey's no good to keep the Devil away,' said Dame Trot. But Grandfather did not want to talk about such things. Sam's uncles stared. It was nearly nine o'clock. It was unheard of for folk to be here at that time.

Grandmother returned and went out and brought back a bucket of coal. 'Now then, Betsy love,' said she. 'Follow me.' Dame Trot obediently followed Grandmother upstairs. She led the way to a small bedroom they used to store the finest apples in. There were two old beds in the room. Grandmother had lit a fire in the grate. There was a pile of lavender-scented bedding on the beds. The room was scented with lavender and apples. Fir cones and best coal made a fine fire in the tiny grate.

Grandfather appeared at the door, pale and troubled, a candle in the brass bedchamber stick wavering in his trembling hand.

'Eh, Lucy, tha's wasting good coal,' said he. Then he saw

the beds. 'Th'art not sleeping in here, art? Leaving me alone?' He sounded frightened.

'Just for tonight I am,' said Grandmother simply.

'Without me?' quavered the old man.

'I am,' said Grandmother, some of her old sharpness returning. 'If Duchess o' Pemberly can have a room to hersen to gerraway from her owd man then I can. Just for one neet!'

'But,' said Grandfather, shook to the foundations, 'Duchess o' Pemberly is a lady!'

'So I've heard tell,' said Grandmother tartly.

Grandfather turned away. 'Leavin' me alone to die,' said he.

Grandmother went pale for a moment.

'Us canna afford fires in bedchambers, Lucy. I've no money to waste on coal for thee an' her,' said Grandfather.

Grandmother's face hardened again. When he had gone the two old women drew up the old Windsor chairs to the bright fire. Then Dame Trot dipped in the bag. She took out the big brown book and gave it to Grandmother. The old woman had listened to Grandmother's argument that if she, Grandmother, read the book in her own house, then the Devil would fetch Grandmother. But Dame Trot could not look at the book. She stared at the hot little fire behind the black bars.

She heard the wind moan in the chimneys. Now and again teacups tinkled because Grandmother had made a pot of strong black tea in a huge, fluted, white china teapot she had fetched from the parlour.

Dame Trot heard the grandfather clock downstairs strike midnight. The wind raged in the chimney, sending little red-hot soot particles into the room. Rain rattled on the windows. Grandmother poured more tea, changed the candles, and said not a word. She was a slow reader, having taught herself from the Bible mostly. The pages of the brown book rustled dryly. Dame Trot's jaws chomped rhythmically as she chewed her ancient black apple cores. Now and again she took a lump of sugar from a bowl Grandmother had brought up.

One o'clock struck. Grandmother was becoming paler and paler as she read ... then there was the rich chuckle as

193

elderberry wine was poured ... a mouse began to gnaw in the walls ... when the wind dropped for a moment you could hear the loud snores of the five sleeping men ... the groans of trees ... Grandmother seemed to be turning into an old woman as she struggled to read—a woman as old as Dame Trot.

When three o'clock struck, something shook the farmhouse. The two women spoke for the first time in four hours. 'He's coming,' whispered Dame Trot. 'Nay, Betsy,' said Grandmother weakly. 'If he is, it's to fetch me—or him,' and she nodded in the direction of Grandfather's room. She tried to smile but could not. Her lips shook.

Dame Trot's mother had been able to draw. Grandmother turned pages of hideous drawings of half-decayed skulls full of maggots and shadows; she saw sprays of deadly nightshade, again darkened and tinted with strange disturbing shadowy shapes that candlelight and time made difficult to understand; there were caves with serpents with curved catlike claws crawling out into a dark world where the only light was a cruel, thin, crescent moon. The old witch had been fascinated by the crescent moon. She had made patterns of drawings of the crescent moon, bundles of crescent shapes made to look like claws or horns. One page had some lifelike pictures of faces that Grandmother was sure she could remember as a girl. Perhaps the witch had hated these people, for the faces were scarred with the crescent moon shape and had sores and boils drawn on them. There were drawings of lead miners at work with strange and evil shapes writhing about them, and there was writing in a language that Grandmother could not understand.

But worse, worst of all was a drawing of the Stone in their own Top Pasture. The witch had drawn it big and swollen and wrapped round in the coils of a devilish creature that made Grandmother want to throw the book then and there into the glowing coals. She saw a picture of All Saints' Church burning in a huge fiery jaw that was swallowing the church and Lambton.

At four o'clock, Dame Trot, who had gone to lie down on one of the beds, began to moan in her sleep. Grandmother, white as the wax candle she carried and trembling every bit as much as Grandfather had been doing, tiptoed down to the kitchen and blew up the ashes of the fire with the bellows and made a big fire like the ones Grandfather had been making. She put the kettle on and while she was waiting for it to boil she checked that the back and front doors were locked. She made a pot of lime-flower tea and put the brandy flask on the tray she was preparing. She then took from the candle cupboard an assortment of candlesticks. Tin bedroom ones, an old blue china one, two heavy iron ones, and a bent silver one. She put candles in them and put them on the tray.

Back upstairs she lit all the candles. She put the soothing lime tea on the iron mantelshelf and like Grandfather had been doing for weeks made as big a fire as she could in the tiny grate. She piled coal on till the iron bars glowed red-hot and one of the tiny yellow tiles split with a noise like a gun and woke Dame Trot.

'Eh, Lucy,' said she. 'You shouldna have read them books.'

Grandmother did not reply. She wrapped the blanket round her, sipped the tea: but sleep would not come. Not after what she had read.

Like Sam she prayed for the morning.

Morning did come with an iron-grey cold. Grandmother got up, tight-lipped. She tried to joke as she and Dame Trot washed at the pump. 'Keep them books away from Abel,' said she. 'Devil's supposed to have hid all his gold under yon Stone. Anyone touching it will be took. An' Abel could never resist gold.' She smiled a ghost of a smile. But she was very worried.

Greyness was in the air just as Sam's whining music was in the air. Sam saw the autumn colours had gone and as he got dressed he could see the distant high moors glimmering white with an early snowfall. His body was racked with pain. Looking up at Bow Cross Farm he saw Grandmother waving a white tablecloth.

'Eat that bit of breakfast and see what she wants,' said Sam's mother with anxiety in her voice. Sam grabbed some bread and fat bacon, gulped tea and ran. It was only seven o'clock. What had happened?

Grandmother met him in the lane.

195

'Sam,' said she, 'fetch thy marrer, John. We've got to move yon Stone into the churchyard—or we're done for.'

The wind blew against him as he raced back home to go the long way round. He ignored his mother's wavings and frownings. It was half-past eight when he raced through the cold grey streets to the little row of cottages where John lived.

John was white and pale. He had had his dreams again. 'Off you go to school,' said Mrs Mellor. She was pleased. Sam was the first boy who had ever called for John in a morning.

Out of sight Sam explained to John. Then they ran back again, stopping for breath now and again, keeping the bitter taste of hard running from their mouths by eating the apples Grandmother hastily stuffed in Sam's pockets and eating the black roadside elderberries. They both knew it was a race against unseen danger.

At half-past nine they were in Bow Cross Farmyard. Grandmother and Dame Trot in cloaks and bonnets had a spade each and Grandmother was leaning on a barrow usually used for mucking out the pigs. A big row was in progress round the muck cart. Ted, Jo, Jack and Albert and a white-faced Grandfather were shouting at the two women.

'It's living with thee all these years, it's turned her barmy!' shouted Jack to Grandfather. He was red with rage. Even his neck was red. Grandmother, for the first time in her married life, had not cooked breakfast. Jack was missing the hot sweet tea, the porridge, the cream, the fried oatcakes, sausages, eggs and bacon. He stamped and swore like a toddler in a rage.

Grandfather walked round in circles.

'Tha'll never dig out yon Stone on thy own, mother,' laughed Albert.

'It's not women's work. It'll kill thee,' said Ted to his mother.

'Aye,' said Grandmother. 'And it'll kill me if I dunna dig out yon Stone. So both ways tha'll go without thy breakfast, my Jack.' Grandmother, Dame Trot, Sam, and John began to walk through the gate and up the muddy sheepwalk to the Stone. Sam kept thinking—if only we are not too late. At last—they were doing something . . . would they be able to do it in time?

But even at this late hour Grandmother could not resist doing what had held Sam up all through this terrible year. She had to have her say about something that had nothing to do with the Stone and its evil. She turned round and shouted to her sons and Grandfather. 'Aye,' she shouted through the cold air. 'I can see now who thinks about me. I'm just here to cook and clean and wesh and mend thy clothes. I should have left ye all to the Devil under this Stone!'

Her sons could only stare. Grandfather's face went as cold and white as the clouds hanging round the snow-capped high moors.

'Bloody hell,' said Jack and banged off to the pigs.

'Well I'm danged,' said Ted and stumped off to the hayricks.

'Well, I'll go to hell and back,' said Albert.

None of them believed Grandmother or thought of getting their own breakfast. Only Jo stood still. Jo was Grandmother's youngest son now that Edgar was dead. He was the tallest and biggest of Sam's uncles. If you had tortured Grandmother to say who was the least likeable of her sons she would not have said Jo. She would not have said any of them . . . but she nagged at Jo the most. He rarely brushed his hair and often it lay in hay-dusty, greasy coils on his collar. He let his beard and moustache grow wild. The Lambton lasses, while impressed by his strength, said he smelled like a horse. Grandmother was endlessly telling him to clean his boots. Sometimes his brothers refused to sit with him at the table and threatened to drag him to the pump. He spoke rarely. But just as he had made a long speech on Saturday, he made another now.

'I'll give thee a hand, mam,' he said to Grandmother. She stared at him.

Perhaps Jo had seen something when he found John, Jessie, and Sam on Saturday. The big adder had scared him. It was the best thing that could have happened, for Jo was a fast, tireless worker. He marched up to the Stone with a shovel and a spade and began to dig. John seized a spade and helped. But Sam found that now he was close to the Stone his ears were ringing with that shrill music and his hand hung limp. 'Oh God,' he thought, 'please don't let anything happen!'

'Canst hear yon music and see magic blue fire?' said Sam aloud.

Dame Trot stared at Sam's body, twisted and hunched.

'Eh, Lucy,' said the old woman. 'Thy Sam's been got. By All Saints, Lucy, we're too late. To think I never noticed the lad had got the evil eye on him and him in me cottage only yesterday. I mun be getting old, Lucy.'

Grandmother said nothing but looked on at John and Jo grimly. A gust of wind carrying swirling beech leaves and sleet buffeted her. She turned from the stinging wind to see her other sons coming across the muddy pasture. 'Mother, if tha's set on shifting t'owd stone, us'll do it while tha gets us breakfast,' said Jack with his usual grin. And Grandmother went. It was difficult to break the habit of a lifetime.

'Be quick,' said she. She looked at Sam. Then she went. Her sons stood round the Stone and began to dig. John helped to make the soil into a neat mound. As for Sam the weight of the terrible music seemed to thunder in his ears. Once or twice he staggered at the impact of it. He watched in fear and trembling while his uncles dug deep and became to Sam's eyes knee-deep in a blue fire. Yet it seemed only he could see it ... just as it seemed only John saw the shadow things and the devils. And as they dug the music throbbed in his head and every blow of the spade twisted his body further.

'I canna stand it,' he muttered.

'I'm an owd 'ooman,' muttered Dame Trot. 'I should've seen the evil eye was on him. Devil'll have him before us gets to church.'

Grandmother fried eggs, bacon, sausages, bread, mush-rooms, oatcakes in the big black pan, but not to her usual perfection. Her eyes were outside on the window as though she was expecting something to happen. She was. Once she dropped a whole slice of bread in the fire, an unknown thing for her.

She gave Grandfather some bread to toast on the long, black, toasting fork, for the terrified, bewildered old man had sought refuge by the blazing fire. The toasting fork shook so much that he too lost all the bread to the fire.

'You shouldna meddle, Lucy. You shouldna meddle ...
everything belongs to the Devil up here ... yon Stone does ...
t'Devil's in charge round here!'

'You should have said something,' said Grandmother.

'I tried ... I tried ...' said the old man pitifully. 'Thee an'
my lads allus laughed at me.' He coughed weakly. 'Aye.
T'Devil's in charge ...'

'Then it's about time someone stood up to him,' said
Grandmother. 'You've been frit all thy life Abel, and never
told me ...'

'You laughed,' said Grandfather. 'Thee an' Jack.'

There was a long pause. Grandmother seemed to have
something in her eye that made it water a deal, a speck of
soot perhaps or a crumb. Then she put her sons' breakfast
out to keep warm. She kissed the old man. He was drinking a
cup of water with a leaf in it. She hurried out to where her
sons were waist-deep in a large hole. She saw Sam being sick.
And she heard a thrush trying out his next year's spring song
in the silvery wet ash trees. All the leaves had gone. She could
see the spire of All Saints' Church. The bird and the spire
gave her courage. She did not notice Sam, doubled with pain,
as the Stone, like a decayed long tooth stump, was loaded on
the muck cart.

'I'll go wi'out me breakfast. I'll wheel it to church,' said Jo.
This silenced his brothers again. They began to feel there was
something wrong.

It made a strange procession. Jo wheeling the muck cart,
John steadying it, and Grandmother and Dame Trot in cloaks
and bonnets behind. Then Sam, trailing and ill. Dame Trot
kept looking at Sam and muttering, 'Devil's got him. Aye. He
has. He has an' all. He's the one, poor lad. He'll be took, the
lad will. Devil'll want one of us before us gets to church ...
he's the one.'

Sam felt himself caught in a net of blue painful fire. Even
when the muck cart's iron wheels whispered over the fallen
ash leaves or over the pulp of a mass of conker leaves, it
sounded like thunder to him. When the wheels shuddered
over the old turnpike, he could have screamed with agony.
And when he saw the evil green leaves of the new deadly
nightshade plants by the cave he was sick again.

199

'He's not got much longer,' whispered Dame Trot.

Then Sam saw that the Stone was weeping a dark bloodlike moisture from the ugly carved eye. And that eye was watching him. 'That eye,' he said to Jo. 'It's sending out ... blood ... its blood.'

'It's just muck and moisture,' said Jo. 'Stone's allus do when weather turns right cold after a warm spell.'

But the eye filled with the dark stuff and the angle of the cart tilted it to an evil flickering crescent. And that eye grew in Sam's mind and his breath came in gasps and his heart beat faster and faster as Dame Trot knew it would. On Lambton Bridge they heard the eerie sound of the tenor bell softly ringing itself again.

'It's ringing for thee, Sammy Walton lad,' muttered Dame Trot. 'We took this Devil's Thing too late. It's done its worst. Tha's a-gonna, Sammy Walton.' Her muttering was lost in the crunch of wheels.

Sam had to stop. He could go on no longer.

Grandfather sat and watched his sons, ravenous and raving with hunger, eat their breakfasts noisily. Then he managed to get to his feet and he leaned on his crook. 'I'm going to go and see what a mess tha's made in me Top Pasture,' said he. 'None of yo' lads can dig a hole proper.'

His sons ignored him as usual. Their breakfast was three hours late. But Grandfather had to go and look in that hole. There was a story his father had told him once about Devil's gold, a story that he had told nobody ... He walked slowly up the sheep walk, rutted with boots and the muck cart. The spades and shovels had been thrown aside on the wet, grey, cold grass. 'Careless buggers, my lads,' said Grandfather. 'Idle too.'

He seemed to be afraid of looking in the hole, as though he were remembering something else his father had told him. Then he stepped in the black hole and took a spade. He dug deep.

Then he put his hand to his eyes and cried out.

It began to rain heavily as the little procession began to wheel the cart over the cobbles of Lambton. Grandmother was almost carrying Sam. Sam heard the deep thunder again and felt the needles of hail and sleet. The rumbling muck cart brought people to cottage and shop doors and the men shovelling away the litter and straw of yesterday's market came to stare. Jo and John were red with shyness. Not Grandmother.

'Morning to thee, Nancy Clay,' said she cheerfully, at the same time helping the twisted and hobbling, tortured Sam. 'Turned out a nasty day for gawping at folks, hasn't it?' Mrs Clay turned away muttering.

'I'd be ashamed to have a son as mucky as Jo Walton. He's like a gypsy,' said she, going into a shop quickly.

'Stop the cart for Mrs Turner, our Jo,' said Grandmother sweetly, propping Sam against herself. 'She's not seen enough yet. Tek a good look, love. Now, hast seen enough?'

They reached the churchyard. The Archdeacon had been inspecting a crack in the nave wall. He was sure he could feel the stones vibrating. He saw the procession coming up the steep path. He began to rush down the wet path, slippery with wet lime leaves, his cloak flapping in the wind and alarming the jackdaws.

'Take away that heathen idolatrous monument AT ONCE, do you hear me, my good woman,' he boomed. He had never been disobeyed in his life. 'GO! Take it back. It is befouling God's little acre. I will have no monuments to devilry here.'

Sam knew the Archdeacon of old. It was the final blow. He slumped over a table-like grave top.

The wind ruffled and a crescent of dark water in the evil eye gleamed with triumph.

Grandfather's sight cleared. He had looked for a moment into a seemingly bottomless pit where a vast coiled creature waited with wide jaws, waiting for him. It was an old dream he had had since he was a boy. Strange he should have it now while he was awake. There was a rustle and a big adder slithered away. It must have been that that he had just seen. He aimed a boulder at the sluggish snake and missed.

201

It crawled away to more secure quarters for the winter. Grandfather dug wearily and slowly. Then his spade struck metal.

'Eh, by gum!' said Grandfather, feeling better than he had for months. He stirred the soil and found a pile of metal. He unearthed a small gold bowl, a gold bracelet, a gold ring, and coins. He peeped over the rim of the hole, not unlike a cuckoo in a nest, to see if his sons were watching him. Then he put the treasure in his smock.

'By gum,' said he. He trotted down the muddy path. 'It's nowt to do with me,' he said aloud. 'It weren't me that dug up Devil's Stone. They did. They'll be took. Devil'll tek them. Aye, he will. I just found t' gold. I just came across it, casual-like. Aye, that's what happened. Aye, that 's it. Aye, by gum!'

He found Albert, well fed and good-tempered, wiping his mouth on the back of his hand.

'Pigs are looking badly,' said Grandfather. 'Tha's not feeding them right. I'll look after them till Chrissymas.' He went in the sties. Moving the pigs expertly with his boot, he pulled out a heap of stone from the wall. He uncovered a pot of sovereigns he had hidden. He pushed the treasure in the hole. He put a big pile of straw and dung in front.

But he had not put all the treasure in the hole. He had had to keep one small gold article. He could not resist gold. And this bit of gold was still shining and bright after a thousand years or more in the soil. Grandfather spat on it to make it shine more.

'Real gold, tha knows,' said Grandfather to the nearest pig.

Had he looked at the article with his reading magnifying glass he would have seen a finely wrought, small, gold serpent, wickedly coiled and with ruby eyes that seemed to have an evil life and fire in them. But Grandfather thought it was a kind of gold ring.

He put the evil thing in his waistcoat pocket next to his heart.

'Go!' boomed the Archdeacon.

'Nay, Your Reverence,' said Grandmother. 'It needs to be here on holy ground. Tip it out, our Jo.'

202

And Jo tipped it out muddy and shining. The Archdeacon stamped his patent leather boots in the wet leaves. Then the church clock struck eleven. A gleam of pale lemon sunshine turned the Stone and church to a dull gold. A robin sang in a lime tree—there had been no birds in the churchyard since September. The jackdaws went back calmly to the belfry—they had kept leaving it when there was an earth tremor coming. Sam sat up and rubbed his eyes.

Nobody had seen Dame Trot creep slowly up the steps to the church porch. She sat down on the ancient stones that were piled in the south porch, stones as old as the one just brought to join them. She heard the bells.

'I were wrong,' she gasped. 'Them bells is for me. I'm getting old. I were wrong. The Stone took Edgar Walton. Now it's taking me. But it'll get another ... Sam Walton ... it needs three ... Devil needs three lives ... Sammy Walton ... mebbee ...' Nobody heard her.

Then Dame Trot cried out, 'Mam!' and her breath came in violent gasps. She smiled a little despite the painful breathing. Then her smile turned to one of pain, fear, and horror.

Then all was silent in the sunlit musty south porch. Dame Trot was smiling now but still. There was just the sound of the jackdaws' claws on the leads of the porch roof.

She had died alone with nobody to heed her warning words that another life must go.

Chapter Two

Sam had no clearly understood reasons to dread Hallowe'en now—but he did. True, he could feel at peace in the woods now. Rain, wind, thunder had passed. A carpet of fallen mahogany and golden leaves covered the ground in the woods, hiding the old shafts and secret caves. The bare trees, brown and black without their leaves, stretched to a warm, faint blue sky. Sam dared to walk in the woods again and was almost at peace ... and yet ... now and again there would breathe out a faint breath of ice-cold air, so faint that it hardly disturbed the drifting beech leaves that had covered the deadly poisonous, deadly nightshade growing by the cave. Yet ... the web of evil had gone but something remained like the evil smell in a witch's kitchen after a spell is finished. A ghost of the evil was there still ...

Sam tried to tell John about his feelings while they were building a huge bonfire together for November 5th. They were building the fire in the field of a farmer not far from the church—John had worked for the farmer sometimes. Sam and John now found they got on well together: John liked to go to Bow Cross Farm with Sam where Grandmother fed John on rabbit pies, apple dumplings, cheese and pickled onions, and her own dark sweet, pickled walnuts. Grandmother found it a treat to feed up John who appreciated her cooking far more than Grandfather and her sons.

'I just dunna feel right,' said Sam to John as they admired the big fire they had built together.

'It's all tha's been through,' said John, smoking comfortably and leaning up against the bonfire. 'Things are all right now. Dunna thee worry. There's been no more earth tremors since us moved that Stone—an' I'm sleeping better than I have since I first saw that bloody Stone! Dunna thee worry, Sam.'

He passed Sam his pipe and stretched out in the late sunshine. But the thought of Hallowe'en still sent a shiver up Sam's spine.

If Sam was not convinced the danger was over, Grandmother was. She no longer worried or felt sorry for Grandfather. As for Grandfather, he kept drinking the tea he made from the plant he had found near the cave: behind the little gold snake in his waistcoat pocket he kept feeling a squeezing breathtaking pain.

Sometimes when he thought Grandmother was not looking Grandfather would take the little gold snake out and stare at it and rub his body where the snake had lain, for the pain was so great.

'What's that tha' keeps fixing thy eye on, Abel?' asked Grandmother one day.

'Aye, er no,' said Grandfather, putting the wicked snake back in the pocket over the pain. 'It's nowt! It's a penny wi' two Queen's heads on,' lied the old man hastily.

'Gerraway,' said Grandmother, busy with a rook pie for John. 'Fancy that! First time I've seen a penny shaped like a gold worm.'

'Eh?' said Grandfather.

'I said if tha doesna turn thy bum from that fire it'll burn.' Grandmother bustled about. Things seemed back to normal she thought. She was wrong.

Soon after that she walked down the old road to Lambton. She walked alone past the cave where the deadly nightshade hid under the leaves; her boots crunched lightly on the crisp leaves in the sunshine of Saint Luke's Little Summer, as she called the lovely weather. She looked neither right or left. She thought the curse had vanished. She was going down to the undertakers to order a fine marble tombstone for the spot where Dame Trot was buried in the churchyard.

Sam and John had helped Grandmother spell out the inscription she wanted.

IN MEMORY OF ELIZABETH TROTTER WHO DIED 13 OCTOBER 1883 WHILE RIDDING THE PARISH OF A GREAT NUISANCE

'Eh, tha canna put that, Lucy,' Grandfather had said. 'That's not rate.'

'I can,' said Grandmother. 'Our Sam and John spelled it for me. An' it's going on my gravestone after I've finished thee off!' She stared at him grimly. Now the danger was gone she was as brisk and quick-tongued with him as ever.

'I'm nonna paying,' said Grandfather, rubbing his body under the snake where the pain twisted and turned as though the snake was eating him alive.

'Thee can pay,' said Grandmother, 'all that gold tha's got.'

'Tha's a witch, Lucy. Tha knows too much!' Like all people with a guilty secret he thought Grandmother knew more than she really did about the hidden treasure. 'Reading them books has made thee a witch!' he shouted.

'Aye. That's not the first time I've been called a witch this year,' said the old lady calmly.

Then Grandfather had moved to the table to eat—to take his turning, twisting, snakelike pain away. Then he began his endless talking of nonsense that so tried Grandmother's patience at mealtimes.

'Aye. Dame Trot's dead, 'er is. Aye. She is that. She were old. Rate old. Aye. She were old when I were young. If she hadna died on Saturday she'd have died another day. Yon lump of beef's a big tidy bit for the middle of the week, Lucy. I've no gold to pay for meat joints for thee and my idle lads. Aye. Dame Trot's dead. Aye. Us all dies some day. Some die afore others. 'Er heart stopped beating when her died. It does, tha knows, Lucy. Stop grinning, our Jack. She'll be in her coffin now, six feet down now. Aye. Us all ends up in the churchyard, some early some late.'

And the wicked gold snake lay in his pocket and the pain grew worse.

Grandmother, trembling with rage at the old man's talk, accidentally did something she'd wanted to do for fifty years. She let slip the bowl of mashed potatoes on the old man's head. He sat there too stunned to carry on, potatoes piled on his head while the deathly pain under the little gold snake from under the Stone racked his body.

Hallowe'en came closer and closer.

'I still dunna feel right,' said Sam to John one night as they sat on the railway bridge, smoking pipes after school. John often came as far as Bow Cross Farm with Sam, to eat some of Grandmother's cooking. John was fit and well with no dreams or fear. But Sam still had pains in his head and felt shivery down one part of his body. And Hallowe'en would not leave his mind. A train chugged under the bridge, its wheels screaming and squeaking and they heard the hiss of steam. The porters rushed to open the doors and both boys, looking down on the platform, were amazed to see Grandfather step out.

He had been secretly to Derby to see a lawyer and get him to sell the gold he had found under the Stone. Sam and John watched him climb the wooden steps of the foot-bridge that led to the road; he clutched the gold snake, for the pain was so vicious under it. He had nobody to meet him; he had left the farm secretly. He saw the two boys.

'Give us a pipe, lads. I'm spent. I've no money for baccy. I'm a poor old man with nowt left!'

Sam and John grinned and nudged each other. They trudged through the golden woods, Grandfather puffing and wheezing on John's pipe; he kept stopping to look and listen. Like Sam he felt there was still something not quite finished.

'I want thee to write a letter,' said the old man to Sam when they reached the farmhouse. He led them into the damp

207

smelling, cold north parlour where the window looked to the hill where the Stone had been. Grandmother disliked the room, preferring the sunny south parlour that looked out to her flowers. In this damp little room a small rug half-covered the red and black tiles and a huge oak bureau stood against the damp-speckled wall. Grandfather rummaged in the desk and found quill and ink.

'By gum, I feel badly,' said the old man suddenly.

'So do I,' said Sam. They both stared at each other, fear in their eyes.

'I know what us'll do,' said the old man, and fetched two slices of Grandmother's bread. Then he pulled open a drawer in the desk with much heaving and grunting and drawer squeaking and took out an old Bible. He carefully ripped two pages from the Bible and put the brown, damp-speckled pages between the bread.

'Best medicine out, bread an' a page from t'Bible,' said Grandfather. 'My old dad used to tell us.'

Sam tried the damp, mildewed paper and chewed it: neither Sam nor Grandfather felt any better. They were both aware of a deeply hidden threat and danger that they could no longer even sense clearly.

'Let's do the letter, lads,' said Grandfather weakly.

Sam had to write with a goose quill and muddy brown ink, fifty years old. The letter was to the British Museum. Grandfather had lied to the lawyer and told the man the treasure had always been in the family. The lawyer told him to write to the Museum and he, the lawyer, would send the treasure there: then the Museum might buy the ancient gold.

'Write "Dear Sir",' said Grandfather, holding the candle high over Sam so that Sam's head was a black bobbing shadow on the desk lid.

> ' "I hope this finds thee as it leaves me an' thy horses are
> in fine fettle. I have telled Obadiah Salt the lawyer,
> him by the Church in Derby with a peg leg between
> the spice shop and the clockmaker to send thee some
> treasure that belonged to me dad and to his dad and
> his dad and his—" '

('What treasure?' asked John. 'Keep thy big neb out of Walton's business,' growled Grandfather, hand on his pain. The quill scratched on ...)

> ' "Obadiah Salt says thee will send me gold in exchange for the treasure. I need the gold as me barns have burned down and life is hard and my lads never help me—" '

('That's not true Grandfather,' protested Sam. 'Hold thy rattle!' snapped Grandfather. 'Thee write. I'll say.')

> ' "I send thee my compliments. My wife Lucy is middling to bad and only to be expected at her age.
>   Your humble servant,
>   Abel Walton." '

With his hands shaking Grandfather sealed the letter with red sealing wax. Sam addressed it to the British Museum, London. Then they went through to warm themselves and eat ham and celery, freshly dug and washed clean by Ted. Both Sam and Grandfather felt as cold as ice.

The golden weather vanished. Gales and winds screamed and roared in the woods as Hallowe'en approached. Grandfather had taken to the fire. He was sitting there on the morning of Hallowe'en: it was a cold, wet morning with rain beating at the windows and the wind moaning and chuckling in the chimney.

The postman, gleaming and shining and black in his rain-wet uniform, brought a letter to Grandfather. Grandmother gave the postman some hot sweet tea. Grandfather stood in front of the fire with the letter ... inside was a cheque for £1,000, enough to buy another farm with. Grandfather stared and stared. Grandmother and the postman gossiped comfortably. Grandfather stared so long that his smock caught fire.

'Lucy! Lucy! Devil's got me! He's behind me. I stole his treasure! He's come!'

'He allus comes for them with guilty secrets,' said Grandmother, beating out the flames.

'It must be an important letter, Mr Walton,' said the postman.

'It's about the price of bulls in Stockport,' said Grandfather feebly. He thought his time had come.

'That's strange,' said the postman. 'It said "The British Museum" on the envelope and it has a London postmark.'

'Nowt's straightforward in this house,' said Grandmother to the postman.

On that night of Hallowe'en, 1883, Grandmother realized indeed that nothing in life was straightforward and life was forever full of mystery. At eight o'clock, Grandfather, clutching at his waistcoat where the wicked gold snake lay, climbed the stairs and called feebly for Grandmother.

'There's gold under them floorboards ... and it's for thee,' said Grandfather to Grandmother, white and terrified.

'I know, love,' said Grandmother gently. She held the old man's hand as he lay weak and ill on the bed, staring at the window where the rain still clawed and blew in the storm.

'Tha's worked hard for it, Abel,' said Grandmother softly. 'Aye. Tha worked hard for it, lad.' She called him lad as she had fifty years ago when they were first married. Her eyes were full of tears.

A loud gust of wind thumped at the window. 'Canst hear the wind keening?' asked Grandfather. 'My dad allus said ... allus said ... ' He was fighting for breath now. Suddenly the old man slipped back in time to when he and Grandmother were young and newly wed.

'I'll go an' see to them sheep an' get them out of that storm ... ' said Grandfather, his eyes bright as they had been when he was young. 'Thee can stay with thy baby ... '

'Aye,' said Grandmother. Her lips trembled and her eyes swam in tears as she played her last game with Grandfather. 'Aye ... I'll get thee some supper when tha gets back.' And through her tears the game came true. Grandmother no longer saw on the patchwork quilt the trembling white-faced old man. She saw the man she had married with eyes of ice blue like Sam's and a thatch of golden hair. He was tall and strong and had promised to make her the

210

richest farmer's wife in all of Derbyshire. And he had.

'I've made thee rich,' said Grandfather.

'Aye,' said Grandmother, licking away a falling tear.

Then pain twisted the old man's face.

'Canst hear, Lucy? Devil an' his horses ... They're coming ... me dad said they'd get me if I were bad ... he allus said Devil's coach used this road and went in by cave in woods ... it's a bad place here, Lucy ... us should've moved.'

A gust of wind blew small grains of ancient soot down the chimney. A tile grated as though something were on the roof, listening and waiting by the chimney. For a moment in the wild night Grandmother thought she heard the sound of galloping horses.

'Gold for thee,' whispered Grandfather.

Grandfather died in Grandmother's arms.

Sam had had a horrible day. He had been sick and sweating. He opened his bedroom window. Cold, sweet, night air rolled into his room. The storm had passed. The clouds had rolled away from the hills. The stars were wind polished and needle sharp. Over the hill where the Stone had been shone the constellation of Pegasus, square and friendly. The wet, bare trees gleamed with star-shine. An owl hooted. The world, the woods, the hills were his again. There would be pheasants' eggs to poach in spring and newts to catch in the ponds. He knew the old magic had been laid to rest for ever.

He leaned on the sill and drank in the cold air. Then, wiping his rain-wet hands down his nightshirt he fell into a deep drenching sleep, the like of which he had not had for a year or more.

But it was not as deep as the death sleep of his Uncle Edgar, his Grandfather, or Dame Trot. He had been spared.

He slept on.

Chapter Three

Grandmother wept. It was the thought of the mashed potatoes. She should have been more careful.

'Dunna thee weep, mother,' said Jack. 'You did all you could and more. He'd have tried the patience of a saint, him and them daft owd tales of his.'

'They wunna daft, Jack,' said Grandmother softly. But the cart that was carrying Grandfather's coffin to All Saints' churchyard was rumbling over the cobbled streets of Lambton and nobody heard her.

Early in December of that year Jack was taking the dog for a walk. He noticed a pile of dust and bones by the cave. The dog backed away, snarling, his hair rising. As Jack kicked at the pile with his boot, the east wind scattered the dust. It left behind one large claw. Jack bent and picked it up. It was a claw shaped like the crescent moon. Jack thought it was a wild cat's. But Jack had little imagination so he threw it in a hazel bush and carried on his walk in the moonlight.

Soon after, Grandmother bought Dame Trot's cottage, a fine cottage under the dirt and neglect. She forgot her grief in scrubbing out the stinking cottage. Jack went to work as a shepherd on a farm near Sheffield. Albert went to work in an iron works near Chesterfield and earned more in a week than Grandfather had given him in a year. Jo went to work in the Duke of Pemberly's stables. Ted was going to stay on at Bow Cross Farm till Lady Day next year when he was going to take a farm near Ashbourne. He wanted to get away. The farm was Ted's but he did not want it. So Sam and his father and mother took on the tenancy, for Sam's father was Grandfather's second son and had the next choice.

Sam had a bedroom with curtains now: for the first few nights he had a fire in the little grate, for Grandfather had left a great amount of coal. Sam liked his little room, though the fireplace had a cracked tile ... his mother lit a fire because the room smelled of apples she said.

Sam and his father grew stronger. Bow Cross Farm was a bigger, easier farm to farm. Sam's mother organized everything including the little garden that had been Grandmother's. Grandmother had packed it with flowers and herbs and vegetables in a glorious carpet of rich colour—but Sam's mother wanted a path and a sundial. Sam helped her clear it.

As he was doing so he uncovered a slab of stone. It was surrounded by the green and white spears of the snowdrops, just beginning to show through. It said

JACOB WALTON 1840

'It were thy Grandfather's brother,' said Grandmother when Sam asked about it. Sam and John and Jessie had called for cake and milk at Grandmother's cottage after school.

'He hanged himself. He were like thee, Sam, and John. He saw things and felt things nobody else could. It got too much for him ... vicar said he would have no suicides buried in churchyard ... he said Jacob had been taken by the Devil.'

Going through Grandfather's clothes the day after the funeral Grandmother had found the little gold snake. It seemed to burn her hand; it reminded her of a drawing in the old books.

213

She wanted to be rid of it. So she had put it in an envelope and addressed it to the Duke of Blackdon. It was like the snake on his family shield. Grandmother did not even put who it was from. She never wanted to see the wicked little carving again. She never did. Others did, however ... but that's another story.

Frost and cold, pure and calm, came as Christmas approached. Sam, John, and Jessie had been to look at the old Stone in the churchyard. They were on their way to Grandmother's cottage, one Sunday night before Christmas. She had invited them to tea.

The Stone lay on the frosted grass under a gaslamp, sparkling with rime and frosted dust. It looked cold and lifeless. The foul monster on it seemed little more than whorls and carved circles filled with hoar frost.

John kicked it. Then they turned their backs on the Stone and the snow-dusted spire where the stars of winter sparkled in the midwinter sky. Their boots crunched the snow as they made their way down to Grandmother's. The bells pealed out from the spire, ringing the people to evensong, for the bell tower was safe and repaired again. They ran the last bit, sliding and shouting to the bells and stars and clinging to gaslamps to stop their speed.

Grandmother had lit twelve fine, white, wax candles above the tongue, ham, jellies, jams, plum cake, and bread and butter piled high on the old pale blue willow-patterned plates she had brought from Bow Cross.

'What did tha do wi' them old books of Dame Trot's, Mrs Walton?' asked John, his mouth full of mince pie.

'Lit me fires with them,' said Grandmother. 'Only thing to do, John.'

'Dost think all them things were true, Mrs Walton?' asked Jessie, pressing firmly in her mouth, with two fingers, some iced cake.

There was a long silence. The fire crackled. The bells pealed out. Grandmother filled their cups and then went to the window that looked out to the church and looked up at the great spire soaring up to the stars. One silver star gleamed brighter than the rest just above the snow-dusted steeple.

'I dunna know ... I dunna know ... perhaps folks don't know what goes off under their noses ... I never did.'

Then she cut them all a slice of her iced Christmas cake that had icing as white as the snow on the snow-dusted spire out under the stars.

The Stone lay in the churchyard, where it had been left, for the twelve days of Christmas. Snow drifted against it and softened its stark outline: frost filled the weird carvings with ice flowers and ferns. The Stone was sleeping in the churchyard as the old legends said it would.

Early one January morning in 1884, before the grey dim light of a winter's morning had reached the Stone, two men carted it away after loading it into their cart by the north gate of the churchyard. They had been ordered to do so by a rich and powerful man who lived nearby and had heard about the Stone. He was interested in devil worship and witchcraft and began to plot and plan how to use the Stone for his own selfish and wicked ends. You can read how he used the Stone for his dark purposes in the next book THE DEVIL FINDS WORK.